THE GUIDE TO GOING VIRAL

ALSO BY BRENDAN KANE

ONE MILLION FOLLOWERS:
How I Built a Massive Social Audience in 30 Days

HOOK POINT:
How to Stand Out in a 3-Second World

THE GUIDE TO GOING VIRAL

The Art and Science of Succeeding on Social Media

BRENDAN KANE

AMARYLLIS
An imprint of Manjul Publishing House

AMARYLLIS

An imprint of Manjul Publishing House Pvt. Ltd.
• C-16, Sector 3, Noida, Uttar Pradesh 201 301, India
Website: www.manjulindia.com
Registered Office:
• 2nd Floor, Usha Preet Complex, 42 Malviya Nagar,
Bhopal 462 003 – India
Distribution Centres
Ahmedabad, Bengaluru, Chennai, Hyderabad,
Kochi, Kolkata, Mumbai, Noida, Pune

The Guide to Going Viral by Brendan Kane

Original English language edition published by Hook Point, LLC.

This paperback edition first published in 2026
Second impression 2026

ISBN 978-93-5543-573-6

Printed and bound in India by Repro India Limited

Praise for The Guide to Going Viral

"As long as I've known him, Brendan has been on the cutting edge of social media. The Guide to Going Viral *is a must-have manual for outshining the noise. Brendan equips you with the essentials to grab attention, hold it, and cultivate trust with an audience."*

—**Prince EA**, filmmaker, inspirational speaker, author; 23M across platforms

"I've been doing social media for four years now, and I've grown over a million followers each on TikTok, Instagram, Snapchat, and Facebook. On TikTok, I have over 19 million followers. My brain either works very similarly to Brendan's, or perhaps, we arrive at the same conclusions to growth strategies, because it's what just works. I can validate the techniques and strategies used in Brendan's book because I've used many of them to grow my following, and I've also learned a lot more from Brendan's book that I'm excited to apply.

"It's difficult to find real experts in this field, but Brendan is the real deal, and the advice he gives . . . works. Be patient when trying to grow your social media, work hard, and make sure to follow GOOD advice. The Guide to Going Viral *is just that."*

—**Alex Stemp**, photographer and video creator; 23M across platforms

"After reading and implementing Brendan's first two books, there was a drastic increase in the quality and structure of my videos. My social media accounts more than doubled in size, and I was able to leave my day job to become a full-time content creator, so I was delighted to see that he had written another book.

"The Guide to Going Viral *is a deep dive into the exact process of creating videos that can be viewed by millions of people. I found the research and analysis sections particularly useful, and in the short time since reading the book, I've found that this has helped streamline my process. There are real nuggets of gold throughout, and I especially like that the book is tailored to both long- and short-form videos. I firmly believe this is the best social media book I've ever read, and it will be the go-to book for content creators around the world. Quality over quantity!"*

—**Ben Newell**, author and video creator; 2.7M across platforms

"In today's micro-attention landscape, breaking through the noise can feel impossible. Brendan Kane's latest book is a game changer. His proven methods to capture and retain attention make The Guide to Going Viral *a must-read for anyone sharing content on social media today."*

—**Sally Newell Cohen**, ICANN SVP, global communications;
former COO at Toastmasters

"In today's world, grabbing attention is like mining gold—and it's getting tougher every day. That's why The Guide to Going Viral *is a game changer for anyone who wants to shine online—whether you're building a business or boosting your personal brand. Having worked alongside Brendan Kane, I've witnessed his methodical magic firsthand. He demystifies the viral code, showing that it's not about beating an algorithm that's out to get you. His approach is simple, practical, and yes, even fun. Ready to go viral? This is your playbook."*

—**Florencia Andres**, five-time bestselling author;
founder of Easy Launch Academy

"Brendan takes the mystery out of why some videos work and others do not, removing the fluff and hype, and revealing the science behind what grabs our attention—and most importantly, what keeps it. This book is a literal master class for any creator who wants to stop guessing at what will work and instead create and post with more confidence."

—**Heather Parady**, content creator and show host

"The Guide to Going Viral *is more than a title, it's a challenge that you can finally accept with the knowledge in this book from Brendan. In a world where it's almost impossible to get a person's attention, Brendan Kane does a masterful job of going into the detail you need, in a way we can all understand, to get your signal above the noise. As the Sleep Doctor, I devoured this book, and I'm putting its principles into practice daily."*

—**Michael Breus, PhD**, bestselling author,
internationally renowned as "The Sleep Doctor"

"Brendan's expert strategies pave the way to achieving your social media aspirations and beyond. Unleash your potential to create a brand, drive sales, or establish influence with the invaluable insights offered within these pages."

—**Luke Wahl**, vice president of unscripted, Nickelodeon, and former executive producer at *Sports Illustrated*

"What Brendan has been able to achieve on social media is extraordinary! And he's done this multiple times across multiple platforms. What's crazier? He shares his secrets. Read this now!"

—**Chris Do**, Emmy Award–winning designer, director, CEO and chief strategist of Blind; founder of The Futur; 3.6M across platforms

"Brendan's expertise in grabbing attention is unmatched. If you're feeling lost in a sea of competition and struggling to make your mark, look no further. Dive into his latest book, The Guide to Going Viral, *for instant access to practical tools and strategies that can set you apart today."*

—**Dean Sheremet**, professional chef and content creator

"When I first met with Brendan, I told him that I didn't know more than 500 people, so how was I going to get more than 500 views? 100 million views later, I've learned that data analysis combined with content you are proud of is the real secret."

—**Dr. Erin Nance**, cofounder and CEO of FeelBetr Health

"I think to be at the top of an industry, you have to be obsessed with it and study it. Brendan Kane lights that fire with this book and sets you off with a new set of tools to go get at it! I honestly love his insights and how he organizes his research. It makes it easy to apply to your life and sparks new ideas. Thanks, Brendan!"

—**Lenay**, singer/songwriter; cofounder of XOX Studios; 19M across platforms

"Brendan is a wonderful writer and has an absolute gift for understanding marketing. His ability to simplify something so essential while drawing readers in and making it compelling for them is a masterpiece. The world of viral content is full of uncertainty, but Brendan generously and fascinatingly shares his proven formula to elevate visibility and distinguish oneself from others. Brendan equips you with workable strategies, tools, and insights essential for visibility."

—**Marisa Peer**, speaker, author, founder of RTT, trainer of 19,000 therapists

"If you want to get people lining up to do business with you, this book is for you. Viral content is a marketing miracle most people only wish for. Brendan has ripped back the curtain to reveal a formula that dramatically improves your odds of being seen by millions of potential customers."

—**Daniel Priestly**, entrepreneur; author of *Oversubscribed*

"The Guide to Going Viral *is an essential resource for competing and succeeding in The Attention Economy. Brendan's battle-tested strategies and insights are a must-have for every social media creator."*

—**Ernest Lupinacci**, founder and CCO,
Ernest Industries; founder and creative director, Anomaly

"Brendan reveals effective strategies to ignite interest in your brand or business within our always-on society."

—**Jon Jashni**, founder of Raintree Ventures; former president and chief creative officer of Legendary Pictures, where he oversaw the development and production of films such as *Kong: Skull Island*, *Warcraft*, *Godzilla*, *42*, and *Pacific Rim*

To those with talent, intellect, and a pure heart whose voices are being suppressed or ignored: may this book be your guide to amplifying your voice, finding your power, and making a positive impact on the world.

TABLE OF CONTENTS

INTRODUCTION

GOING VIRAL IS NOT A MERE STROKE OF LUCK; IT'S A SCIENCE

In a world where more than 4,800,000,000 content creators churn out billions of pieces of content daily, the competition for recognition is fierce. In this landscape, where social media reigns supreme and every brand and individual vies for attention alongside the likes of Kim Kardashian, MrBeast, Gary Vee, Cristiano Ronaldo, Jimmy Fallon, and teenage influencers, how can you rise above the noise and win the battle for attention?

Well, welcome to the world of content virality, where luck takes a back seat and science takes the wheel. Since 2005, I've been on a mission to unravel the mystery behind making content go viral for the largest brands, celebrities, and individuals worldwide. In 2007, I pioneered the first-ever influencer campaign on YouTube, setting the stage for groundbreaking strategies to come. Over the years, I've overseen $200 million in marketing spend and have collaborated with major corporations such as MTV, Viacom, *Vice Magazine*, Paramount Pictures, Ikea, and Skechers shoes. My expertise extends to building digital platforms for renowned figures like Taylor Swift, Rihanna, and Adriana Lima. Additionally, I am the founder of the social media agency Hook Point. Some of you may also recognize me as the author of the internationally bestselling books *One Million Followers: How I Built a Massive Social Audience in 30 Days* and *Hook Point: How to Stand Out in a 3-Second World.*

Before we dive into the powerful tools I've developed during my career, let's address some common myths about social media. Many people enter this competitive arena with misconceptions that obscure a clear understanding of what it truly takes to succeed.

TOP SEVEN SOCIAL MEDIA MYTHS DEBUNKED

Many people hold certain beliefs about social media that lean more toward myth than reality. When I first start working with a client and debunk the top seven social media myths, they often find some of these truths surprising. This section aims to clear up the most common misconceptions, offering insights that could challenge your current understanding of social media. Ready to uncover the truth? Let's dive in.

Myth 1: Extensive Experience Is Necessary for Social Media Success

Does success on social media really require years of digital expertise? Discover how newcomers can also achieve viral success with the right strategies.

Common Belief: The prevailing view is that only those with a wealth of digital experience can achieve social media success, potentially sidelining those new to the field.

The Reality: In reality, effective strategies and adaptability are more crucial than extensive experience. The Viral Content Model, which you will learn in this book, demonstrates that success is accessible even to novices who are willing to learn and apply its principles.

Behind the Myth: Intimidation from witnessing experienced influencers' success can be disheartening for beginners. However, social media is constantly evolving, offering opportunities for new creators to succeed with fresh and innovative content.

Success Stories: Examples such as leatherworker Tanner Leatherstein, with 1.7 million followers across TikTok and Instagram; and hand surgeon Dr. Erin Nance, with 700,000 followers on TikTok, both started with minimal social media experience and achieved significant success, challenge the notion that extensive experience is required. Everyone begins with zero followers and zero views when they first join these platforms. I started at this level too, which is one of the reasons I've spent the past 19 years developing the learning presented in this book—to help people succeed. Even MrBeast, the top influencer in the world, began his journey alone in a bedroom at the age of 13. At Hook Point, we often find that working with marketing experts who have years of experience can be challenging because there's a lot of unlearning that must be done. They must move away from outdated methods and tactics that are no longer relevant for success on social media.

Key Insights: Success on social media is driven by the ability to engage and connect with an audience through compelling content, not the duration of one's experience. The Viral Content Model emphasizes strategic storytelling and audience interaction.

Actionable Strategies: Adopt the Viral Content Model to produce content that resonates with your audience, focusing on strategic learning and adapting based on platform insights and audience feedback. This book will guide you through these steps, regardless of your experience level.

Myth 2: Success on Social Media Requires High Costs and Large Teams

Is the secret to viral success on social media really tied to how much you spend and the size of your team? Let's unpack this myth and discover what truly drives content to go viral.

Common Belief: There's a widespread belief that achieving viral success on social media necessitates significant investment in high-end equipment and large production teams.

The Reality: In truth, the essence of viral success on social media lies more in the power of storytelling and audience connection than in the scale of resources. Viral hits have often been created with minimal equipment, such as smartphones, and without the support of a large team.

Behind the Myth: This misconception persists due to people's familiarity with well-produced TV shows and films. Despite having seen tons of viral content on social media that feature modest production value, many still mistakenly associate high production values with social media success. In reality, a lot of viral content has been created with nothing more than a smartphone. The essence of virality lies in the content's ability to connect and engage, not in the polish of its production.

Success Stories: Content creators like Hunter Prosper, with 8.3 million followers across Instagram and TikTok, who approaches strangers on the street with just an iPhone; and Robert Croak, with 1.1 million followers on TikTok, who films walking listicles (i.e., walking down the street while listing advice), are great examples of how simple, genuine interactions can captivate millions. Along with others who use minimal setups, such as The School of Hard Knocks, with 1.9 million followers on Instagram, that interviews people on the street with a basic microphone. These creators demonstrate that impactful content does not require hefty budgets or big teams. Many Viral Formats that you'll learn about in this book thrive on the simplicity achievable with just a smartphone and genuine human interaction.

Key Insights: The true drivers of social media virality are engaging narratives and authentic connections, not high costs or large teams. Modern audiences value great storytelling, which can be delivered without a hefty price tag or a big team. Social media algorithms favor content that holds viewers' attention through relatable narratives, emotional connection, and genuine engagement over slick production.

Actionable Strategies: Focus on harnessing the storytelling potential within your reach. Utilize the technology at your disposal, such as smartphones, and affordable editing tools to craft content that resonates. This book guides you through creating impactful content without reliance on expensive equipment, emphasizing storytelling and communication techniques that foster genuine engagement over production value.

Myth 3: You Must Be on Every Social Media Platform

Is being active on every social media platform the key to social media success? Let's explore why a more focused approach might be more effective.

Common Belief: Many believe that to maximize their online presence and engagement, brands or individuals must maintain active profiles across all available social media platforms. This belief is rooted in the assumption that being everywhere at once is the key to digital marketing success.

The Reality: The belief that spreading oneself across every social media platform guarantees greater success is a misconception. Each platform is uniquely designed, with distinct content formats, user interfaces, and engagement behaviors. While many people use multiple platforms, they consume content differently on each due to these design elements, which is why the effectiveness of your social media presence depends more on how well you tailor your storytelling to the specific consumption behaviors of each platform.

Behind the Myth: The persistence of this myth is likely influenced by the visible presence of major brands and celebrities on multiple platforms. This widespread visibility reinforces the "more equals better" commonsense approach, where more frequent exposure is often mistaken for greater effectiveness. This strategy, often reiterated by some social media experts, may have found success in the earliest days of social media, when there was less content and fewer creators on the platforms, making it easier to gain traction by simply posting more.

Success Stories: Numerous brands and individuals have achieved remarkable success by focusing their efforts on a single or a limited number of platforms.

- For example, MrBeast, who has 260 million subscribers on YouTube compared to 18 million on Facebook, initially focused solely on YouTube. He mastered its nuances before expanding to other major platforms.
- Another example is Joe Rogan, who initially focused all his energy on YouTube. His success on this platform made him the world's most prominent podcast host, leading to a lucrative $100 million deal with Spotify in 2020. Recently, Spotify renewed its partnership with Rogan under a new multiyear contract potentially worth as much as $250 million, which also includes provisions for his show to appear on competing platforms like YouTube and Apple Podcasts. Despite this expansion, Rogan rarely shares clips on Instagram and does not maintain active TikTok, LinkedIn, or Facebook accounts for his podcast.

By focusing on platforms that best suit their content style, creators emphasize the value of depth over range in their social media strategy.

Key Insights: Spreading resources too thin across multiple platforms can lead to diminished content quality and thus audience engagement. Success in social media marketing comes from understanding the unique characteristics of each platform and creating tailored content that resonates with the specific design and consumption behaviors of the platform.

Actionable Strategies: Instead of trying to maintain an active presence on every platform, choose one that you enjoy working on, which reflects your content style. Invest time in understanding the nuances of this platform, and tailor your content strategy to leverage its specific features and audience behavior. While it's fine to post content on other platforms, focus your primary efforts on mastering *one*.

Myth 4: Frequent Posting Guarantees Social Media Virality

Can posting content frequently guarantee viral success? Uncover the truth behind content frequency and audience engagement on social media.

Common Belief: There's a common misconception that the key to going viral on social media is to post as frequently as possible.

The Reality: Virality on social media doesn't depend on posting frequency, but rather on the quality of content and how deeply it holds the audience's attention.

Behind the Myth: The myth arises from the mistaken belief that social media algorithms prioritize quantity over engagement. While this might have been somewhat true in the early days of social media when there were fewer content creators and less content, the landscape has changed dramatically. Today, with billions of content creators and an overwhelming amount of content for the algorithms to select from, merely posting frequently without focus on quality is ineffective. Only once you've mastered a Viral Format that works for you—which you will learn about in this book—should you consider increasing your posting frequency.

Success Stories: Creators who achieve viral success often do so with infrequent, yet highly engaging content. This approach emphasizes strategic, impactful posts over a haphazard approach to content creation. For example, Mark Rober typically posts a video once or twice a month; MrBeast, in his early days, would post only one video a month;

and Veritasium limits its output to two to three videos per month on YouTube.

Key Insights:

- Algorithm preferences: Contrary to the myth, social media algorithms favor retention and interaction, focusing on viewer engagement duration rather than posting frequency. It's the quality of storytelling that captures and holds attention, not the frequency of posts.
- Quality engagement: The most successful viral content resonates deeply with audiences through well-crafted storytelling, rather than sheer volume of posts.

Actionable Strategies: Shift your content strategy focus from quantity to quality. Concentrate on creating content that genuinely engages and resonates with the masses. Use storytelling techniques and Viral Formats to enhance engagement and viewer retention.

Myth 5: My Business Isn't Sexy Enough to Go Viral

Think your industry is too niche to go viral? Let's challenge the idea that only "sexy" businesses can capture the viral spotlight.

Common Belief: Many entrepreneurs think that their businesses, especially in fields like tax accounting, legal advice, or other specialized areas, lack the general appeal necessary for viral success on social media. They often view these industries as too niche or "unsexy" to attract widespread attention.

The Reality: The idea that only glamorous or inherently exciting industries can achieve virality is a misconception. Viral success often relies more on how content connects and resonates with the audience than on the industry's surface appeal.

Behind the Myth: This myth persists due to the underestimation of storytelling power and the disbelief that any topic can resonate emotionally with the masses. There's a common misconception that the nature of an industry could limit its widespread appeal.

Success Stories: Examples debunking this myth include:

- Clear Value Tax, which has two million subscribers, offers insightful tax advice on YouTube.
- Graham Stephan, a finance adviser with 4.7 million subscribers, shares financial tips for millennials on YouTube.
- Erika Kuhlberg, a legal expert with a combined 14 million followers, simplifies legal concepts on TikTok and Instagram.
- Ben Newell, who has 1.5 million followers, builds terrariums—a type of miniature ecosystem in sealed containers—for plants and small land animals like frogs, ants, and turtles.

These examples show that perceived "unsexy" topics can capture and engage a vast audience.

Key Insights: Viral success often comes from creating compelling stories that build tension and curiosity, which creates a narrative gap that keeps viewers engaged until the resolution. This approach holds attention effectively, regardless of the industry's perceived appeal.

Actionable Strategies: To achieve similar success, use the "generalist principle" by considering how you can weave a story around your niche that engages viewers until the end. If you're unsure how to use the generalist principle and craft compelling narratives within your niche, you've come to the right place. This book will teach you exactly that. Continue reading to discover Viral Formats that will help you structure your stories in extraordinary ways.

Myth 6: Hashtags Guarantee Visibility

Are hashtags really the magic bullet for getting noticed on social media? Let's discuss how the role of hashtags has evolved in the algorithm era.

Common Belief: Popular hashtags are often seen as a magic bullet for ensuring that posts get seen on social media.

The Reality: Hashtags have lost much of their power to boost visibility due to the evolution of social media algorithms, which now prioritize retention and engagement.

Behind the Myth: Once a tool for standing out, hashtags are now less effective amid the current volume of content on social media platforms.

Key Insights: Social media platforms are designed to highlight content that captures and retains attention, not just posts with trending hashtags.

Actionable Strategies: Content creators should focus on the quality of their narratives and the resonance of their posts, rather than using hashtags as a primary strategy.

Myth 7: Virality on Social Media Is Pure Luck

Is going viral on social media just a matter of luck? Let's break down the strategic planning that truly drives virality, dispelling myths of randomness.

Common Belief: Many believe that achieving virality on social media is akin to winning the lottery—a matter of sheer luck rather than strategic planning.

The Reality: Contrary to this common perception, virality is most often the result of meticulous research, planning, and a deep understanding of storytelling and audience engagement, making it more of a science than a game of chance. A detailed examination of viral content often shows intentional design and strategic execution, demonstrating that virality can be systematically planned and replicated with the right storytelling tools.

Behind the Myth: The myth likely stems from the sensational stories of overnight success and the emergence of individuals who defy the conventional image of fame, such as MrBeast. These creators, who differ from the traditional film and TV stars, may give the impression of attaining virality by mere luck, which reinforces this misconception. Yet, the experiences of creators like MrBeast illustrate that such success is far from random. It is the culmination of a deliberate process and extensive learning about the intricacies of crafting a truly viral video. The Viral Content Model detailed in this book unveils the structured approaches behind achieving widespread recognition, challenging the notion that virality is unpredictable and random.

Key Insights: Virality follows principles that can be learned and applied. It involves understanding social media user behavior, leveraging data to inform content creation, and developing narratives that captivate and retain viewer attention.

Actionable Strategies: Rather than attributing social media success to luck, adopt strategic models and tools to significantly increase your content's viral potential. The Viral Content Model outlined in this book serves as a comprehensive guide to achieving planned virality. By focusing on storytelling and communication techniques, you can produce content that resonates with the masses and achieves viral success.

INTRODUCING THE VIRAL CONTENT MODEL

Now that we've dispelled some common misconceptions, let me introduce what I've discovered actually works—the Viral Content Model. This model was developed at my social media agency, Hook Point, based on years of meticulous research and practical application. Designed to master the art of virality on social media, this model has already generated tens of billions of views and secured over 100-plus million followers. Our consistent and impactful strategies have established us as leaders in the industry.

As I explained in the final myth, one of the most powerful truths that has emerged from my years of research and experience is that creating viral content is not a mere stroke of luck; it's a science. And in this book, I'm thrilled to share that science with you. Together, we'll delve into the inner workings of social media algorithms, learn how to craft content that the algorithms love, and uncover simple yet effective strategies to achieve consistent virality using the revolutionary tools developed by my team: the Hook Point Viral Content Model, Viral Formats, and the Communication Algorithm.

Our approach is rooted in a fundamental understanding of how social media algorithms function, making it effective across all social media platforms regardless of any changes they undergo. When the algorithms favor your content, they'll eagerly share it with as many people as possible, exponentially expanding your reach.

Imagine your content not just reaching a few thousand, but tens or hundreds of thousands, or even millions, of people. The impact on your brand's success and bottom line would be extraordinary.

In this book, you'll master the innovative tools mentioned above. By doing so, you'll maximize your investment of time, money, and energy, fueling the growth of your brand and business and increasing your market share.

To achieve maximum results with the algorithms, focus on three core pillars:

1. **Grabbing attention.** Rising above the noise is crucial. If you can't stop someone from scrolling past your content, they'll never see your message.
2. **Holding attention**. Providing maximum value to your audience is key. This isn't about clickbait or trickery. Substance is vital, as you want people to engage with and crave more of your content.
3. **Monetizing attention.** Your content strategy needs to align with your business goals and objectives. A thoughtful and strategic approach not only fuels business growth, ensuring that the investment of time, money, and resources pays off but also helps avoid creator fatigue and burnout.

Throughout this book, you'll discover how to break away from outdated methods and deprogram your thinking about media and content. By adopting the proven methods shared within these pages, brands and content creators can start producing innovative and effective content that genuinely resonates with audiences. This approach to viral marketing at scale isn't about resorting to silly cat videos or pranks unrelated to your brand. Instead, it's focused on mastering storytelling techniques that align with your business goals and objectives.

Understanding the right creative process and aligning content with audience preferences can pave the way for consistent and predictable virality, setting individuals and brands on the path to success in an otherwise challenging and ever-changing social media landscape. Importantly, regardless of your subject matter or expertise, anything can be made to go viral. For instance, tax advice has gone viral with Clear Tax Value, real estate with Ryan Serhant, legal advice with Erika Kullberg, leather craftsmanship with Tanner Leatherstein, blenders with Blendtec, terrariums with Ben Newell, hand surgery with Dr. Erin Nance, and finance with Graham Stephan.

This Book Is for You If . . .

. . . your goal is to achieve success with social media, which entails generating a substantial number of followers, sales, engagement, and views. This information is useful for a diverse range of individuals who are eager to break through the noise and create innovative and effective content on social media, including:

- **Forward-thinkers:** Those who want to master the skills and strategies for viral content creation.
- **Aspiring influencers:** Individuals who want to become influencers and are looking for tangible, applicable content creation skills to stand out in a competitive landscape.
- **Media buyers:** Professionals who wish to boost their brand's visibility by leveraging their knowledge and training in viral content creation.

- **Small-business owners:** Entrepreneurs who need effective tools to reach their customers and gain a competitive edge in the market.
- **Marketing managers:** Those in managerial roles who need to update their skills to keep up with the ever-changing social media landscape and regain mastery over their fields.
- **Social media managers:** Professionals who want to elevate their company's online presence and get their ideas noticed by mastering the art of viral content creation.
- **Entrepreneurs and solopreneurs:** Individuals running their own businesses who seek to make their content stand out in the crowded digital space.
- **College students:** Current students and recent graduates who'd like to gain an extra edge in finding top-tier jobs and build a creative portfolio of viral content.

The skills you will obtain through this book include:

- Understanding and avoiding outdated traditional approaches to digital marketing.
- Authentically communicating with an audience, eliminating the influence of cognitive biases.
- Applying the Viral Content Model, Viral Formats, and the Communication Algorithm to create content that resonates with large audiences.
- Using effective tools to measure content performance and make data-driven creative decisions.

- Interpreting and replicating creative nuances in original content.
- Conducting thorough research and analysis of content performance drivers.
- Creating viral content that captures the attention of general audiences and stands out in the attention economy.

Overall, this book provides a comprehensive learning experience, blending theory and practice, to empower you with the skills and knowledge you'll need to succeed in the dynamic world of social media content creation. You'll walk away with a foundation to successfully repeat virality for the rest of your life.

Mindset: Keep an Open Mind—Deprogram and Adopt a Counterintuitive Perspective

"Hook Point's method is a true revelation! As an Emmy Award–winning radio and TV host, I thought I knew all there was to captivate an audience. But after attending their training sessions, I realized that everything I previously thought about social media marketing was wrong. It's like being introduced to music modes such as Dorian, Phrygian, or Locrian. Suddenly, you see the direct path that opens your eyes, and you realize you just need to focus on this one thing and everything becomes so much simpler! That's exactly what Hook Point's model did for me—it transformed the way I connect with my audience, and now, I can't imagine going back to my old ways. It's a game-changer!"

—**John Tesh**, *Emmy Award–winning radio and TV host*

As we delve into the truth of viral content creation, let me be candid with you. Much of what you've been told about using hashtags, content calendars, posting times, and following trends has been a waste of time. Many so-called social media gurus aren't actually experts, and their advice usually doesn't lead to the desired outcomes they tout. The reality is, creating consistent viral content demands dedication and hard work, much like mastering any skill in life. Although the approach you'll learn in this book may be nuanced, it has the potential to revolutionize your brand or business when you wholeheartedly invest in the process.

To help you stay the course, I encourage you to remember why you chose to read this book in the first place. Learning how to captivate audiences about your brand or business is invaluable. Social media is a powerful space where you and countless others spend significant time each week. Posting there has the potential to draw millions of eyes to your content, impacting your business and life profoundly. Therefore, it's crucial to approach this book with a beginner's mind—as a willing student absorbing information from moment to moment.

Most people who embrace this process enjoy success. Hand surgeon Erin Nance, MD, went from zero to 200,000 followers in two weeks and has generated nearly 100 million views on TikTok. Currently she has over 700,000 followers. DIY expert John Malecki grew his average views from 100,000 to more than one million per video on YouTube. Leatherworker Tanner Leatherstein attracted an impressive 1.7 million followers and 100 million organic views across TikTok and Instagram, and sold out of his goods. Applying this model to Katie Couric's content while she was at Yahoo! led to over one billion views. As for comedian Stuart Mitchell, after a year of using this method to find success on social media, he has consistently generated videos with over one million views, significantly impacting his ticket sales and even propelling his career down unexpected and exciting new paths.

These clients improved their performance and experienced life-changing results because they put in the work and spent time honing their craft. Creators like MrBeast even say that even after his first three years of fully dedicated time to creating videos they still needed improving: "I'm still learning things every day; 10,000 hours is three years of 10 hours a day . . . that's not enough time to master something. After three years, my videos were awful."[1] If you shy away from doing the work, you won't find the success you desire. It's that simple. Just like mastering any skill in life, creating viral content requires dedication.

Your success in implementing the knowledge from this book hinges on one crucial factor: your openness and willingness to adapt your current process to the simple, yet not easy, approach that I'm about to share with you. Again, this method is entirely different from anything you've encountered before, breaking away from traditional norms and preconceived notions about digital success. However, if you embrace this process and commit to following the guidance, the results will be well worth the effort.

Here are four principles that will help you adopt a learner's mindset:

1. **Capitalize on social media's expansive reach.** Recognize that traditional specific audience targeting isn't sufficient for consistently generating organic viral content. Instead, aim to craft content that appeals to a wider audience. Take a cue from Gucci's strategic pivot: they expanded beyond their niche of high-end consumers to market luxury

1 Mina, "MrBeast Challenges Conventional Wisdom on Mastery: '10,000 Days, Not Hours,'" MrBeast News, Sept. 27, 2023, https://mrbeastburger.io/mr-beast-challenges-conventional-wisdom-on-mastery-10000-days-not-hours/#google_vignette.

streetwear on social media, amassing a vast new customer base, which increased sales by 45 percent in one year.[2] It's also crucial to remember that algorithms prioritize maximizing viewer retention and engagement. To align with this approach, identify viral content, study its allure, and weave compelling elements into your own content.

2. **Invest in the process, and embrace the learning curve.** Allow sufficient time and energy to study the platform you want to grow on, and refine your content creation skills. Recognize that significant results may take months or longer to materialize.
3. **Stay committed and persistent, even when immediate success feels elusive.** Trust the process and continue putting in the work.
4. **Realize that each piece of content on social media tells a story.** Develop the craft of storytelling to captivate your audience and maintain their engagement with each post. By mastering this method, your content will not only capture hearts but will also get the algorithms working in your favor.

Throughout this process, I'll help you break free from traditional thinking and deprogram the way you view media and content. By embracing change and adopting a fresh perspective on social media, you can unlock the science of virality and potentially transform your brand or business.

---

2 Florine Eppe Beauloye, "When Streetwear and Social Media Hype Win Over Luxury Fashion," Luxe Digital, March 10, 2023, https://luxe.digital/business/digital-luxury-reports/when-streetwear-and-social-media-hype-win-over-luxury-fashion/.

If you're ready to challenge your preconceptions, embrace this new approach, and put in the work, then this book is for you. I hope to see one of your videos in my feed, amazing the world with your brilliance. Let's embark on this journey together and create something extraordinary!

PART I

THE HOOK POINT VIRAL CONTENT MODEL

CHAPTER 1

DECODING VIRALITY: THE SCIENCE BEHIND SOCIAL MEDIA SUCCESS

Social media is both a blessing and a curse. It's a blessing because it democratizes communication, enabling anyone to pull out their phone, record, and share content globally. However, it becomes a curse when it allows creators to bypass the meticulous learning and strategic approach typically required in film production, music composition, television, and book writing. As a result, social media often features content that lacks the structured storytelling essential for viral success, leaving creators puzzled about why their content goes unnoticed.

To address this challenge, this book primarily focuses on social media video creation, although the Viral Content Model, Viral Formats, and the Communication Algorithm you'll learn about here can be applied to any type of social media content. We emphasize video because it generally performs better with the social media algorithms due to its higher retention rate compared to other formats. In other words, videos typically keep viewers engaged in ways that photos and text simply cannot match, increasing both engagement and the time spent on the platform, which are key goals for social media companies.

Building on this foundation, this book will teach you the Viral Content Model, a creative process designed to perfect storytelling on social media and achieve genuine success. At the heart of this model is the use of "formats"—video storytelling frameworks that enable creators to strategically incorporate their brands, identities, stories, or ideas. These structured templates provide a consistent narrative backbone, giving content the best chance to break through and connect with the masses. Top formats act as flexible canvases, allowing for the sharing of unique messages and creativity, akin to the three-act structure in film, the verse-chorus format in music, teasers and tags in TV, or the Hero's Journey in literature. Every industry relies on a proven formula to structure and enhance creative output.

Understanding the difference between fleeting social media trends and enduring formats is crucial. Trends may capture attention temporarily, but formats provide a lasting blueprint for content creation. Recognizing and applying these formats is essential to enhancing your online presence and achieving lasting impact.

At Hook Point, we've noticed many content creators chasing virality without a proper understanding of formats or misusing them due to a lack of subtlety in their approach. This is because there are numerous formats available, some tailored to specific platforms, so you need to learn how to recognize and leverage these formats for success. Learning the intricacies of formats is as critical for creating impactful social media videos as it is for producing a great film. Fortunately, my team excels at identifying effective formats that captivate the masses. We've devoted thousands of hours to analyzing billions of views and tens of thousands of videos on social media, uncovering and breaking down the nuances of these formats—insights we share in this book. Our goal is to underline the critical role of formats in creating impactful content and to offer a new lens through which to view social media storytelling.

Just as a recipe or a blueprint is indispensable in cooking and construction, formats act as essential blueprints for content creation, ensuring that they capture the audience's attention. For instance, the "Two Characters, One Lightbulb" format effectively debunks misconceptions, demonstrated by "Are You Eating Puppy Portions?" by @ EmilyHackettFitness, which attracted over seven million views. In this video, Hackett entertainingly debunks the myth that counting calories is necessary for weight loss. This example illustrates how a format can transform common content into something both enlightening and shareable.

Throughout this book, I'll be referencing many videos and documents. If you'd like to enhance your learning experience and get a clear visualization of the topics discussed, you can view all video links and resources here: **http://guide.hookpoint.com/**.

In Part II of this book, we'll delve deeper into formats. For now, start recognizing them in your feed. Properly applying these formats can transform your content, propelling it toward virality. Success, however, demands more than mere recognition. Ninety-nine percent of those who attempt to use a format without proper research and implementation might fail. But those who diligently apply the Viral Content Model and utilize Viral Formats can nearly guarantee their success.

Beyond Industry Borders: The Generalist Approach to Capturing Attention on Social Media

To stand out amid the noise and capture attention, you need to adopt a generalist approach. By "generalist approach," I mean that many companies and brands often make the mistake of solely focusing on competing with their direct industry rivals. But on social media, it's crucial to remember that you're not just competing with peers from your sector. You're in a virtual arena where a personal finance company is not only up against other financial firms but also faces competition from every baking tutorial, beauty tip, travel vlog, and DIY enthusiast out there. It's not just about who offers similar services or products—it's about who can capture the audience's limited attention span. To stand out, you must think outside the box; it's essential to ground your content in broader interests, crafting content hooks and narratives that resonate with a wider audience, all while maintaining authenticity and insight with your core audience.

An excellent example of this generalist approach is Graham Stephan's YouTube channel, which is geared toward teaching millennials about finance. Instead of producing a technical video on car financing—a topic that might only resonate with finance enthusiasts—he widened his reach with the enticingly titled video *How I Bought a Tesla for $78 Per Month.* This clever framing appealed not just to finance buffs but also to anyone intrigued by snagging a great deal, owning a Tesla, or simply discovering how he managed to achieve it. It's this type of creative repackaging—combining niche expertise with widespread interests—that allows content to shine in the crowded arena of social media, transforming what might garner 1,000 views into a sensation with more than 8.5 million.

Imagine this scenario: You open a social media app, and the algorithm is tasked with determining the first 15 posts you will see, drawn from a pool of approximately 150,000 or more potential pieces of content. In this situation, 99 percent of the content from this pool has no chance of being seen, even if the users follow you. Given this challenging environment, it's not enough to excel only within your specific category or vertical; you must outperform content across *all* verticals. Therefore, seeking inspiration and innovation beyond your immediate industry becomes not just beneficial but crucial.

Algorithms: The AI Man, the Myth, and the Legend

There are many myths surrounding algorithms. Frustrated content creators often wonder if the algorithms are designed to suppress their content to force them to use paid media for visibility. Let me debunk this myth right away: if that were true, no content would ever go viral, and successful influencers wouldn't exist without spending on ads.

So what do algorithms really do? *They're engineered to prioritize content that captures and sustains users' attention for as long as possible.* Social media platforms are designed to keep users engaged on their platform for longer durations so they can serve them as many ads as possible—maximizing user retention is their primary business objective.

Think about it: the longer someone stays on a platform, the larger amount of content they consume, providing more opportunities for ads to be shown. Attention-grabbing content fuels these social media engines, and it's our collective eyeballs that determine what kind of fuel is fed into these platforms. Without our attention, platforms can't serve ads, and without great content, we won't stay engaged. Therefore, creating content that the algorithms love becomes the key to getting our content seen.

As a brand owner and content creator, your goal is to craft content that not only grabs attention but also retains it longer than all the potential posts the algorithm can serve up to your audience each time they open the app. When you meet the algorithm's standards, it will eagerly serve your content to its users, amplifying its reach. You may not be able to defeat the algorithm, but you can collaborate with it.

Drawing from extensive experience and testing, I've found that *there's only one proven method to become an expert at creating algorithm-friendly content.* It involves researching top-performing content formats, carefully crafting content based on that understanding, analyzing its performance, and refining it accordingly.

Now, I don't want you to just take my word for it. MrBeast, one of the most successful content creators in the world, with more than 300 million subscribers across his social media platforms, concurs with this method. When asked how he learned to consistently create viral content, MrBeast shared:

> Most of my growth came after I graduated high school. I somehow found these other four lunatics. Three of us were college dropouts, one was a high school dropout. We were all super small YouTubers, and we basically talked every day for a thousand days in a row and did nothing but just hyper-study what makes a good video, what makes a good thumbnail, how to go viral. We would call them daily "masterminds." We'd just get on Skype every morning and, some days, I'd get on Skype at 7am, and I'd be on until 10pm, and then I'd wake up and do it again. We'd take a thousand thumbnails, and see if there was a correlation between the brightness of the thumbnail and how many views it got, or videos that get over 10 million views, how often do they cut the camera angles? We

> were very religious about it. So that's where most of my knowledge came from. I surround myself with these lunatics, and every day, we didn't do anything. We had no life. We all had 10 to 20,000 subscribers when we met, and by the time we stopped talking, we all had millions of subscribers. We all hit a million subscribers within a month of each other, which is crazy.[3]

As you can see, MrBeast and his fellow YouTubers dedicated themselves to daily "masterminds" for more than a thousand days, obsessively analyzing what makes videos go viral. Their relentless pursuit of knowledge and unwavering commitment to understanding the intricacies of successful content creation eventually led them to massive success. Such dedication and attention to detail played a pivotal role in their journey to becoming viral sensations.

While not everyone may have the luxury of investing a thousand days in exhaustive research, fear not. I feel your pain. At Hook Point, we've harnessed our extensive experience and expertise to develop a creative model that reverse-engineers virality across any social media platform. My goal is to provide you with foundational elements of this model, ensuring that you consistently stand out amid the noise and captivate your audience.

Winning Trust with Social Network Algorithms: A Comprehensive Guide

In today's digital world, algorithms govern the visibility and virality of content. These intricate systems, used by social media platforms, determine what content is displayed in our feeds. Here's an in-depth

3 Jeremy Utley, "To Grow Like Mr. Beast, Gather Lunatics," *Medium*, March 30, 2022, https://medium.com/paint-pipette/to-grow-like-mr-beast-gather-lunatics-a2eadf626667.

look at how these algorithms function and how you can navigate them to achieve online success:

THE NATURE OF ALGORITHMS

Social media algorithms are designed with one primary goal: retaining users on the platform for as long as possible. Think of an algorithm as a cautious friend you're trying to impress. A new friend will introduce you to small groups of their friends initially. The algorithm does the same by exposing your content to a select audience first. If this initial audience resonates with what you've shared, the algorithm broadens its reach.

SEEDING: AN ANALOGY

Imagine that you're a gardener planting seeds. The growth of these seeds hinges on factors such as soil quality and sunlight. Similarly, the "seeds" of your content are first "planted" among a smaller audience. If this group interacts positively, indicating good "soil conditions," the algorithm "plants" your content among a larger audience, letting it grow and flourish.

THE GROWTH CURVE: FROM FEW TO MILLIONS

When well-known creators like MrBeast post content, the algorithm trusts its appeal, given his track record, seeding it to millions immediately. But newcomers shouldn't get disheartened if their initial reach is limited. Creating and sharing content that consistently engages viewers can gradually earn the algorithm's trust, widening the audience reach.

REBUILDING TRUST

Cookie-cutter content with low watch time will reduce visibility over time. If your content doesn't resonate with the initial viewers it's been shown to, the algorithm will stop sharing it. Yet, a dip in performance isn't irreversible for your account. By analyzing audience preferences and adapting—meaning creating a new, better piece of content that has mass appeal—you can regain algorithmic trust. Remember, these algorithms aim to optimize user experience. Align your content with this goal, and trust will follow.

THE INTRICACIES OF VIRALITY

Many people believe that virality is a product of luck or a massive follower count. However, the reality is more complex. A large number of followers doesn't guarantee heightened visibility or engagement in today's digital world. For instance, on platforms such as Instagram, research indicates that only about 10 percent of followers might view a specific post.[4] Numerous big brands or influencers, despite their vast followings, often experience a mismatch between their follower count and actual engagement. Their brand's reputation propels their social presence; and due to their widespread recognition, people follow. However, a high follower count doesn't always equate to high viewership and engagement.

On the other hand, social accounts by creators with fewer followers can create content that fundamentally drives their business. Their

4 Susan Saurel, "Only 10% of Your Followers See Your New Post: How to Beat This Algorithm?" *Short Stack,* June 16, 2022, https://www.shortstack.com/blog/only-10-of-your-followers-see-your-new-post-how-to-beat-this-algorithm/.

expertise in social media storytelling results in genuine engagement and a growing customer base.

PAID GROWTH VS. ORGANIC VIRALITY

Organic virality arises when users genuinely engage with and share content. Maintaining a steady organic reach can be challenging, which is why platforms offer paid opportunities to seed your content to new people. But if the content doesn't have inherent appeal, even paid pushes can fall flat. Crucially, paying for promotion on a piece of content that doesn't have the ability to generate genuine engagement might even reduce organic reach in the future. Nevertheless, once your content demonstrates organic success, paid promotions can bolster its impact. For viral content that has reached a standstill, paid promotions can reignite its spread, especially if that content is generating leads or sales.

UNLOCKING VIRALITY: CRAFTING COMPELLING CONTENT THROUGH RESEARCH AND ANALYSIS

The secret to virality lies in creating content that keeps viewers' attention on your content, a skill you'll hone through the research and analysis techniques detailed in this book. It's essential that your content not only captivates but also connects with a wide audience. The more time people spend watching the entirety of your videos and actively engaging with your post via likes, comments, and shares, the higher the likelihood that algorithms will boost its reach.

Navigating the maze of social network algorithms is no easy task. At their core, these algorithms prioritize consistent user satisfaction and experience. For content creators and brands, this means creating content that incorporates performance drivers and utilizes a compelling Viral Format.

Is the Business Driving Social Media, or Is Social Media Driving the Business? Why You Shouldn't Follow Apple's Strategy

Many clients approach my team and me with the hope of emulating content from popular businesses and celebrities. At face value, this appears to be a solid strategy, but there's more beneath the surface. Consider Apple: although they have more than 31 million followers on Instagram, their videos only average around two million views. On YouTube, where they boast 18.5 million subscribers, their videos gather between two and five million views each. However, it's worth noting that many of Apple's YouTube videos, such as *A Guided Tour of iPhone 15 & iPhone 15* Pro, with 31 million views, are boosted with paid promotions. The evidence? It has only 68,000 likes. In comparison, Mark Rober's *How to Escape a Police Sniffing* Dog, with a similar view count of 27 million, has 608,000 likes.

A general rule of thumb is that videos on YouTube should have at least 1 percent of their view count in likes. TikTok, on the other hand, typically sees a higher ratio, with likes averaging between 5 and 10 percent of views. Although Apple's numbers may seem impressive, they're quite modest given the brand's global prominence, especially when factoring in the paid media they put behind their videos. For a brand of Apple's caliber, these numbers are surprisingly low.

Now, it's tempting to attribute Apple's and Amazon's follower counts to their content quality. However, that's not the full story. Their global brand recognition draws audiences to their social media platforms, not necessarily the potency of their content. Understanding this nuance is important for anyone using social media as a growth tool.

Also, companies such as Apple and Amazon invest billions in off-platform advertising. For instance, Amazon's 2022 advertising budget hit a record-breaking $20.6 billion,[5] while Apple allocated $1.8 billion in 2020.[6] This heavy investment undoubtedly impacts their social media traction.

The performance of major brands like Apple and Amazon underscores why they aren't good references for content creators to mimic. These larger brands often apply traditional creative strategies to social media, a platform that demands a unique approach. To truly excel on these platforms, brands should craft content specifically tailored to them, instead of merely repurposing conventional methods. One could argue that their content does little to boost product sales or drive new subscribers. Instead, people gravitate toward these pages out of product love, not content infatuation.

On the other hand, consider the fashion influencer who calls herself Bestdressed. Despite only having 3.7 million subscribers on YouTube, her videos average well over two million views. On Instagram, with 1.5 million followers, she averages around 100,000 likes—the metrics on both platforms surpass Apple's. This difference

---

5 Bradley Johnson, "Amazon's Ad and Promo Spending Topped $20 Billion in 2022, A New Industry Record," *Ad Age*, Feb. 8, 2023, https://adage.com/article/datacenter/amazon-ad-and-promotion-spend-topped-20-billion-2022-new-record/2468861#:~:text=Amazon's%20ad%20and%20promo%20spending,2022%2C%20a%20new%20industry%20record&text=By%20Bradley%20Johnson.,Published%20on%20February%2008%2C%202023.&text=Amazon%20in%202022%20powered%20up,annual%20spending%20by%20any%20marketer.

6 Justin Parker, "How Much Does Apple Spend on Advertising?" Zippia, April 24, 2023, https://www.zippia.com/answers/how-much-does-apple-spend-on-advertising/.

highlights the necessity of discerning why people follow a particular account. Evaluating views and interactions can reveal if it's the content, brand loyalty, or a blend of both that attracts audiences.

Social Media Is a Science: Harnessing Data for Success

In the realm of science, progress is driven by centuries of iterative testing (small, gradual changes or updates to a product based on insights), meticulous data analysis, and accumulated knowledge. But in content creation, there's a tendency to discard the plethora of accessible data, choosing instead to chase after pure originality.

Consider the process of developing a new drug: It's not based on mere trial and error or gut feelings. Instead, pharmaceutical companies follow the scientific research process. They thoroughly study existing medicines, understanding which ingredients have been successful and which ones have failed. Then they use this knowledge to develop winning formulas.

In contrast, when developing content, many prioritize originality in storytelling, believing it will drive their success. Although innovation is crucial, overlooking the vast data bank available is a missed opportunity. But it's not just about numbers. A significant portion of our research-driven model is rooted in qualitative analysis—gathering, organizing, and interpreting quantitative data to reveal elements that are driving performance in content. Although striving for fresh ideas is commendable, many have explored similar concepts—with varying outcomes. As such, we should treat past efforts as valuable learning experiences. The core of our work together will involve identifying content that genuinely resonates with the masses, as well as what falls flat. This qualitative, research-based insight will steer your content creation, empowering your social media strategy with storytelling that captivates the masses. In the digital age, data is invaluable, but understanding the story behind the data is equally pivotal.

Target with the Generalist Principle: Go Beyond Your Core

Identifying a target audience is undeniably essential for any brand or business. However, hyperfocusing on just that audience with your social media content can limit your opportunities when aiming for consistent viral breakthroughs. My goal is to guide you in crafting content with universal appeal. This content can be packaged and framed in a way that resonates with the masses yet retains a subtext and core message that engages and motivates your target audience. Although this strategy may seem counterintuitive to some marketers, it's the most effective approach for consistently going viral on social media. Although succeeding with niche messaging is possible, it can be quite challenging and relies heavily on luck. As a primary strategy for organic social media, I don't recommend it.

As a marketer, your goal is not just to engage existing fans but also to achieve continued growth and attract new fans and customers to your brand or business. This means appealing to those who are already familiar with your brand as well as to those who have no prior knowledge of it whatsoever. By catering to both groups, you can maximize the reach and impact of your content, significantly increasing your chances of success.

Although you may have a target audience in mind, if you carefully examine your current social media content, you'll likely find that the highest-performing content doesn't solely cater to that specific target audience. For instance, let's say your target audience is women aged 35 to 55. If you analyze the highest-performing post that reaches that demographic, you'll notice that its success stems from appealing to the masses. *The key is to create content that can be enjoyed and valued by anyone, without losing the subtext that is important to your core target audience.* By producing content with a universal appeal, you position yourself to not only capture and hold the attention of the masses but also to prompt algorithms to share your content with people beyond your existing followers. This amplification results in heightened engagement, bolstered brand awareness, and ultimately, business expansion.

Neuroscience professor and lab director Andrew Huberman, PhD (hubermanlab on Instagram), is an example of a creator with an extremely niche subject matter, yet he has incredibly high-performing content that often surpasses more than a million views. His success can be attributed to the fact that he has engineered his content to have mass appeal—it can enhance and improve anyone's life—without watering down his expertise. By choosing broad topics such as screentime or sunlight exposure, which hold relevance to almost anyone, Huberman's content garners significant viewership.

Another prime example of the value of appealing to the masses is world-famous podcast host Joe Rogan. If you look at some of his most successful episodes, you'll discover that they comprise interviews with individuals discussing niche topics that typically involve specialized terminology and jargon. One such episode is his conversation with Jimmy Corsetti, an independent researcher behind the YouTube channel "Bright Insight," which explores ancient mysteries and lost civilizations. Although Corsetti might be a recognized name among his fans, the average Rogan listener likely isn't familiar with him or his detailed investigations.

In their episode, they explore Corsetti's theory of the Lost City of Atlantis—a topic unfamiliar to many. Rogan takes the approach of assuming that his audience has limited knowledge on the subject and provides an opportunity for them to learn something new. Although Corsetti's core audience would undoubtedly enjoy the episode, Rogan ensures that it's accessible to everyone. His generalist approach, combined with his genuine curiosity, propelled this episode to be viewed more than 10 million times on YouTube alone. By adopting this inclusive mindset, Rogan successfully makes even the most esoteric subjects accessible to a vast audience.

Going Viral vs. Converting

Some of you may already be familiar with my book *Hook Point*, in which I explained that successful marketing at scale requires you to develop a strategy to grab attention to stand out from the vast sea of content out there. Then, you need to hold that attention by having substance, so that people receive value from your content. From there, you can maximize attention by monetizing it effectively.

Although some argue that focusing solely on virality is not as crucial as concentrating on conversion rates—such as generating sales or leads—it's essential to understand that the goal of the method presented in this book aims to achieve both virality and increased sales. While achieving a 50 percent conversion rate on a video with 1,000 views is impressive, this approach is geared toward reaching hundreds of thousands to millions of views consistently. At this scale, even a modest conversion rate can yield substantial results, as the exposure to a larger audience increases awareness and potential conversions. Furthermore, this expansive reach bolsters a robust retargeting audience for your paid media efforts.

A practical example to support this approach comes from recent data shared by TikTok. This video hosting service highlights the merits of an "always engaged" approach, which combines organic and paid content while engaging creators to help brands realize unique business objectives. This holistic tactic empowers brands to be dynamic and involved on the platform, fostering increased brand affection, recall, and resonance.

Consider these illuminating statistics from TikTok that emphasize the potency of a combined organic and paid content approach:

- **The Power of platform-specific content creation:** 79 percent of TikTok users gravitate toward brands that exhibit prowess in content creation specific to the platform, implying that integrating content types showcases your brand's proficiency beyond just ad campaigns.
- **Doubling up on ROAS (return on ad spend):** When brands combine organic activity with paid media on TikTok, they experience a noticeable boost in their ROAS.
- **Influential creators:** One-third of TikTok users have been persuaded to make purchases based on recommendations by platform creators, suggesting the merit of collaboration with creators alongside individual brand promotions.
- **Escalated brand awareness:** Content diversity can supercharge brand awareness, with TikTok recording a staggering 173 percent uptick in brand top-of-mind awareness after two brand content exposures.
- **Amplified brand affinity:** Post ad viewing, organic content sees a 20 percent spike in brand likability.
- **Boosted brand recall:** Preceding an ad with organic content can elevate brand recall by up to 27 percent.
- **Augmented brand relevance:** After ad exposure, organic content relevance surges by 18 percent, as per user feedback.

In essence, a balanced blend of organic and paid content on platforms such as TikTok can supercharge your brand's outcomes. The platform's users are noticeably more responsive to advertising when they perceive a brand's commitment to both organic and paid content creation.[7] Additionally, the insights gained from your analysis and research on organic social media can be directly applied to your conversion strategies. Most people don't realize that their targeted advertisements need to compete with organic content in users' feeds, just as organic content does.

Focus on Winning One Platform at a Time

My team and I like to categorize content into two primary types: short form and long form. Short-form content usually ranges from 15 seconds to three minutes and is primarily found on platforms such as Instagram, TikTok, YouTube Shorts, and Facebook. In contrast, long-form content, which is typically 20 minutes or longer (with some of the best content extending to hours), is more prevalent on platforms like YouTube.

Prioritizing one platform at a time is key. By mastering content creation on one platform—say, Instagram—you establish a foundation. From there, branching out to other platforms becomes a logical next step. For those focusing on short-form content, our advice is to zero in on one platform for optimization and benchmarking, while also considering cross-posting onto other platforms. To illustrate this concept, if your primary platform is Instagram and you've tailored your

7 Matt Southern, "7 TikTok Stats Shows Impact of Combining Paid & Organic Content," *SearchEngineJournal*, May, 31, 2022, https://www.searchenginejournal.com/tiktok-organic-paid-stats/452577/#close.

content for it, this content can be repurposed and shared on TikTok and YouTube Shorts. It's essential to note that results may vary across platforms, given the distinct consumption behaviors inherent to each. Once you have a solid grasp of your primary platform, you can explore adjustments for other platforms or even consider a distinct content format tailored to each one.

Traditional Approaches to Content Creation Don't Work: The "Commonsense Model"

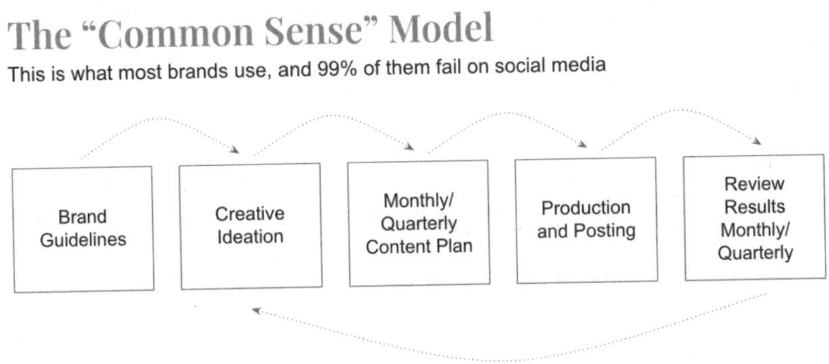

When it comes to content creation, 99 percent of brands follow what I call the Commonsense Model. This widely adopted approach usually starts with creating comprehensive brand guidelines, which comprise elements such as the brand's chosen colors, tone, mission statements, and more to establish the brand's identity. Once these guidelines are in place, they become the bedrock upon which all content creation is based.

Following this approach, marketing teams begin brainstorming sessions for their monthly or quarterly content plans. From there, they move into a production phase, often producing content in batches. For instance, they might curate a series of 20 videos, all meticulously scheduled for release at 9 a.m. EST on predetermined dates over the course of a quarter. Once the designated month or quarter comes to an end, they review the results to assess the performance and impact of the content they shared.

On the surface, this approach seems logical and well structured. However, it often leads to repetitive and stagnant outcomes. The absence of data-driven insights, regular experimentation, and a continual feedback mechanism means that brands often produce content that fails to captivate or engage their audience. This leads to sporadic success that appears more by accident than design—without any sustained growth, improvement, or learning along the way.

By failing to take the time for proper analysis, the Commonsense Model forces marketers to rely on luck. When content underperforms, the initial response is to assume that there's a need for better ideas. But how do you refine ideas if you don't know where they faltered? Was the idea flawed at its core, or did the execution not do it justice? Was the video's introduction lacking, or was it the way the story was told? Without analyzing and learning from each content piece, determining areas of improvement becomes a guessing game.

Instead of producing a bunch of videos all at once, it's better to pace yourself. A smarter creative model involves analyzing the performance of a single video in depth, discerning its strengths and weaknesses, and harnessing those insights to shape the next piece. Although this approach certainly slows down the content production cycle, it encourages a culture of reflection and deliberate creation. It champions understanding audience preferences and prioritizes the quality of content over mere volume.

Prioritizing quality in content creation is crucial, given that the algorithms determining content visibility and popularity aren't swayed by sheer quantity. Instead, they favor user engagement and retention. The longer a viewer watches and engages with your content, the better its performance. By channeling resources—whether it's time, money, or creative energy—into crafting fewer but more impactful pieces, you not only foster better engagement but also position your brand for sustained growth in the long run.

The Viral Content Model

To help you avoid relying on mere luck, allow me to introduce the Viral Content Model, a systematic approach that saves you time, resources and money:

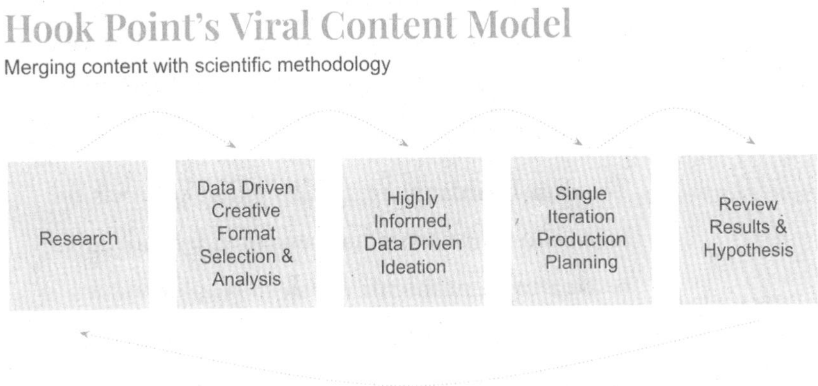

UNDERSTANDING KEY TERMS

Before we dive into the steps in the Viral Content Model, it's essential to familiarize ourselves with some key terms:

- **Formats:** These are video storytelling structures that serve as frameworks into which creators can strategically insert their brands, identities, stories, or ideas. These structures offer a consistent narrative framework, guiding content presentation to resonate with the masses. Top formats offer a versatile canvas for creators to insert their messages and creativity.

- **Performance drivers:** Elements in a video, or their combinations, that specifically influence the performance of a video either upward or downward. Only elements that have a clear impact on performance are considered drivers.
- **Qualitative analysis:** This involves gathering, organizing, and interpreting quantitative data to reveal elements that are driving performance in content. Some examples of performance drivers that we discover through qualitative analysis include:
    - » **Communication Design:** The arrangement of visual and auditory elements of a video in a way that creates a clear and effortless cognitive experience for the viewer.
    - » **Tension Building:** Storytelling that compels the viewer to know what happens next by indicating or creating a problem, which in turn generates anticipation for a resolution.
    - » **Contrast:** The juxtaposition of two or more items that can direct the viewer's attention, create curiosity, or support storytelling. On social media, contrast can be found in the storyline, visuals, or delivery.

    (We will go more in-depth into all these performance drivers and more, later in the book.)

- **Storytelling elements:** These are techniques that creators use to craft compelling narratives. On social media, these elements support traditional story arcs comprising an introduction, conflict, rising action, climax, and resolution. Almost any tactic that supports traditional storytelling can be adapted for use in social media content. Storytelling elements often, but not always, serve as performance drivers. For instance, techniques such as tension, suspense, irony, humor, and subverting expectations can amplify content impact.
- **Video nuances:** These refer to the intricate details of a video, encompassing aspects such as lighting, script structure, story hooks, composition, the attire of the creator, and much more. When particular nuances consistently appear in top-performing videos but are absent or rare in low-performing ones, they can be identified as performance drivers.
- **Tactic:** In content creation, every element that you can see and hear—words, music, visuals, story structure—is considered a tactic.
- **EOV:** The Effect on the Viewer (EOV) refers to the impact that a tactic or tactics have on those viewing the video. It's a performance driver that focuses on intangible yet powerful experiences for the audience. The content moves them emotionally through dramatic storytelling, reversal of expectations, surprise, change of perspective, or an overall "gut punch." Some common examples include gaining clarity, sparking curiosity, or feeling satisfied.

- **Hypothesis:** In the realm of content analysis, a hypothesis proposes that a specific content nuance—whether audio, temporal, visual, or storytelling—has a positive or negative impact on a piece of content's overall performance. To validate a hypothesis, you must compare top-performing (designated as "Gold") content with low-performing ("Bronze") content, looking for consistent patterns. If a specific content element predominantly appears in the Gold content and is absent from Bronze content, the hypothesis stands validated, confirming that the element in question enhances video performance.
- **Gold content:** This category represents the pinnacle of performance within its format, outshining typical results. Think of this as the standout, breakthrough viral content that garners exceptional attention. To discern what contributes to its viral success, we identify and analyze its performance drivers, contrasting them against low (Bronze) and baseline (Silver) performers to spot similarities and differences in performance drivers among these groups. Limiting our analysis solely to Gold content could potentially exaggerate the importance of certain nuances.
- **Silver content:** This tier signifies the baseline number of views that a creator (or creators within the same format) consistently achieves. The number of views for Silver content approximates the value that appears most frequently within our content sample. (In statistics, this most common value is also called the "mode.") We use this mode value rather than the mean number of views to define Silver content because

extremely viral or poorly performing videos could skew the mean, leading to misclassification.

- **Bronze content:** This category denotes content that falls below a creator's or format's median view count. In comparison to their baseline and breakthrough content, the view count for Bronze content would be disappointing for the creator.

That's a lot of information, so here's a condensed list of key terms for your reference:

- **Formats:** Frameworks guiding content presentation to engage the masses.
- **Performance drivers:** Elements influencing a video's upward or downward performance in terms of views, watch time, and engagement.
- **Qualitative analysis:** Gathering, organizing, and interpreting quantitative data to reveal elements that are driving performance in content.
- **Storytelling elements:** Techniques supporting traditional story arcs, such as tension or humor, enhancing content impact. These are often found to be performance drivers.
- **Video nuances:** Details such as lighting, attire, script, and so on, influencing video performance.
- **Hypothesis:** Proposes specific content nuances affecting a video's performance.
- **Gold content:** This category represents the pinnacle of performance within its format, outshining typical results.

- **Silver content:** This tier signifies the baseline number of views that a creator (or creators within the same format) consistently achieves.
- **Bronze content:** This category denotes content that falls below a creator's or format's median view count.

It's crucial to remember that our assumptions about content, formats, and their performance should be treated as hypotheses and not facts. A common misconception is thinking that content featuring cute puppies will automatically go viral. This oversimplification halts deeper analysis, often leading to underwhelming content performance. If the mere presence of cute puppies were the recipe for virality, every puppy video would be a viral hit. This is where the iceberg analogy comes into play: most only witness the top 1 percent of cute puppy videos going viral, missing the 99 percent below the surface that don't make the same impact.

Steps in the Viral Content Model

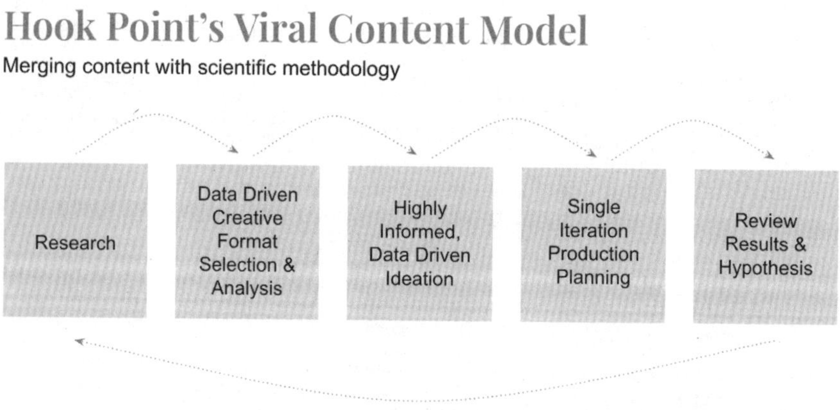

1. **Research:** Starting with preliminary research, we aim to understand the nuances of the social media landscape and spot creators and format directions that hold significant potential and have proven to consistently go viral.

2. **Creative and data-driven format selection and analysis:** Based on our research, we first select a format that shows the potential for success. Then, we delve deeper into the top (Gold), average (Silver), and bottom-tier (Bronze) performers within that format. For example, contrasting videos with two million views against those that have 10,000 in the same format reveals the key distinctions for their varying performances.

   Through a comprehensive analysis of numerous videos, we begin to identify consistent patterns. These patterns serve as the foundation for developing hypotheses about the essential elements that can propel a video to viral status within a particular format. They also highlight elements to steer clear of. With this knowledge in hand, we transition to the ideation (coming up with ideas) phase.

3. **Highly informed, data-driven ideation:** Here, we generate around 20 potential content ideas, based on the format we've identified and informed by what we've discerned about performance drivers within that format. From this pool of ideas, we carefully choose the one with the most potential based on our assessments.

   A standout advantage of our approach is our method of prioritizing and ranking ideas. We've established a structured scale of 1 to 5, where 1 represents the strongest ideas with the most possible chance for virality, and 5 represents those ideas with less potential. Our guiding principle leans on qualitative data (elements that are driving performance in content) and rigorous research, pushing aside personal opinions and preferences. This allows for a more straightforward evaluation of each idea's potential for success. We will dive deeper into the ideation process later in the book.

4. **Single-iteration production planning:** Also, instead of batch-producing a large amount of content, a one-at-a-time approach is adopted, primarily to test hypotheses effectively. The best idea from a list is then selected, produced, and posted.
5. **Reviewing results:** The results are reviewed, and if the video goes viral, fantastic! We can keep creating videos within that format as long as we stick to the hypotheses that have been validated. Moreover, it is easier to come up with new ideas using the same approach because of the deliberate effort that lead to the success of the initial post. If, on the other hand, a video doesn't gain traction, we must critically assess our execution. By comparing our video with a top-performing (Gold) reference from our research, we can determine if our video matches the standards set by the successful reference. If our video *does* match those standards yet still underperforms, it signals a need to revisit our research and develop new hypotheses.
6. **Reiterating the process with new insights:** Every iteration offers invaluable insights, furthering our learning and honing our approach.

Our Philosophy: The Need for a Predictive Approach

Central to the Viral Content Model is vigorous research. We invest significant time in analyzing which storytelling formats are effective and *why* they resonate. All creative ideas must be deeply rooted in research and qualitative analysis. This is why my team and I consistently prioritize quality over quantity. We steer clear of chasing fleeting trends or sticking to arbitrary posting schedules like "Throwback Thursday." Instead, our focus is on critically assessing the performance of each individual piece of content. By doing so, we validate our understanding and application of insights gleaned from research. This feedback is indispensable, directly informing the next piece of content we work on, thereby perpetuating the cycle of research, analysis, and ideation.

The Viral Content Model vs. the Commonsense Model

The Viral Content Model stands in stark contrast to the Commonsense Model introduced earlier in this chapter. The latter prefills a month's content calendar in advance, leaving minimal opportunity to learn from and refine each individual post. In this setup, content creation becomes a risky endeavor, often resulting in a series of underperforming or even unsuccessful posts. What makes matters worse is the lack of insight gained from these failures. On the other hand, the Viral Content Model adopts a dynamic, research-oriented approach emphasizing qualitative analysis, which leads to continual improvement and a higher probability of viral success.

Branding and Its Impact on Performance

Another area where our approach diverges from the Commonsense Model is in the integration of branding. We incorporate branding into our content tactfully, and only after identifying the formats and qualitative nuances that resonate with audiences on a large scale. Additionally, we rigorously assess how the inclusion of branding elements influences content performance.

Initially, our strategy leans toward creating content that's minimally branded to prioritize virality. After ensuring that the content can indeed capture attention and go viral, we then integrate branding elements to evaluate their impact on performance. For instance, if we can generate a million views on a video using a specific format without a brand logo, and then see a 75 percent drop in performance upon introducing that logo, it's clear that the logo is detrimental to engagement. Armed with this insight, we then experiment with different methods of incorporating vital branding elements in ways that don't detract from performance.

Effect on the Viewer: Make People Care

In viral content creation, the primary goal is to discern what genuinely captures and piques the interest of your audience. At Hook Point, we emphasize the elements that profoundly affect and influence the viewer. We term this the EOV (Effect on the Viewer). The EOV represents the intangible impact or feeling that viewers derive from content. For example, viewers might be intrigued by the value promised in a video's meme card (text caption boxes that appear at the top or bottom of a video on Facebook, Instagram, or TikTok).

- However, the EOV should not be confused with a tactic—the tangible method or tool employed in content execution. Tactics include every element you can see and hear, such as words, music, visuals, and story structure. Although these tactics lead to an effect on the viewer, they are not the same thing. For instance, displaying a meme card in a social media video is a tactic. The EOV resulting from this tactic, on the other hand, can vary. Such text can evoke feelings of intrigue, inspiration, confusion, challenge, indifference, or reassurance in the viewer. Without understanding the intended EOV, simply deploying a tactic might not achieve the desired impact. Also, multiple tactics can be used to achieve the same EOV.

To excel in content creation, it's important to align the tactics to achieve the intended EOV. By doing so, creators ensure that the tangible elements of their content (tactics) resonate with viewers in a meaningful and impactful way (EOV). If, during your analysis of a format, all the top videos feature text on the screen but you don't consider the impact that this text has on the viewer, then your observation of "text on the screen" becomes meaningless.

There are various techniques for creating tension, and you can do an in-depth analysis to discover them, but most brands don't take the time. Instead, they use primitive methods or fall into the copycat syndrome, where they see a text box in a high-performing video and assume that it drove performance, when it was actually the EOV of that tactic that created the impact. When brands attempt to replicate the success of top creators, they often borrow concepts from their videos; yet when their own video fails to generate the expected traction, confusion arises. Many don't realize that the success of top creators comes from carefully studying and using storytelling methods that deeply connect with their audience. It's not solely the concept driving their success; the finesse with which the idea is executed is equally as important.

When it comes to execution, you don't need fancy strategies or complex camerawork. What matters is understanding how your content will impact your viewers—the emotions it evokes and the inspiration it provides. Surprisingly, you can profoundly inspire and move your audience with subtle tactics that have an immense effect.

For example, let's look at creator Hunter Prosper, who has more than 6.3 million TikTok followers. He simply asks strangers on the street thought-provoking questions, and his videos average a million-plus views each. Prosper's tactics are quite simple: he captures real people's genuine responses to thought-provoking questions such as "Who was your greatest love, and why did you fall in love with this person?"

What's fascinating is that his videos are technically straightforward, yet they have an enormous impact. He only needs one camera (most likely an iPhone), because Prosper doesn't appear in his videos. Through trial and error, he learned that his presence detracted from the power of others' stories. When, instead, he let the story and the responder take the spotlight, his videos' success skyrocketed.

Prosper also skillfully captures the audience's attention right from the start by beginning his videos with captivating moments that evoke strong emotions in those he interviews. Whether it's a gasp or a glimpse of nostalgia in their eyes, these subtle yet powerful moments draw viewers in, leaving them craving more. As you watch, you can sense the tension in the performance right away, and you care about witnessing the outcome.

EXERCISE: BEGIN THE PRELIMINARY RESEARCH PHASE

Now it's *your* turn to embark on phase one of the research process! Dive into social media platforms such as YouTube, TikTok, and Instagram reels to start observing content that's gaining traction. As you explore, try to identify a successful Viral Format. Remember, a format is different from a trend—formats are reusable storytelling structures for content, while trends are often fleeting and subject to change. To pinpoint a successful format, visit the creator's account of the video that caught your interest. Check if they consistently use that format and have at least five to 10 videos using it with high engagement rates. Take note of any specific elements that captivate your interest and make you want to watch the videos till the end.

Next, explore content that isn't performing well but uses the same storytelling format. To find low-performing content, delve into the profile of a successful creator you come across. Assess their overall content performance numbers, and find videos that aren't performing as strongly as their regular posts.

By actively engaging with social media, over time you'll gather real-time information and gain a better understanding of what works and what doesn't. This hands-on approach will lay the groundwork for your ability to craft content that resonates with audiences and has the potential to go viral.

CASE STUDY: CRAFTING VIRALITY: HOW CRAFTSMAN TANNER LEATHERSTEIN TRANSFORMED INTO A DIGITAL SENSATION

Introduction and Background: Tanner Leatherstein, an exceptionally talented leather craftsman, faced the challenge of competing against established luxury brands. Turning to Hook Point, his goal was clear: educate people about quality crafted leather goods, and immerse them in an unforgettable tactile experience.

Challenge: The task was to carve a niche for a smaller brand, making it a compelling alternative to legacy luxury brands. Although Leatherstein and his team were passionate, they had little experience in the vast landscape of social media. Operating on a tight budget meant that they couldn't invest heavily in paid advertising, so they aimed for organic growth but didn't know where to begin.

Solution: Our team guided Leatherstein through a comprehensive approach encompassing several key strategies:

1. **The core of storytelling:** We delved into the principles of storytelling and authentic marketing, emphasizing the Viral Content Model and the Communication Algorithm (which is detailed in Part III of this book). Leatherstein learned how to captivate vast audiences by leveraging broad psychological patterns and communication styles.
2. **Research and format selection:** Together with Leatherstein, we researched creative-content avenues and identified his core storytelling format: "Is it Worth It?" Here, Leatherstein deconstructs luxury leather goods, such as high-end Louis Vuitton handbags, to determine their true worth in relation to their market price.
3. **Iterative content creation and testing:** We familiarized Leatherstein with the foundational elements of the Viral Content Model. This encompassed guiding him on research techniques, utilizing references, integrating the proper ideation process, and emphasizing the importance of iterative testing throughout his content development journey.

4. **Generalist approach:** To reach the masses, Leatherstein used a "generalist" approach that extended beyond his usual leatherworking niche. His innovative "Is it worth it?" format proved to be a hit, sparking curiosity among a diverse group of viewers. Even those with no prior interest in leather goods found themselves engrossed in his videos, such as when he dissected a Chanel handbag to evaluate its value. This strategy not only intrigued a general audience but also appealed to potential customers deeply invested in the world of leather goods. By focusing on the universal appeal of quality and value, Leatherstein's content became a bridge between leather enthusiasts and the public at large, creating narratives that were universally engaging.
5. **ASMR integration:** Capitalizing on the intrigue of ASMR (autonomous sensory meridian response)—referring to the feeling people get in response to certain video and audio stimuli—we advised Leatherstein to enhance the sensory experience of leather crafting, catering to enthusiasts of both leather crafting and ASMR.
6. **Strong opening hooks:** To ensure sustained viewer engagement, we emphasized the importance of compelling video openings. By suggesting that consumers might be overpaying for luxury brand items, Leatherstein found that his content became widely appealing.

Results: Leatherstein's transition from offering niche leatherworking tips and stale video ads showcasing his leather goods to deconstructing well-known brands' top products led to remarkable growth. This success was not a matter of luck but the result of a deep understanding of storytelling, virality, and human psychology. There was a significant increase in brand awareness, which contributed to a dramatic increase in online sales. Visits to his company's website, PEGAI.com, soared from 10,000 to 100,000 visitors per month. This exposure also led to features in prominent publications such as the *New York Times*, the *Financial Times*, *The Cut*, *Daily Mail*, *Yahoo! Sports*, and the *New York Post*. In addition, Leatherstein has gained a 1.7 million followers across TikTok and Instagram, with an impressive 100 million organic views. The venture has been so successful that he has established a new business to capitalize on the extensive community he has built.

Conclusion: Leatherstein's transformative journey from a novice in social media to a viral sensation demonstrates that extensive prior experience isn't a prerequisite for success with this model. For businesses eager to augment brand visibility and make a substantial impact, Leatherstein's story provides inspiration.

CHAPTER 2

THE RESEARCH REVOLUTION: UNLOCK THE SECRETS TO VIRAL CONTENT

Research is your ultimate superpower when it comes to crafting viral content. Although it may seem time-consuming at first, this approach actually saves a ton of time in the long run. Imagine producing 100 videos with each generating 10,000 views, compared to producing just one video that generates a million views. Additionally, diving into research can be both enlightening and enjoyable. As you begin discovering content that inspires you, and delve into the reasons behind its allure, you'll develop X-ray vision with respect to the mechanics of content creation. This newfound understanding will grant you the ability to shine brilliantly amid the sea of four billion other content creators out there.

Your research isn't merely about counting views, likes, or comments. While quantitative data can tell us if a video was popular, it doesn't reveal the deeper story. This is where our qualitative approach shines. Rather than just asking "How many?," it delves into the "Why?" Why did a piece of content resonate? What storytelling elements captured audiences' attention? It gives us insights into the underlying reasons for a piece of content's success or lack thereof. In this chapter, we'll focus on these qualitative factors, equipping you with the skills to unravel the narrative threads that weave the most engaging stories.

Incorporating Marginal Gains

Our approach reflects that of the British cycling team's use of marginal gains, as highlighted in James Clear's book *Atomic Habits*. Led by Sir Dave Brailsford since 2003, British cycling has conducted exhaustive research to refine every aspect of their performance. This includes enhancing training regimens and dietary plans, improving the aerodynamics of equipment, and boosting sleep quality for optimal recovery. The research and composition of massage gels has also been refined to expedite muscle recuperation. Furthermore, they investigated the use of customized bike seats tailored to each rider's physiology, which significantly enhanced comfort and efficiency during races.

This research-first methodology uncovered numerous opportunities for minor yet significant improvements. Implementing these insights led to incremental, cumulative enhancements, catapulting British cycling from underperformers to world leaders. Their success reveals the impact of disciplined, research-driven strategies.

When integrated into a social media strategy, this principle of prioritizing in-depth research followed by methodical testing and thoughtful application can significantly boost your digital presence.

By adopting a comprehensive research approach that encompasses an understanding of diverse formats and the nuanced drivers of communication performance—both positive and negative—you set yourself up for success in the competitive arena of social media, aiming for your own "gold medal."

Finding and Comparing Formats

Formats are video storytelling structures that serve as frameworks into which creators can strategically insert their brands, identities, stories, or ideas. These structured templates offer a consistent narrative framework, guiding content presentation to resonate with the masses required for viral breakthroughs. Top formats offer a versatile canvas for creators to insert their messages and creativity. For instance, a format such as Visual Metaphor (explained in depth in Part II) can be applied across diverse topics but retains its recognizable structure.

Understanding formats is crucial for organizing your content research effectively. It's essential to compare content within the same format, focusing on clusters with common structural, narrative, or thematic elements. This method enhances your ability to analyze not only the effectiveness of each format but also the specific qualitative components that contribute to their success.

A simple way to grasp the concept of formats and how to use them is by drawing a parallel with movies. The identical three-act structure, or format, is used in almost every film to craft both an Academy Award–winning movie and the worst one you've ever seen. What sets the two apart isn't the structure itself, but rather, the *qualitative components* such as dialogue, acting, cinematography, pacing, and tone. Similarly, in content creation, it's vital to compare videos within the same format to identify which qualitative elements make some stand out over others.

You can also think of a format as a study system. If scientists wanted to do research on how pollution affects rivers, they wouldn't examine lakes, oceans, and creeks. These are all bodies of water, but they're dissimilar enough from rivers that including them would greatly influence and muddle the results. In the same way, funny cat videos and how-to content both appear on Instagram, but comparing them against each other would be pointless and render our analysis meaningless.

Begin by identifying content formats that consistently deliver excellent performance. Look for patterns of success with a single format across various content creators' accounts, ensuring that each creator has at least five to ten successful examples of using a specific format. This approach helps to distinguish formats that are genuinely effective from those that might have been one-time hits or a fleeting trend. Once you've identified such a format, delve into breaking down its performance drivers. Our approach typically starts with format identification, followed closely by the analysis of such drivers.

Cross-industry analysis can provide valuable insights as well. For example, examining how lawyers and doctors use certain content formats can offer perspectives applicable to different fields, such as tax accountants or real estate agents. In niches with limited successful examples, broadening your research scope may be necessary. Such an approach is effective because it emphasizes the context and qualitative elements driving success, rather than focusing solely on the content itself.

Be aware of different baseline view counts for various format types. For example, music videos are wildly popular, and high-performers may receive billions of views. In contrast, fitness videos cater to a smaller audience; perhaps their high-performing content may receive hundreds of thousands to millions of views. In other words, a super performer in fitness content may get the same number of views as a low performer in music content. If you don't take this into consideration, you may incorrectly identify some of the fitness content as low-performers. This misclassification would create a domino effect, causing you to miss key performance drivers in your analysis.

Step-by-Step Process for Finding Formats for Your Research: TikTok and YouTube

To find formats for your content on TikTok and YouTube, try these steps:

- **Keyword search:** Enter keywords related to your field, or even unrelated ones, into the TikTok and YouTube search bars. Remember, you're searching for formats, not just topics. Use ChatGPT and Google to discover additional related keywords. Examples include "Real Estate," "Product Reviews," "Dog Training," "Business Coach," and so on.
- **Identify viral videos:** Focus on videos with high view counts. Visit the creator's page to see if they have more content in similar formats. If the first account isn't fruitful, return to your search and look for another viral video. If your initial keyword doesn't pull up viral videos or creators, try using a different, related keyword.
- **Keyword combinations:** Mix topical keywords with format-specific ones for diverse results. For example, combine

"Nutrition" (topic) with "Challenge" (format), or "Cooking" (topic) with "Hacks" (format).

- **General format keywords:** Enhance your topic searches with these format category keywords that can help you identify popular content structures within your topic area:
    - Hacks
    - Challenge
    - Tutorial
    - Competition
    - Skit
    - Reaction
    - Vlog
    - DIY
    - Explainer
    - Interview
    - Man on the street
    - Worth it
    - Satisfying
    - Versus (vs)

FOR INSTAGRAM

Instagram's search functionality differs from TikTok and YouTube, requiring a different approach to find content formats. Use these strategies to navigate Instagram effectively and identify popular content formats for your use:

- **Use the mobile app:** Search for content using the Instagram mobile app, not the desktop browser, for optimal functionality. Click on the Search icon, type in what you want to search for, and tap Search.
- **Navigate to reels:** After searching, you'll see options like "For you, accounts, audio . . ." at the top of the screen. Scroll horizontally through these options to find "reels" at the end and select it to focus on the reels feed.

- **Checking view counts:** To see how popular a video is, tap on it and visit the account's reels page. Look for videos with high view counts, as they indicate popular formats.
- **Manual scrolling:** Since there's no way to sort videos by performance on Instagram, manually scroll through and take note of the performance of each video. Consider keeping a record for better analysis.
- **Identify repeatable formats:** Watch multiple videos from the same account to see if they consistently use a particular format. This will help you understand which formats are repeatable and potentially successful.

In Part II of this book, I'll reveal some of Hook Point's favorite Viral Formats that you can use to inspire your own content, but for now, keep in mind that there's a plethora of different formats out there—hundreds, in fact. Your favorite content creator probably uses one or two consistently. Once you truly grasp the intricacies of the importance of the qualitative elements that enhance a video's performance through your research, you'll be able to find success within a specific format. If you're feeling a little overwhelmed by the prospect of conducting research yourself, my team at Hook Point offers custom research services for clients. To learn more, please visit: http://guide.hookpoint.com/.

Selecting Creators or Formats to Analyze

To commence your research, begin by choosing either a specific creator or a content format that draws your interest. It's important to focus narrowly, particularly if a creator utilizes various formats. Only analyze one format at a time to maintain clarity in your research.

Once you've selected a creator or format, prepare to document your findings. Identify two to four social media channels that are relevant to your research needs. Prioritize content from the platform you intend to engage with most—whether it's Instagram, YouTube, TikTok, or some other one. This targeted approach will ensure that your research is directly applicable to your intended use.

Copy and paste the content you select into a table like the one below:

Channel Name	Platform	Link
Mark Rober	YouTube	[URL]

CRITERIA

The pages you select should meet these criteria:

1. **Consistent high views:** Content should consistently receive hundreds of thousands to millions of views. For example:
    - *Good candidate:* A creator whose videos consistently get one million views.
    - *Bad candidate:* A creator with one video that has 20 million views but normally only receives 10,000 views or fewer.
2. **Success not based on status:** Avoid content whose success is tied to celebrity, brand identity, or other nonreplicable factors. Consider whether their success is due to

replicable strategies rather than a one-off success or their social/business status.

- You can include brands that use social media to drive brand awareness and growth, such as Duolingo on TikTok.
- Exclude major brands or celebrities like Apple or Lady Gaga, whose identities drive their social media success.

3. **Organic performance:** Focus on content whose performance is organically driven rather than driven by large media spends. Content primarily driven by ads typically has a likes-to-view ratio below 1 percent.

Categorizing Content by Performance: Gold, Silver, and Bronze

To conduct our qualitative research process, we developed a system called Gold, Silver, and Bronze (GSB). To utilize this system, start by identifying a content creator or format. Then, document your observations within a research sheet, for which we typically use Google Sheets. For example, look at the research sheet that my team created to analyze a creator named Dylan Page, who operates the number-one news account on TikTok. **Remember, you can view all resources and videos throughout the chapter at: http://guide.hookpoint.com/.**

THE GUIDE TO GOING VIRAL

	A	B	C	D
1		VIDEO	VIEWS	PAGE
2				
3		Please let me know if there is a soundcloud track or account	7,500,000	Dylan Page
4		191 Mass Shootings In 127 Days… 💔	8,000,000	Dylan Page
5		US is running out of money	8,000,000	Dylan Page
6		Bus Driver Passes out	8,500,000	Dylan Page
7		The UK officially Crowned King Charles Today! 🇬🇧 #coror	8,400,000	Dylan Page
8	Gold	This Is Reportedly Serbias First School Shooting 💔	9,900,000	Dylan Page
9		What do we think about this??	31.000.000	Dylan Page
10		Explosion at laundry store!	12,000,000	Dylan Page
11		Is it worth it or not??	10,000,000	Dylan Page
12		What do we think about this?? #nicolabulley	15,400,000	Dylan Page
13		Komodo dragons venom on pieces of meat!	26,000,000	Dylan Page
14		What do we think about this?!	17,300,000	Dylan Page
15		What do we think about this??	14,000,000	Dylan Page
16				
17		It's the sharks for me!	2,500,000	Dylan Page
18		What do we think??	2,200,000	Dylan Page
19	Silver	Damn well… onwards I guess!	2,800,000	Dylan Page
20		https://www.tiktok.com/@dylan.page/video/715779475720З	2,600,000	Dylan Page
21		What do we think about this??	2,100,000	Dylan Page
22		Which was your favourite?!	2,400,000	Dylan Page
23				
24		Anyone have "germ bomb" on their 2023 bingo card?	1,100,000	Dylan Page
25		Is this exciting or just weird?	1,300,000	Dylan Page
26		Has the uprising begun?	1,300,000	Dylan Page
27		Thoughts & prays are with their families 💔	1,000,000	Dylan Page
28		What do we think of this?!	1,300,000	Dylan Page
29		Is this a step forwards or backwards??	1,200,000	Dylan Page
30		Will Kanye stick to not saying A WORD for an entire month?	1,100,000	Dylan Page
31	Bronze	You can never be too prepared for the apocalypse! AD #z	700,000	Dylan Page
32		Which was the strangest?! P2 in the morning!! #fyp	399,000	Dylan Page
33		No.1 is just too much!	342,000	Dylan Page
34		We believe them or nah?	193,000	Dylan Page

E
NOTES
"Fastinating research shows the human Y chromosone, which essentially makes men.. men. is slowly disappearing" -What does this mean for humanity?
-"Dashcam moment shows the moment a man killed 9 people at a mall yesterday" -Big implications and impact -What happened -Connects to the fact at the end that there was 191 Mass shooting in 127 days
-"It has just been revealed that the U.S. government will hit their debt ceiling and run out of money in less than a month" -Big implications for everyone
-"we have just got some new information about the 13 year old boy that carried our serbia's first mass shooting in 7 years"
-"KSI Finally followed someone on TIkTok, but the only person he followed was me" -Why did that happen, what's going to happen
-"This is why you always need to check your pockets before you put your clothes in the tumble dryer" -COuld have killed the person, major damage
-"This is the excuciating surgery that short guys are gettting to be taller" -What is the surgery, why would some pay that much
-"There are now only 10 minutes unaccounted for in the mysterious disspareance of UK dog walker, Just listen to how strange this one is"
-Takes a boring experiement and applies it to the viewer (implicaiton)
-"This is terrifing footage showing what would happen if you were bitten by Komodo Dragon"
-Africa is splitting apart -Talks about tectonic plates Big implications of future of humanity
"The WHO has just urged a urgent waring of germ bomb aft Sudan invaded" -There is no language about how this would affect the average person -It seems far away and disconnected from my reality -There isn't really a lot of curisosity in what could happen next
-At least 64 people have just been killed in a brutal passenger plane crash in Nepal
-"just to round out the strangest year, alcholchics will be given Ketamine"
-"Kanye West has confirmed he is one of the lads by partaking in no nut november"
-"Today I googeld what are some of the strangest cases of real life xombies -The hook is the potential of a story insteaf of a promise of a story -Ad at the end
-"Here are 5 of the strangest animals you probably never knew that existed" -Not directly applicable
"Today I googled what is the worst prision in the world" Gooc through list of 5
"Today I learned that in 2003 the most mysterious and unexplained remains of a mummified of a six intch tall skeleton was discovered in a ghost town in chile's dessert" -Strange

KEY FINDINGS
Instill in the viewer's mind "What could happen?" (Promise of story) Dylan's top performing content always builds your curiosity within the intro hook segment. His hooks either foster the question of "What could happen?" "Why did that happen?" or "How did that happen?" This in turn creates a promise of story for the viewer. Whereas in his low performing content, the intro of the videos are mere statments that fail to build curiosity and often involve listicles or merely reading out facts of a news story. For example U.S. is running out of money (8M) instills in the viewer "Could the US actually run out of money, and what would happen?", Dissapearance of UK Dog Walker (15.4M) creates curiosity in the viewer about what could have happened to the dog walker. Komodo dragons venom (26M) showcases a shocking visual that makes the viewer ask "why is the meat corroding like that?" etc. Versues the low performers, Thoughts & Prays are with their families (1M) simply states what happened without making the viewer curious. And No1. is just too much! (342k) is a listicle that doesn't inspire a promise of a story.
Big Implications & Directly Applicable To Viewer (Generalist Principle) Dylan Page's top performing content often involves stories that discuss big implications for the viewer or humanity as a whole. The way he frames his stories and stresses these implications often results in making the story feel more directly applicable to the viewer than just any other random news story. For example Africa is Splitting Apart (17.3M) opens up with a line that seemingly impacts the entirety of Africa and humanity as a whole "Africa is splititng apart." This is a huge implication for the people in africa and across the world due to the economy, trade, potential disasters etc. He qualifies this futher and then reveals Africa won't fully split for millions of years as he is talking about tectonic plate movement. Compared to The Strangest Animals (399k) which is a list of strange animals, but the viewer is wondering "Why should I care, how does this apply to me?"
Dramatization Dylan's framing of topics is key to his overwhelming success. He will take concepts that may not be top of mind for many people and find a way to inject drama into these story lines. He will also curate music and adjust his delivery to be more serious and impactful at key moments. This in turn makes the information feel more important. For example in Komodo dragons venom on pieces of meat! (26M) the actual subject is a an old experiment that on it's own is interesting but is not very impactful or dramatic. Dylan frames the video as "This is terrifing footage showing what would happen if you were bitten by Komodo Dragon." This framing makes this experiment directly apply to the viewer and the use of the word "terrifying" adds to the drama as well. Additionally there is a slight slow piano track in the background which helps the further this effect in a subtly way. However in the low performer: What do we think of this (1.3M) the subject is merely framed as absurd instead of potentially having dire consequences. There is also a lack of descriptive adjectives, the script is mostly facts, and his delivery is not very dramatic.
Light hearted personality moment + Connecting with the viewer Most news organizations fail to connect with the average viewer and gain a social media audience because their language, scripts, and overall delivery feel too disconnected and uptight to most people. Instead of the feeling that a organization is delivering this news, Dylan's content feels more like a friend telling us the pressing news we need to or want to hear. Part of his authenticy and why viewer's relate to him is his little bits of playful commentary and adressing what we think or our "head voice." For example in "Y Chromosone disappearing" (7.5M) Dylan cracks a couple jokes in between data and addressing what the viewer may be thinking. He says "Can't we just get through 2023" referring to all the other crazy news stories and the viewer likely being overwhelmed with all the newsworthy events. He also mentions "Not the worst time to be a man!" in a joking manner. These little moments humanize Dylan and showcase his personality which seperates him from many other newscasters.

Within this research sheet, data is categorized into three performance tiers:

1. **Gold content:** This category represents the pinnacle of performance within its format, outshining typical results. Think of this as the standout, breakthrough viral content that garners exceptional attention. To discern what contributes to its viral success, we identify and analyze its

performance drivers, contrasting them against low and baseline performers to spot similarities and differences in performance drivers among these groups. Limiting our analysis solely to Gold content could potentially exaggerate the importance of certain nuances.

2. **Silver content:** This tier signifies the baseline number of views that a creator (or creators within the same format) consistently achieves. The number of views for Silver content approximates the value that appears most frequently within our content sample. (In statistics, this most-common value is also called the "mode.") We use this mode value rather than the mean number of views to define Silver content because extremely viral or poorly performing videos could skew the mean, leading to misclassification.
3. **Bronze content:** This category denotes content that falls below a creator's or format's median view count. In comparison to their baseline and breakthrough content, the view count for Bronze content would be disappointing for the creator.

Note: These tiers aren't tied to specific view counts; instead, they're relative within a format and not across all content. As you comprehensively analyze a format, you'll discover different baseline view counts for various format types, and you'll establish the characteristic view count range for each tier.

When selecting a creator or format for your study, begin with identifying the Gold high-performing videos. Subsequently, investigate the Bronze low-performing ones, and then proceed to the Silver-ranked videos. Your analysis will primarily compare high-performing (Gold) and low-performing videos (Bronze) videos. However, you need to understand the creator's average performance (Silver) to accurately identify these categories. Analyzing Gold versus Bronze videos makes it easier to pinpoint the tactics and performance drivers that result in different EOVs and helps you understand how they influence the videos' overall success. As you gain more experience, you'll become adept at identifying the differences in videos categorized as Silver from Gold and Bonze. However, it is better to start with the more distinct contrasts.

Consider the number of subscribers or followers on the creator's page as an initial metric. Although it's not a definitive measure, it offers a glimpse of the account's reach. Analyze accounts with consistent viral potential, and avoid those with minimal followers, such as accounts with only 30,000 followers, which may not have demonstrated consistent virality. Exercise caution with accounts created by big brands or celebrities, as their popularity may be attributed to offline fame, not the content's quality.

Applying this analysis to your content is possible, but until you experience substantial growth, keeping tabs on other creators' performance is a smart strategy. This will provide insights to refine your content strategy.

In your analysis, closely examine the view count for each post or video within the chosen format. For instance, a creator might regularly achieve between 100,000 and 300,000 views, with occasional spikes reaching 600,000, or even surpassing one million (Gold). In such scenarios, the expected (Silver) range for this creator would be 100,000 to 300,000 views. Additionally, note the content pieces that underperform (Bronze), such as those only amassing 10,000 or 15,000 views. Some creators may consider boosting their content to increase views, but it's essential to understand that top creators typically rely on organic reach and engagement.

Overview of Information to Include on Your GSB Sheet

As you gather your references of videos or posts, you'll organize them into a GSB sheet. Here's an overview of the type of information that will be included on this sheet:

- **Tier:** Indicate which GSB category the video belongs to based on its performance.
- **Video (link, title, and summary):** Provide the URL of the video or post for reference, the title of the video, and a brief summary of the content and its theme.
- **Page:** Note the name of the creator's page.
- **Video views:** Record the number of views the video has received.
- **Notes:** Add any specific observations or notes you have about the video's content, structure, or style.
- **Key findings:** As you dive into videos from each tier, it's imperative to note recurring themes or patterns. Here's a checklist of some elements to look out for; however, keep in mind that this is not an exhaustive list. At Hook Point, we have a library of over 1,000 performance driver key findings to select from, but we typically narrow it down to three to five per format. Here are just a few aspects to consider:
    - » *Common elements:* Are there recurring symbols, characters, or props?
    - » *Storytelling techniques:* Analyze the structure. Is there a specific pattern, like a problem-solution format?

» *Pacing:* Is the video fast-paced throughout, or does it have moments of pause? How does this impact viewer engagement?

» *Tonality:* What is the mood of the video? Upbeat, dramatic, melancholic, or humorous?

» *Environment/setting:* Where is the video shot? Indoors, outdoors, studio, or on location?

» *Opening sequence:* Pay close attention to the first three seconds. What is used to grab the viewer's attention immediately?

» *Lighting:* Is it consistent? Does it vary based on mood or setting?

» *Cadence:* Listen to the rhythm of speech or music. Is it steady or does it vary?

» *Camera techniques:* Any noticeable trends in camera movements, angles, or focus?

A Step-by-Step Data Entry Process for Filling Out a GSB Sheet

Let me walk you through the step-by-step process for filling out a GSB sheet. For a video walkthrough and to download a template of the GSB sheet, go to: http://guide.hookpoint.com/.

STARTING WITH A BLANK SHEET

A blank GSB sheet looks like this:

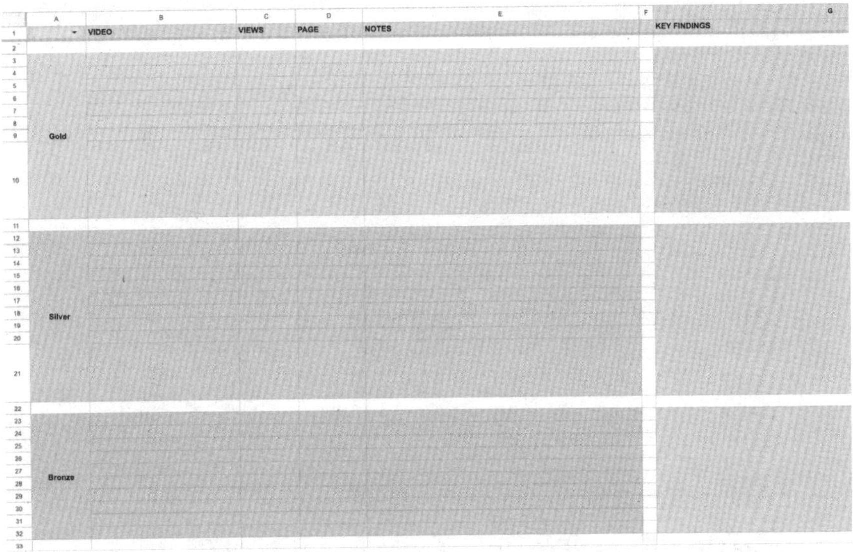

ENTERING DATA FOR GOLD TOP PERFORMERS

Next, from your references, identify and document the Gold top-performing content.

On the GSB sheet:

- Enter the video title in the VIDEO column under the Gold section, and hyperlink it using Command + K (Control + K on Windows).
- Record the page's name in the PAGE column.
- Note the number of views in the VIEWS column.
- Enter the number of followers/subscribers in the FOLLOWERS/SUBS column.

After entering data for Gold performers, the GSB sheet will look like this:

	A	B	C	D	E	F
1		VIDEO	VIEWS	PAGE	NOTES	KEY FINDINGS
6		Roger Federer made $600M Dollars OFF c	934,000	Codie Sanchez		
7		Logan Paul is work 245 Millionaire	2,700,000	Codie Sanchez		
8		50,000 a month from pig farming	1,400,000	Codie Sanchez		
9	Gold	Making 150k study music	1,100,000	Codie Sanchez		
18	Silver					
23					Repeat the same process as the Gold, except here you pulling out the really low under-performers. Videos with noticeably low numbers	
27	Bronze					
32		Refraction AI	13,300	Codie Sanchez		

IDENTIFYING LOW-PERFORMING BRONZE VIDEOS

Next, identify low-performing Bronze videos, and record their statistics.

	A	B	C	D	E	F
1		VIDEO	VIEWS	PAGE	NOTES	KEY FINDINGS
3		How the famous Cake Boss scaled his bus	2,500,000	Codie Sanchez		
4		How this man made $300 million selling ba	1,300,000	Codie Sanchez		
5		10,000 a month naming babies	1,300,000	Codie Sanchez		
6		Roger Federer made $600M Dollars OFF c	934,000	Codie Sanchez		
7		Logan Paul is work 245 Millionaire	2,700,000	Codie Sanchez		
8		50,000 a month from pig farming	1,400,000	Codie Sanchez		
9	Gold	Making 150k study music	1,100,000	Codie Sanchez		
12		MrBeast Pays His Janitor a Million A Year	532,000	Codie Sanchez		
18	Silver					
21					Now you're going to repeat the process one more time--but this field is the typical number this creator regular gets--not the average, but their baseline performance.	
23		Two chess fans created a $100M company	53,000	Codie Sanchez		
24		Gwyneth Paltrow's 250 million company	82,600	Codie Sanchez		
25		Justin Bieber sold his music catalogue for $	63,000	Codie Sanchez		
26		Rolls Royce is Recession Proof	82,000	Codie Sanchez		
27	Bronze	Power Washing: Good ASMR, Great Busin	19,400	Codie Sanchez		
28		This guy is taking on Jeff Bezos and winnin	57,000	Codie Sanchez		
29		95k Jeans	42,100	Codie Sanchez		
30		How to make $525M selling water	61,000	Codie Sanchez		

IDENTIFYING SILVER BASELINE PERFORMERS

Then, determine the Silver baseline content, and document their statistics.

	A	B	C	D	E	F
1		VIDEO	VIEWS	PAGE	NOTES	KEY FINDINGS
2						
3		How the famous Cake Boss scaled his bus	2,500,000	Codie Sanchez		
4		How this man made $300 million selling ba	1,300,000	Codie Sanchez		
5		10,000 a month naming babies	1,300,000	Codie Sanchez	-Unexptected and a little weird -Seems easy -Big number hook	
6		Roger Federer made $600M Dollars OFF c	934,000	Codie Sanchez		
7		Logan Paul is work 245 Millionaire	2,700,000	Codie Sanchez		
8	Gold	50,000 a month from pig farming	1,400,000	Codie Sanchez		
9		Making 150k study music	1,100,000	Codie Sanchez		
10					Now that you have all the references collected, it's time to fill out the notes sections. This isn't a summary, but you're jotting down things you notice, especially the effect on the viewer (suprise, dismay, satisfying, perceptions overturned), tactics (hooks, pacing, music choice) that elicited that effect, and anything else that could be driving or hindering performance.	
11						
12		MrBeast Pays His Janitor a Million A Year	532,000	Codie Sanchez		
13		This Founder makes $10 Million A Year wit	579,100	Codie Sanchez		
14		Yellowstone is making 100 million	407,100	Codie Sanchez		
15		How to own $150M in self storage units	153,000	Codie Sanchez		
16		AeroSmith members 100 Million Guitar Her	286,000	Codie Sanchez		
17		Making Billions From Used Car Vending M	274,900	Codie Sanchez		
18	Silver	Duckweed	216,000	Codie Sanchez		
19		Meal Worms	313,000	Codie Sanchez		
20						
21						
22						
23		Two chess fans created a $100M company	53,000	Codie Sanchez		
24		Gwyneth Paltrow's 250 million company	82,600	Codie Sanchez		
25		Justin Bieber sold his music catalogue for $	63,000	Codie Sanchez		
26		Rolls Royce is Recession Proof	82,000	Codie Sanchez		
27		Power Washing: Good ASMR, Great Busin	19,400	Codie Sanchez		
28	Bronze	This guy is taking on Jeff Bezos and winnin	57,000	Codie Sanchez		
29		95k Jeans	42,100	Codie Sanchez		

ANALYZING GOLD PERFORMERS

Watch Gold performer videos to find common elements among these top videos, noting any recurring patterns or tactics that may contribute to their success.

Document any observations in the NOTES column, or use a separate document if preferred.

	VIDEO	VIEWS	PAGE	NOTES	KEY FINDINGS
Gold	How the famous Cake Boss scaled	2,500,000	Codie Sanchez	-Remeber this show "Cake Boss"? Well he turned his entire business into an automated vending machine bussiness making him millions -Automated -Making millions -Cake vending machines -It makes sense, costs 1,000,00 ot invest in a full service bakery so why not spend 10k-50k to get a vending machine -Intergrating technology to bussines	**Specificity & An Individual's Story** Top performing content is focused on specific stories of success rather than the idea of success in a broad category. In fact, every gold video featured includes a case study based on one person's individual story aside from pig farming video. When the viewer hears that this story is real and is attributed to a singular individual, this promises the viewer that it is possible and the video is not some empty suggestion without proof. For example Logan Paul is worth 245 Million (2.7M) centers around Logan Paul only, not the hundreds of employees behind the bussiness and not the general suggestion of becoming an influencer/creator, and then releasing a huge consumer brand. By discussing Logan Paul, viewers can relate to a story, as it was actually pulled off. A counter example is Power Washing: Good ASMR (19k) where Codie Sanchez discusses the unusal occupation of ppower washing, but instead of covering an individual's story, she covers what she finds so appeal about the bussiness without any proof. Refraction AI (13k), 95k Jeans (42k), Rolls Royce is Recession proof (82k), and Two Chess fans (53k) all miss the nuance of an individual's story.
	How this man made $300 million se	1,300,000	Codie Sanchez	-I just read about a guy who made 386,000,000 selling ugly carrots and bruised bannas -Big number hook	
	10,000 a month naming babies	1,300,000	Codie Sanchez	-Unexptected and a little weird -Seems easy -Big number hook	
	Roger Federer made $600M Dollars	934,000	Codie Sanchez	-One simple but unexpected decision resulted in millions -Big number hook	
	Logan Paul is work 245 Millionaire	2,700,000	Codie Sanchez	-Codie mentions she didn't expect this -Big number hook	
	50,000 a month from pig farming	1,400,000	Codie Sanchez	-She frames pig farming in an absurd and simple process -Big number hook	
	Making 150k study music	1,100,000	Codie Sanchez	-Emphasizes the simplicity -Big number hook	
Silver	MrBeast Pays His Janitor a Million /	532,000	Codie Sanchez	-Absurd salary for a janitor -Promise of a story -Big number	
	This Founder makes $10 Million A Y	579,100	Codie Sanchez	-Seems attainable -Big number	
	Yellowstone is making 100 million	407,100	Codie Sanchéz	-Absurd but doesn't seem attainable -Big number	
	How to own $150M in self storage u	153,000	Codie Sanchez	--Big Number hook -Doesn't seem absurd	
	AeroSmith members 100 Million Gu	286,000	Codie Sanchez	-Unexpected practice -Big Number hook	
	Making Billions From Used Car Ven	274,900	Codie Sanchez	-Unexpected practice	
	Duckweed	216,000	Codie Sanchez	-Communication heigharchy/hard to read text -Different backdrop -Energy doesn't shift much -Doesn't lead with an indiviudal	
	Meal Worms	313,000	Codie Sanchez	-Doesn't lead with an indiviudal	
Bronze	Two chess fans created a $100M cc	53,000	Codie Sanchez	-General/empty promise, "Want to make 100 million like these guys did" versuses "X Person made $Y by doing Z" -Expecteded bussiness practice	
	Gwyneth Paltrow's 250 million comp	82,600	Codie Sanchez	-Doesn't seem attainable for the average Joe -Expected story	
	Justin Bieber sold his music catalog	63,000	Codie Sanchez	-Not attainable -Expected answer	
	Rolls Royce is Recession Proof	82,000	Codie Sanchez	-Luxury companies are successfull during a recession -Doesn't feel replicable, expected for many	
	Power Washing: Good ASMR, Grea	19,400	Codie Sanchez	-No big numbers -Very general, no specificity	
	This guy is taking on Jeff Bezos anc	57,000	Codie Sanchez	-No big numbers -Feels difficult for the average person -Poor audio -Explanation doesn't feature anything unexpected	
	95k Jeans	42,100	Codie Sanchez	-Not focused on an individual, feels too general -While an absurd stat, most people do not imagine themselves at the bottom of the sea seatching for jeans (doesn't seem easy)	
	How to make $525M selling water	61,000	Codie Sanchez	-Story is fairly well known -	
	Refraction AI	13,300	Codie Sanchez	-Company mentioned instead of individual -Poor audio -Story is to be expected, ttech start up	

TESTING HYPOTHESES WITH BRONZE VIDEOS

Evaluate whether patterns identified in Gold videos also appear in Bronze ones to determine if they are significant performance drivers:

- If patterns are found in both Gold and Bronze videos, they may not be key performance drivers.

- Patterns exclusive to Gold videos likely contribute to high performance, whereas those exclusive to Bronze videos may detract from performance.

COMPILING KEY FINDINGS

In the KEY FINDINGS section:

- List the core performance drivers based on your analysis.
- Support each hypothesis with examples from both Gold and Bronze tiers, demonstrating the effect of these drivers on video performance.

This structured approach ensures that you'll systematically capture and analyze performance data across different content tiers, enabling you to identify the qualitative factors that drive successful social media content.

A fully completed GSB sheet with the Key Findings section filled out will appear as follows:

	VIDEO	VIEWS	PAGE	NOTES	KEY FINDINGS
	How the famous Cake Boss scaled	2,500,000	Codie Sanchez	-Remeber this show "Cake Boss"? Well he turned his entire business into an automated vending machine bussiness making him millions -Automated -Making millions -Cake vending machines -It makes sense, costs 1,000,00 ot invest in a full service bakery so why not spend 10k-50k to get a vending machine -Intergrating technology to bussines	**Perception of being easy** One of the major drivers of this format is framing/picking success stories which have the perception of being easy to do. These are stories where Codie mentions what they did, and most people say to themselves "I could've done that." In the top performing videos, Codie often uses the word "automated" a lot, by simplifying these stories with such language, it almost seems like these individuals are making free money. In addition, a lot of the top performers feature **underdog** stories. Whether it be the average Joe that noticed a gap in the market, or somone who came up with an innovation. These individuals don't seem to be perceived as successful or accomplished before their big idea. If it is a well known figure, Codie provides the viewer with someway to let them see part of themselves in the figure. For example in How this man made $300 million selling bad apples (1.3M), the premise is extremely simple and when Codie gets into the story, she mentions that Ramesh was able to buy this produce for "pennys of the dollar" which implies anyone could do something like this with little capital, no need to be rich. On the otherhand, low performers often seem difficult to accomplish and would require a lot of capital and dedication. Take 95k Jeans (42k) which would require you to dive to the bottom of the ocean and stumble across a random pair very old jeans, or Gwyneth Paltrow's 250 million company (82k) which requires a celebirity presence. Another low performer like Two Chess Fans (53k) required a partnership with several people and an intial investment of $50k.
	How this man made $300 million se	1,300,000	Codie Sanchez	-I just read about a guy who made 386,000,000 selling ugly carrots and bruised bannas -Big number hook	
	10,000 a month naming babies	1,300,000	Codie Sanchez	-Unexptected and a little weird [illegible] -Big number hook	
	Roger Federer made $600M Dollars	934,000	Codie Sanchez	-One simple but unexpected decision resulted in millions -Big number hook	
	Logan Paul is work 245 Millionaire	2,700,000	Codie Sanchez	-Codie mentions she didn't expect this -Big number hook	
Gold	50,000 a month from pig farming	1,400,000	Codie Sanchez	-She frames pig farming in an absurd and simple process -Big number hook	
	Making 150k study music	1,100,000	Codie Sanchez	-Emphasizes the simplicity -Big number hook	

12	Silver	MrBeast Pays His Janitor a Million /	532,000	Codie Sanchez	-Absurd salary for a janitor -Promise of a story -Big number	**Specificity & An Individual's Story** Top performing content is focused on specific stories of success rather than the idea of success in a broad category. In fact, every gold video featured includes a case study based on one person's individual story aside from pig farming video. When the viewer hears that this story is real and is attributed to a singular individual, this promises the viewer that it is possible and the video is not some empty suggestion without proof. For example Logan Paul is worth 245 Million (2.7M) centers around Logan Paul only, not the hundreds of employees behind the bussiness and not the general suggestion of becoming an influencer/creator, and then releasing a huge consumer brand. By discussing Logan Paul, viewers can relate to a story, as it was actually pulled off. A counter example is Power Washing: Good ASMR (19k) where Codie Sanchez discusses the unusal occupation of Power Washing, but instead of covering an individual's story, she covers what she finds so appeal about the bussiness without any proof
13		This Founder makes $10 Million A Y	579,100	Codie Sanchez	-Seems attainable -Big number	
14		Yellowstone is making 100 million	407,100	Codie Sanchez	-Absurd but doesn't seem attainable -Big number	
15		How to own $150M in self storage u	153,000	Codie Sanchez	--Big Number hook -Doesn't seem absurd	
16		AeroSmith members 100 Million Gu	286,000	Codie Sanchez	-Unexpected practice -Big Number hook	
17		Making Billions From Used Car Ven	274,900	Codie Sanchez	-Unexpected practice	
18		Duckweed	216,000	Codie Sanchez	-Communication heigharchy/hard to read text -Different backdrop -Energy doesn't shift much -Doesn't lead with an indiviudal	
19		Meal Worms	313,000	Codie Sanchez	-Doesn't lead with an indiviudal	
20						
21						
23	Bronze	Two chess fans created a $100M cc	53,000	Codie Sanchez	-General/empty promise, "Want to make 100 million like these guys did" versuses "X Person made $Y by doing Z" -Expecteded bussiness practice	**Absurdity/Cleverness Element** Absurdity and Cleverness go hand in hand with this format. Cleverness can be defined as something that is unexpected and smart. Absurdity is out of the ordinary, weird, and out of the box thinking. Top performing content in this format often do both. For example 10,000 a month naming chinese babies is unexpected, a bit strange, and yet a smart idea and good example of spotting an opprotunity and ceasing it. This type of content makes you think "Why didn't I think of that!" Some other examples include Logan Paul (2,700,000) where Codie states that he ammassed his wealth by doing something she "didn't expect", This man made $300 million selling bad apples (1.3M) involves a man selling products that "people didn't want" and distributors saw as unsellable. Going against the traditional way things are done and succeeding always presents such individual as clever. In low performers, the actions of individuals is often smart but not unexpected or weird. For example 95k Jeans (42k) and Rolls Royce (82k) both discuss the recession proof business practice of creating luxury products for the wealthy. This concept is not novel nor unexpected, but it is smart. This is not enough. Another example is Two chess fans (53k) where Codie claims "it's one of the smartest plays" but does not talk about the process of what made them different than competitors, rather that they wanted to be the chess company and that they are successful. Nothing unexpected or absurd about that.
24		Gwyneth Paltrow's 250 million comp	82,600	Codie Sanchez	-Doesn't seem attainable for the average Joe -Expected story	
25		Justin Bieber sold his music catalog	63,000	Codie Sanchez	-Not attainable -Expected answer	
26		Rolls Royce is Recession Proof	82,000	Codie Sanchez	-Luxury companies are successfull during a recession -Doesn't feel replicable, expected for many	
27		Power Washing: Good ASMR, Grea	19,400	Codie Sanchez	-No big numbers -Very general, no specificity	
28		This guy is taking on Jeff Bezos anc	57,000	Codie Sanchez	-No big numbers -Feels difficult for the average person -Poor audio -Explanation doesn't feature anything unexpected	
29		95k Jeans	42,100	Codie Sanchez	-Not focused on an individual, feels too general -While an absurd stat, most people do not imagine themselves at the bottom of the sea seatching for jeans (doesn't seem easy)	
30		How to make $525M selling water	61,000	Codie Sanchez	-Story is fairly well known -	
31		Refraction AI	13,300	Codie Sanchez	-Company mentioned instead of individual -Poor audio -Story is to be expected, ttech start up	
32						

The Importance of Classifying Research with GSB

In our analysis, we compare high-, average-, and low-performing content to determine which creative nuances exclusively appear in top-performing content. Simply watching viral videos isn't sufficient; we must contrast them with low performers to identify the similarities and differences between the two groups. If we only watch viral content, we won't be able to determine which elements are driving performance.

For example, imagine we watch five top-performing videos and five low-performing videos in the fitness space. All 10 videos incorporate a trending dramatic song. However, only the five top performers showcase reactions from strangers—bystanders who unexpectedly encounter the fitness activity and display emotional reactions such as awe, shock, or surprise when viewing the fitness enthusiast's abilities. If the trending dramatic song was the sole factor driving virality, all

10 videos should ideally perform similarly, since they all incorporate the song. Yet, this isn't the case. We can infer that the spontaneous reactions from strangers—present only in the top-performing Gold content—play a significant role in making those five videos go viral.

Now, contemplate a scenario where we only watch the five high-performing videos and exclude the low performers from our analysis. In that case, we might mistakenly assume that the trending dramatic song and reactions were equally important.

It's worth noting that, as is typical in research, we encounter outlier content that thrives despite lacking a crucial driver. Generally, we account for outliers by highlighting that multiple drivers often interact to foster success.

For example, let's introduce another low-performing video into our earlier example. This video does feature the "reactions of strangers" driver, consistent with the five top-performing videos. But it lacks close-up shots (another performance driver) that provide clear views of the reactions. Similarly, although key performance drivers might not appear in every piece of viral content, they tend to appear in the majority of cases.

Format Defines Tier

Suppose we're analyzing a hypothetical video with one million views. If this video were part of the larger Omegle Reactions format (a format where musicians engage with strangers on Omegle, a platform similar to Skype for random one-on-one video chats, and then later post these sessions on YouTube), it could be classified as an average performing video. This might surprise you, as you'd think that one million views should place it in the top status (Gold/high performer).

However, our classification is based on how the video performs within its specific format, not across *all* types of content.

In the Omegle Reactions format, which is used successfully by creators such as Marcus Veltri, viral videos often garner more than five million views, with one million views being the average. However, in the context of the "What's Your Favorite Book?" format—one often seen on TikTok and Instagram where librarians and bookstore owners share their favorite books, successfully utilized by creators like D. A. Murray, Joshua Robinson, and Schuler Books—a video with 700,000 views is deemed a top performer. Thus, a video with one million views would be classified as high-performing Gold tier within this format.

How This Works for You

You might believe that 700,000 views, or even slightly below-average performance for the Omegle Reactions format, is an ideal target. However, the goal of this process isn't to necessarily match the exact view count you're researching. Instead, it's about understanding the storytelling elements that drive success for content creators and applying those insights to your content strategy.

Identifying Patterns of Video Performance

Once you've organized your findings into the GSB categories on your research sheet, identifying patterns is the next step. These patterns could be found in elements like the topic of the video, the first three seconds of the video, the design of video headlines, or the thumbnail designs. For example, a common YouTube thumbnail style among all the top-performing Gold videos could indicate a potential performance driver. You should test this hypothesis against the low-performing Bronze videos. If Bronze videos feature similar thumbnails, it indicates that thumbnails alone do not drive performance. This insight would then perhaps redirect your focus to the video titles. When the top-performing videos have common Hook Points or headlines absent in the Bronze videos, it demonstrates that these elements are crucial for driving performance and capturing audience attention.

To see this pattern recognition process in action, let's analyze the YouTube channel Answer in Progress. This channel has amassed more than 1.38 million subscribers and is known for its investigative format, posing compelling life questions and engaging viewers with a mix of on-site discovery, dynamic research, and storytelling that often mirrors the complexity of a conspiracy. Their video *Your City Is Full of Fake Buildings, Here's Why* achieved more than 6.7 million views, featuring a thumbnail with a dramatic facial expression, contrasting colors, and imagery that suggests a deeper story. Combined with a title teasing a conspiracy, it entices viewers into a journey of discovery. In contrast, *The Real Reason Ice Is Slippery* presents a straightforward question with a less captivating thumbnail, leading to a modest 96,000 views.

Further analysis of *I Tried 5 Types of Water (to Find the Best One)* and *Why Japan's Internet Is Weirdly Designed* reinforces these findings. The water video, with its linear and predictable topic, didn't resonate as strongly, achieving 203,000 views. Meanwhile, the video on Japan's internet design, which explores a unique cultural phenomenon, captivated a much larger audience, with 4.6 million views. The stark difference in performance can be partially attributed to the latter video's layered exploration depicted within its thumbnail and title, which implies a story rich in depth and complexity. This is one of the important factors influencing the disparate outcomes.

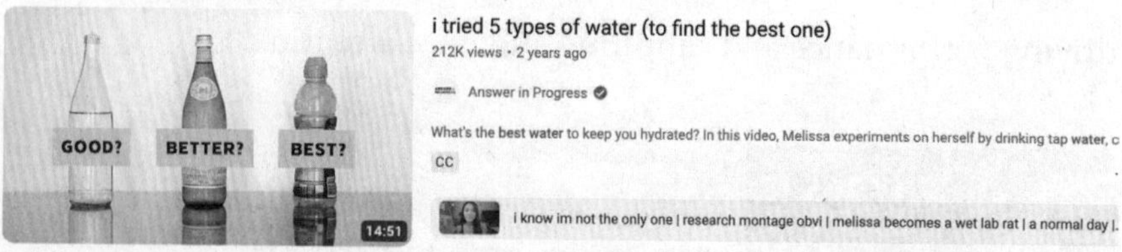

This analysis reveals a clear pattern: High-performing YouTube thumbnails typically include dramatic facial expressions, suggest depth, explore multiple perspectives, and use contrast to create visual intrigue. They pair effectively with titles that ask broad, open-ended questions or make startling statements, prompting viewers to seek answers. This pattern suggests that such thumbnails and titles pique viewers' curiosity, inviting them to participate in unraveling the mystery alongside the host.

Lower-performing videos, by contrast, often lack this narrative promise in their thumbnails and titles, reducing the viewer's need for exploration. They often present the core answer or theme directly, leaving little room for the viewer's curiosity to grow. This analysis highlights the importance of a thumbnail that's not only eye-catching but also complements a title, together weaving the beginning of an engaging story that the video then expands upon. This distinction also points to the value of creating content that invites viewers to join in on the discovery process, fostering a sense of community and shared inquiry.

By integrating these insights, you can refine your approach to thumbnails and titles, adopting the storytelling techniques observed in Answer in Progress. Applying this strategy to new content enables you to evaluate whether a compelling thumbnail-and-title combination significantly boosts viewer engagement and video performance.

During this analysis, you may also observe variations in the look and feel of the video, or the cadence of the speaker. Bronze videos may come across as amateurish, while Gold videos may captivate you and establish a stronger connection with the video creator. Gold videos often incorporate an element of suspense, which becomes apparent when juxtaposing them with lower-performing videos. Additionally, higher-performing videos often evoke curiosity rather than simply offering information, making them more engaging for the masses. You'll also begin to discern which content subjects truly resonate and make people care.

Noticing Patterns across Industries

After identifying initial patterns, it's beneficial to cross-check them with content from a completely different subject area that uses the same format. For this example, let's consider the "Two Characters, One Lightbulb" format, popular among creators such as Mark Tilbury and Erika Kulberg. This format features two characters, often played by the same individual: a novice representing the average viewer who has a common misconception about a topic, and an expert character who clarifies the misconception, leading to an enlightening "lightbulb" moment. If your analysis began with Kulberg's legal videos using this format, you might then explore its use in Tilbury's finance videos. The aim is to discover unique patterns that drive success within each content category.

Although tax and medical videos may perform well by presenting facts and information in an innovative visual style, other content verticals may require a more exploratory and narrative-driven approach. By analyzing different industries using the same format, you gain a more holistic understanding of the diverse patterns and performance drivers across topics. You may even discover that certain performance drivers are universal, transcending the boundaries of specific content areas.`

Understanding Content Potential: Eliminate One-Hit Wonders

When conducting research, it's crucial to look for formats that consistently achieve hundreds of thousands, if not millions, of views. This level of consistent success is a strong indicator of high potential as a place to draw insights for your own content. Even if you come across a video that you like and it garnered 20 million views, further investigation is needed. Visit the creator's profile, and evaluate whether they consistently replicate that level of success with the same format. If the high view count is a one-time occurrence, the potential for using it as a model to help you find consistent performance might be limited.

Leave Your Personal Tastes at the Door

When categorizing content as "good" or "bad," it's essential to clarify that these labels are not simply reflections of personal preferences or subjective opinions, but rather, are metrics grounded in the performance and success of the content, gauged by engagement and viewership. For example, although there may be content creators who don't align with your personal tastes, if they consistently generate millions of views, that's undeniable evidence of a successful content strategy. Our personal preferences shouldn't get in the way of the fact that there's a wealth of knowledge to learn from, based on their approach.

On the other hand, content you love that doesn't garner widespread attention might not be the best yardstick if you want to achieve vast viewership. Most of us enjoy content that resonates deeply with our personal tastes. However, given the diverse interests of the wide viewing audience, the same content doesn't always resonate with everyone. Observing content that achieves enormous viewership should prompt us to figure out why it resonates rather than pass off the audience's interest as mere whims or poor taste. Ultimately, the objective is to discern the patterns and strategies that consistently yield successful content, enabling us to fine-tune our approach.

Cognitive Biases

Assumptions are the beliefs we hold, often rooted in conventional best practices. The essence of analysis, however, is to evaluate the underlying factors that drive content success or failure and understand the reasoning behind it. This is why, when dissecting content, it's imperative to leave space for the unknown and the unexpected, and to challenge our initial assumptions.

Consider, for example, Veritasium's video titled *The Most Common Cognitive Bias*. In it, people are shown a sequence of numbers: 2, 4, 8. Then they're asked to guess the rule behind it. Many quickly think the rule involves just doubling the numbers; so they think of sequences such as 8, 16, 32. But the sequence 1, 2, 3 also fits the rule. The rule is simple: numbers just need to be in ascending order. Most people only see this when they try a sequence where numbers decrease. This is a great example of how we can get stuck on our first guess.

When analyzing content, similar pitfalls occur. It's a common tendency for people to make assumptions prematurely and then not continue to explore further to uncover the authentic reason behind a piece of content's success. Even if you're confident in your grasp of why a particular piece of content has achieved success, it's essential to challenge yourself and continually work to verify your hypothesis.

To truly understand what drives performance, investigate all the underlying factors. Treat your initial ideas as hypotheses, and try to disprove them as soon as possible. When you find a hypothesis that you can't break, you are onto a significant finding, and you can start building content concepts from there.

Tactics vs. Effect on the Viewer (EOV): Avoid the Copycat Syndrome

In content creation, **tactics** are every element that you can see and hear, including the words, music, visuals, and story structure. Although crucial, these tactics alone are insufficient to captivate an audience. Viewers don't engage with content simply because the music was nice, or the lighting was dramatic. Their engagement is much more dependent on the EOV.

The **EOV** refers to the impact that a tactic or tactics have on the viewer. It's a performance driver that focuses on intangible yet powerful experiences for the audience. The content moves them emotionally through dramatic storytelling, reversal of expectations, surprise, change of perspective, or an overall "gut punch." Some common examples include gaining clarity, sparking curiosity, or feeling satisfied.

In content analysis, focusing on the EOV is more crucial than simply replicating tactics. For example, the prevalence of on-screen text in high-performing videos suggests its potential benefit. However, understanding the specific EOV that it generates is vital. Adding text without considering the desired response may not be effective. The objective is to comprehend how top videos utilize text to boost engagement, not to simply mimic their tactics.

My team analyzed Mark Rober's "Watch Me Work" format, where experts share how-to tutorials or skills, and we observed that successful videos in this format generally start with a strategically chosen teaser. These aren't arbitrary clips, but rather, carefully crafted scenes that create a cliffhanger, building tension and anticipation that keeps the audience engaged. The success lies in using the teaser to produce a particular EOV: anticipation.

As an example, take Rober's viral video *World's Largest Jello Pool–Can You Swim in Jello?*, which has more than 138 million views: he begins by speaking from within a Jello pool, then the video cuts to him about to dive in, stopping just before the plunge. This approach not only piques viewers' curiosity but also taps into their emotions, fostering a sense of expectancy crucial to the video's strategic appeal.

Remember, the objective of content analysis is to extract valuable insights from successful content, identify the essential elements driving its impact, and apply those elements to your content to achieve comparable engagement. So, before adopting any tactic, it's essential to consider its potential EOV.

GOLD, SILVER, BRONZE EXERCISE

	VIDEO	VIEWS	PAGE	NOTES	KEY FINDINGS
Gold					
Silver					
Bronze					

To begin, access a blank GSB sheet and view a partially filled-out GSB sheet at: http://guide.hookpoint.com/.

Remember, a fully filled-out GSB sheet will look like this:

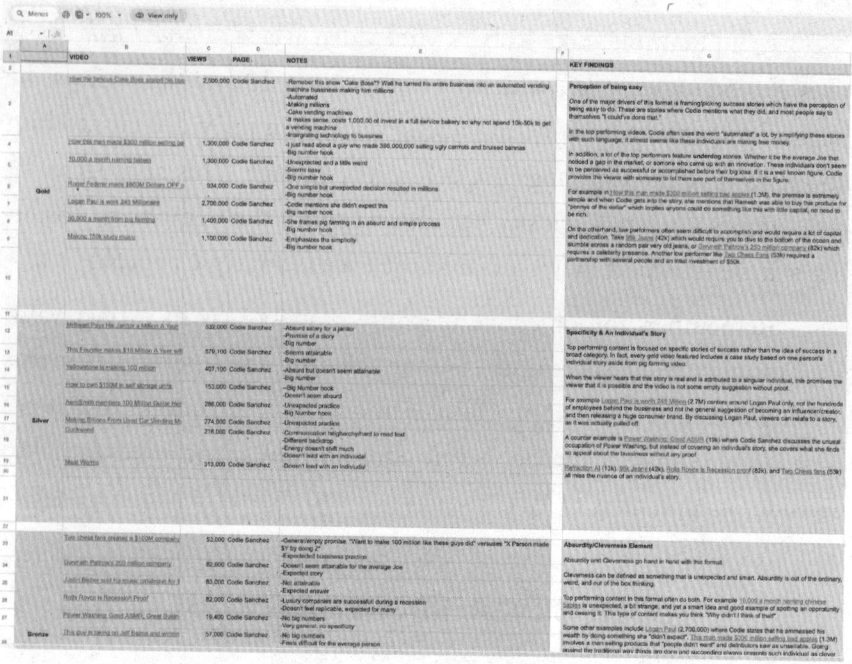

	VIDEO	VIEWS	PAGE	NOTES	KEY FINDINGS
Gold	How the famous Cake Boss scaled his bus	2,500,000	Codie Sanchez	-Remeber this show "Cake Boss"? Well he turned his entire business into an automated vending machine bussiness making him millions -Automated -Making millions -Cake vending machines -It makes sense. costs 1,000.00 of invest in a full service bakery so why not spend 10k-50k to get a vending machine -Intergrating technology to bussines	**Perception of being easy** One of the major drivers of this format is framing/picking success stories which have the perception of being easy to do. These are stories where Codie mentions what they did, and most people say to themselves "I could've done that." In the top performing videos, Codie often uses the word "automated" a lot, by simplifying these stories with such language, it almost seems like these individuals are making free money. In addition, a lot of the top performers feature **underdog** stories. Whether it be the average Joe that noticed a gap in the market, or somone who came up with an innovation. These individuals don't seem to be perceived as successful or accomplished before their big idea. If it is a well known figure, Codie provides the viewer with someway to let them see part of themselves in the figure. For example in How this man made $300 million selling bad apples (1.3M), the premise is extremely simple and when Codie gets into the story, she mentions that Ramesh was able to buy this produce for "pennys of the dollar" which implies anyone could do something like this with little capital, no need to be rich. On the otherhand, low performers often seem difficult to accomplish and would require a lot of capital and dedication. Take 95k Jeans (42k) which would require you to dive to the bottom of the ocean and stumble across a random pair very old jeans, or Gwyneth Paltrow's 250 million company (82k) which requires a celebrity presence. Another low performer like Two Chess Fans (53k) required a partnership with several people and an intial investment of $50k.
	How this man made $300 million selling ba	1,300,000	Codie Sanchez	-I just read about a guy who made 386,000,000 selling ugly carrots and bruised bannas -Big number hook	
	10,000 a month naming babies	1,300,000	Codie Sanchez	-Unexptected and a little weird -Seems easy -Big number hook	
	Roger Federer made $800M Dollars OFF o	934,000	Codie Sanchez	-One simple but unexpected decision resulted in millions -Big number hook	
	Logan Paul is work 245 Millionaire	2,700,000	Codie Sanchez	-Codie mentions she didn't expect this -Big number hook	
	50,000 a month from pig farming	1,400,000	Codie Sanchez	-She frames pig farming in an absurd and simple process -Big number hook	
	Making 150k study music	1,100,000	Codie Sanchez	-Emphasizes the simplicity -Big number hook	
Silver	MrBeast Pays His Janitor a Million A Year	532,000	Codie Sanchez	-Absurd salary for a janitor -Promise of a story -Big number	**Specificity & An Individual's Story** Top performing content is focused on specific stories of success rather than the idea of success in a broad category. In fact, every gold video featured includes a case study based on one person's individual story aside from pig farming video. When the viewer hears that this story is real and is attributed to a singular individual, this promises the viewer that it is possible and the video is not some empty suggestion without proof. For example Logan Paul is worth 245 Million (2.7M) centers around Logan Paul only, not the hundreds of employees behind the bussiness and not the general suggestion of becoming an influencer/creator, and then releasing a huge consumer brand. By discussing Logan Paul, viewers can relate to a story, as it was actually pulled off. A counter example is Power Washing: Good ASMR (19k) where Codie Sanchez discusses the unusal occupation of Power Washing, but instead of covering an individual's story, she covers what she finds so appeal about the bussiness without any proof. Refraction AI (13k), 95k Jeans (42k), Rolls Royce is Recession proof (82k), and Two Chess fans (53k) all miss the nuance of an individual's story.
	This Founder makes $10 Million A Year wit	579,100	Codie Sanchez	-Seems attainable -Big number	
	Yellowstone is making 100 million	407,100	Codie Sanchez	-Absurd but doesn't seem attainable -Big number	
	How to own $150M in self storage units	153,000	Codie Sanchez	--Big Number hook -Doesn't seem absurd	
	AeroSmith members 100 Million Guitar He	286,000	Codie Sanchez	-Unexpected practice -Big Number hook	
	Making Billions From Used Car Vending Ma	274,900	Codie Sanchez	-Unexpected practice	
	Duckweed	216,000	Codie Sanchez	-Communication heigharchy/hard to read text -Different backdrop -Energy doesn't shift much -Doesn't lead with an indiviudal	
	Meal Worms	313,000	Codie Sanchez	-Doesn't lead with an individual	
Bronze	Two chess fans created a $100M company	53,000	Codie Sanchez	-General/empty promise. "Want to make 100 million like these guys did" versuses "X Person made $Y by doing Z" -Expecteded bussiness practice	**Absurdity/Cleverness Element** Absurdity and Cleverness go hand in hand with this format. Cleverness can be defined as something that is unexpected and smart. Absurdity is out of the ordinary, weird, and out of the box thinking. Top performing content in this format often do both. For example 10,000 a month naming chinese babies is unexpected, a bit strange, and yet a smart idea and good example of spotting an opprotunity and ceasing it. This type of content makes you think "Why didn't I think of that" Some other examples include Logan Paul (2,700,000) where Codie states that he ammassed his wealth by doing something she "didn't expect". This man made $300 million selling bad apples (1.3M) involves a man selling products that "people didn't want" and distributors saw as unsellable. Going against the traditional way things are done and succeeding always presents such individual as clever
	Gwyneth Paltrow's 250 million company	82,600	Codie Sanchez	-Doesn't seem attainable for the average Joe -Expected story	
	Justin Bieber sold his music catalogue for $	83,000	Codie Sanchez	-Not attainable -Expected answer	
	Rolls Royce is Recession Proof	82,000	Codie Sanchez	-Luxury companies are successfull during a recession -Doesn't feel replicable, expected for many	
	Power Washing: Good ASMR, Great Busin	19,400	Codie Sanchez	-No big numbers -Very general, no specificity	
	This guy is taking on Jeff Bezos and winnin	57,000	Codie Sanchez	-No big numbers -Feels difficult for the average person	

CREATING YOUR GSB SHEET

Now, let's start by creating your GSB sheet for a top creator in your niche. Focus your initial analysis on creators averaging around one million views. Although those attaining an average of 50,000 views might still offer value, homing in on industry leaders—even if their brand or offerings diverge from yours—unveils potent formats that could propel your content to virality. Realize that achieving consistent viral hits without relying on a tried-and-true format is a steep uphill battle.

KEEPING TRACK OF YOUR DISCOVERIES

Organize your findings using tools such as Excel or Google Sheets, or the blank GSB sheet provided above.

UNDERSTANDING YOUR COLUMNS

When filling out your GSB research sheet, include the following:

- **Video:** Insert a link to the video.
- **Views:** Record the number of views received by the video.
- **Page:** Write down the name of the creator's page.
- **Notes:** Describe the content briefly, including the name and a summary, if needed. An example of a summary is as follows: "Video contrasts a novice character earning $80,000 annually to an expert earning the same but with fewer work hours, ending with a website call to action." Also document specific tactics and observations, and whether they pertain to visual techniques or narrative nuances. This could encompass details from lighting strategies, character interplay, and specific typographical elements.

For example, you might notice how a video strategically uses color contrast to distinguish and amplify distinct messages from different characters. A potential observation could read: "The video employs depth differentiation between the character and the background, utilizing two contrasting colors for text accompanied by emojis. A ring light enhances the lighting, providing clarity. The narrative direction of the video makes the expert's perspective appear both appealing and easily achievable. A noteworthy contrast is drawn between the salaries of the two characters, emphasizing the vast disparity in the effort expended by the novice and expert."

- **Key findings:** This column is central to your analysis. From here, you can draw hypotheses about performance drivers. One of the primary focuses should be on understanding the EOV to identify patterns contributing to a format's success.

Top-performing content frequently incorporates tactics such as teasers, captions, and unique script structures. It's essential not only to identify these tactics but also to understand their impact on audiences, or the EOV. By grasping the core reasons a specific tactic, such as a caption or teaser, resonates with viewers, you can craft content that channels similar emotions in your distinct style, avoiding mere imitation.

It's worth noting that our initial response to content is emotional; it's about how it makes us feel. Yet, during analysis, the focus often shifts predominantly to tactics. Bridging this divide—melding emotional resonance with tactical insight—is crucial in your research.

Some of the key performance drivers influencing success can be "cleverness," "absurdity," "contrast," "making complex topics seem easy," and "leaving viewers wanting more." When you see patterns emerging in top-performing content, it's imperative to thoroughly examine how these elements work—understanding their structure and impact—to effectively apply them in your own content strategies.

To provide clarity, here are a few common examples from our analysis of different formats to guide you in filling out the "Key findings" column:

- **Cleverness:** Cleverness intertwines the smart with the unexpected to create a multilayered impact. Keep in mind the formula: clever = smart + unexpected. Practical applications:

a. *Clever process:* Use dynamic visual metaphors to breathe new life into well-worn topics. When revisiting standard procedures, weave in unexpected elements or rare combinations that intrigue and surprise. For example, consider the use of crumpled paper in a wastebasket to represent trauma, as seen in Dr. Julie's *The Trauma Basket*, which has garnered more than 7.6 million views. Another example can be found in *Hot Ones* interviews, where guests face the challenge of answering questions while eating chicken wings with super-hot sauce.

b. *Clever ideas:* Steer clear of rehashing known content. Brainstorm fresh perspectives on familiar subjects, or ingeniously repurpose everyday items. Link unrelated concepts in novel ways that spark curiosity and insight. For instance, conventional videography techniques can cleverly focus on mundane objects like a spoon or a crumb. An example of this is seen in Grace Wells' *A Very Crummy Commercial*, which has garnered more than 22.4 million views.

c. *Parodies:* Select familiar, topical material for parodies. Exaggerate features to highlight underlying contradictions or absurdities, and balance humor with commentary to craft satire that entertains while it critiques—for example, the *This Is a Generic Brand Video* by Dissolve, which has garnered more than 2.9 million views, effectively demonstrates the company's stock footage library. It critiques the standard business video format while playfully emphasizing Dissolve's distinctive selling points.

- **Absurdity:** Engaging an audience can be achieved through the unexpected and illogical. Absurdity creates a distinctive and memorable experience. Absurd situations are characterized by their nonsensical, peculiarly specific, bizarre, inappropriate, unreasonable, or silly nature, often combining elements that would not normally be seen together. Examples include:

    a. *Novel scenarios:* Content that introduces unusually specific tasks or challenges, such as Areyoukiddingtv's video titled Yes, *Microwaved Is Acceptable* with more than 51.7 million views, which asks students to deliver cooked mac-n-cheese, toss a book, and pour apple juice on themselves. The sheer oddity of these requests commands attention and piques curiosity.

    b. *Provoking genuine reactions:* Absurdity can elicit authentic reactions, as seen in ThatWasEpic's video titled *Cutting People's Earphones, Then Giving Them Airpods,* with more than 53 million views, which features a prank that involves cutting a person's headphone cords. The viewer gets a candid glimpse of the person's emotions, from confusion to shock, providing a raw and engaging experience.

    c. *Escapism through content:* Absurd videos serve as a portal away from the routine, offering viewers an unusual experience that they eagerly consume during their daily scrolls. This can be a potent tool for creators to captivate and maintain an audience's focus.

- **Contrast:** Contrast serves as a dominant driver in video content, whether it's embedded within the concept or exhibited in its presentation. Examples include:
    a. *Scenario contrasts:* Imagine two individuals boasting the same income but their work dynamics are poles apart—one might be entangled in a nine-to-five office routine, while the other enjoys flexibility, working just a few hours from the comfort of home.
    b. *Visual contrasts:* Take a culinary scene where one dish is presented as a gourmet delight, and its counterpart appears bland and uninviting.
    c. *Reality vs. perception:* This could be the contrast drawn between prevailing myths and actual facts, such as demystifying the home-buying process by distinguishing between popular beliefs about financial prerequisites and the real conditions.
- **Make it seem easy:** Top-performing creators have a knack for distilling complex solutions or ideas into easily digestible content. Their approach:
    a. *Simplicity over complexity:* Rather than bombarding viewers with intricate details, they prioritize clarity

and conciseness, ensuring that the information remains valuable.

b. *Showcasing achievability:* By demonstrating that they've reached their goals through uncomplicated means, they inspire viewers to believe that they can do the same.

c. *Effective messaging:* Utilizing relatable phrases can drive home the point. Statements such as "You can still eat more food," "Food doesn't have to be bland," or "You don't need 40,000, just an FHA loan and 7,000," resonate by stripping away the jargon and speaking directly to viewer needs and desires.

- **Leave viewers wanting more:** Effective creators harness the power of curiosity, offering just enough to entice viewers while holding back to maintain intrigue. Their strategies include:

  a. *Teasing future content:* By presenting a fascinating idea without fully unpacking it, creators set the stage for follow-up content, be it a "Part 2" or subsequent episodes.

  b. *Promoting further engagement:* Encouraging viewers to subscribe or follow ensures that they remain in the loop for future content, bolstering platform engagement.

  c. *Highlighting tangible benefits:* Stating specific, desirable outcomes such as "Work from home for 15 minutes a week" or "Enjoy tastier food without breaking the bank" creates a compelling incentive for viewers to return and learn more.

Over time, recognizing these patterns will become second nature, and you won't need to meticulously document each detail. With practice, you'll develop an intuitive sense of what drives the EOV within seconds of watching a video. Although it may initially seem like a lot of work, the more time you invest in the beginning, the easier it will become in the long run.

If, however, you're feeling overwhelmed, you're not alone. Navigating the complexities of doing social media research can be challenging, and it's perfectly normal to seek help. Hook Point works with brands and creators to tailor research specifically for their subject matter and social media goals. For expert guidance without the heavy lifting, discover how we can help at: http://guide.hookpoint.com/.

The key is to focus on identifying high-level concepts and patterns that provide insights into the storytelling elements that work and those that don't. By honing your ability to recognize these patterns, you can streamline your analysis process and make more informed creative decisions. Ensure that you have enough references to draw from when making such decisions. These references can range from a single source to hundreds of examples—whatever amount you need to formulate clear hypotheses and draw actionable conclusions.

CASE STUDY: HOOK POINT ASSISTS HAND SURGEON ERIN NANCE, MD, IN ACHIEVING SOCIAL MEDIA SUCCESS

Introduction: Dr. Erin Nance, a distinguished hand surgeon with a thriving private practice, aimed to highlight her expertise in reality TV through her media company Hands on Media, and to secure a publishing deal for her book. To enhance her viewership and broaden her social media influence, she collaborated with Hook Point.

Background: At the beginning of her digital journey, Nance had no social media presence. Starting from scratch with zero followers and no experience, she faced the daunting task of creating engaging hand surgery content. In the early stages, her videos barely crossed the 500-view mark. But her determination and perseverance paved the way for the growth that followed.

Challenge:. The primary challenge was creating engaging content that highlighted Nance's expertise in hand surgery, designed to go viral and captivate the masses while also boosting her digital visibility.

Solution: In a combined effort, Nance and our team pinpointed the shortcomings in her initial content strategy. We introduced her to a detailed content analysis methodology and strategies for maximizing audience engagement, emphasizing the techniques elaborated in the Viral Content Model. Specifically, we guided Nance to utilize the major communication styles (which you'll learn about in Part III of this book) to create dramatized videos. These videos narrate real moments she experienced as a doctor and fascinating tales from medical literature, serving the dual purpose of entertaining and educating the viewer. Collaboratively, we refined her video presentations to not only reflect her expertise but also to resonate authentically with viewers.

Results: In just a few months, Nance witnessed transformative results. Her videos amassed more than 100 million views, 10 million likes on her content, and her follower count surged to over 700,000. This newfound visibility established her as a leading voice in the field of hand surgery. Several of her videos—each attracting more than 2.5 million views—have propelled her growth, opening doors to new opportunities such as keynote speaking engagements, her first book deal, and discussions with producers about turning her insights into a TV show. Attributing her digital ascent to the combined insights and collaboration, Nance firmly believes in the power of persistence, experimentation, and continual learning in the realm of social media.

In the next chapter, we will delve further into refining your content analysis skills.

CHAPTER 3

THE SUBTLE SCIENCE: THE POWER OF PRECISION IN CONTENT ANALYSIS

In the realm of content analysis, sharpening your ability to understand and evaluate content becomes your secret weapon. This chapter is all about giving you the tools to analyze the content you come across on social media, helping you figure out what works and what doesn't when it comes to getting attention and engagement.

By sharpening your analytical abilities, you'll start to notice the tactics to avoid and the subtle nuances to incorporate into your content strategy. This newfound awareness will empower you to make informed decisions about the direction of your content, ultimately making it more impactful and effective.

Remember, the key lies in your ability to discern between what truly works and what falls flat. Get ready to boost your understanding and fine-tune your content game like never before. Let's dive in and discover the magic behind great content!

Recognizing Performance Drivers

Our brains naturally seek patterns and simplifications to make sense of the world. Imagine frequenting a cozy diner every morning at 8 a.m. You receive excellent service and delicious food from the same friendly staff. Naturally, your experience prompts you to leave a stellar five-star review for this diner based on your positive experiences.

While writing your Google review, you discover a two-star rating, and you're surprised. After some reflection, you realize that your positive experience is specific to the fact that you visit during less crowded hours. As the place gets busier, the quality of service drops due to fewer staff members. This scenario shows how our personal experiences shape our conclusions.

Similarly, when analyzing a piece of content, we often rely on our own experiences and draw conclusions through the lens of what we've seen before. Yet, it's essential to refrain from making hasty judgments based solely on the success of a single video, even if it racks up 20 million views.

Instead, we should broaden our perspective and examine a diverse range of top- and bottom-performing content. Performance drivers—the pivotal factors that influence a video's success or failure in terms of views, watch time, and engagement—often diverge from our initial assumptions. They emerge from objective analysis rather than our personal experiences. By adopting this approach, we gain a deeper understanding of the true drivers that steer content toward success.

Common Downward Performance Drivers

Before we move on to exploring effective upward performance drivers, let's first take a closer look at the typical missteps that often lead to unsatisfactory results. With years of research and analysis under our belt, my team and I have identified several common factors that consistently hinder performance. By recognizing and avoiding these practices, you can steer clear of these pitfalls and position yourself for success. Here are four of the most frequently observed downward performance drivers:

1. **Overt branding:** The traditional thought process involved in focusing on color, palettes, typefaces, and consistency stemming from traditional media doesn't translate well to social media platforms. In the past, when advertisements appeared infrequently in magazines, branding played a crucial role in creating memorability. However, social media operates differently. On social media, users are constantly exposed to a vast amount of content, and their consumption is often passive. So, while rigid branding may appeal to a marketing manager, it doesn't usually resonate with social media users. Viewers don't care about your branding; in fact, noticing that your content is branded will deter viewers. No one ever logs on to social media thinking, *I want to engage with a great branded piece of content.*

   Today, with all the content that is available on social media, most people have become professional content consumers—they have a sixth sense about whether there's an underlying agenda or excessive branding. And yet, many of the most successful corporations in the world make the mistake of failing to notice this and adapt their content to the social media landscape. Even a renowned company such as Starbucks, with its widespread brand awareness, still feels the need to constantly emphasize its logo.

This strikes me as somewhat perplexing, since we're already exposed to the Starbucks logo almost every day, simply by driving around. However, everything they create on social media remains fixated on their brand and logo. This singular focus prevents them from implementing strong narrative structures. They're unable to explore new creative avenues because they're consumed by their brand identity.

2. **Focusing on high production value:** High production value doesn't automatically correlate to success on social media platforms. In many cases, the quality of production elements—such as video resolution, audio clarity, or lighting—is not the primary driver of success or failure. Surprisingly, content created with more modest means often steals the limelight in terms of views and engagement that truly matters.

   Let's take a look: Adidas, a major player with 26 million followers, posts a video centered around the Adidas Adizero shoe: (remember all videos and resources in this chapter can be viewed at: http://guide.hookpoint.com/), and lands a mere 90,000 views. Then, Harrison Nevel, a less-recognized figure with around 44,000 followers, amasses 994,000 views on his shoe-promo video, *Levitating Shoe*.

Adidas's video features beautiful visuals, polished graphics, and well-crafted music. Undoubtedly, a considerable budget was invested in its creation. Yet, despite the finesse and money put into it, the video underperformed, receiving limited viewership and minimal engagement. A closer look reveals that the video is a montage, a visual spectacle that's challenging to understand or connect with when the sound is muted. This greatly works against the video's effectiveness when you consider that approximately 60 percent of users on Instagram and Facebook watch videos without audio.

In contrast, Nevel's video features audio that's overshadowed by loud music, is shot on an iPhone, and has lighting that is less than ideal. But these production limitations don't matter, as the content itself is so compelling. The focus shifts from production value to the value of the content itself. Nevel creates a mesmerizing shoe display that gives off the illusion of the footwear floating and spinning in the air. It's not just visually appealing; it serves a purpose too. Ultimately, Nevel's authenticity trumps Adidas's flashy and heavily branded content.

Nevel's video is also able to grab attention without audio. The easy-to-follow visuals instantly spark curiosity. There's no mystery about the story being told. The communication is linear, and it hooks viewers—and these are drivers that are way more significant than production value.

When communicating your message, it's important to strike a balance between conveying information and providing entertainment value. Many companies mistakenly prioritize high production value, resulting in visually stunning content that fails to elicit a meaningful response from the audience beyond surface-level admiration. The real goal should be to create content that genuinely resonates with people and makes them want to watch.

3. **Using stock imagery:** Stock imagery and video can be an instant turnoff for viewers because it lacks authenticity and conveys a sense of corporate branding. Many brands fall into the trap of using stock content as a cop-out, not investing the necessary effort to differentiate their visuals. However, there's a caveat here. When stock imagery is incorporated into a larger piece of content, such as a vlogumentary or a deep dive, it can help people visualize certain topics and make the video more dynamic. Additionally, when used in an ironic or self-aware manner, stock imagery can also have its place. But generally, people can easily recognize stock photos, and they're uninterested in such generic visuals. It's recommended to prioritize creating unique, original visuals that resonate with your audience over relying heavily on stock materials.
4. **Maintaining consistency and standardizing content:** The idea behind curating a visually appealing grid on social media pages, particularly on Instagram, has led many individuals to meticulously organize their photos, sometimes creating composite images using multiple squares. However, this emphasis on an attractive grid often overlooks the significance of context and engagement. When a single image from such a grid appears in a social media feed, it can feel disjointed and fail to drive

traffic to your page. In fact, posting such images typically leads to poor performance and weakens your standing with the algorithms. Instead, each image that you post should have the ability to stand out individually and actively encourage engagement.

Similarly, efforts to standardize the look and feel of images—a trend often seen on interior design pages—might lead to a cohesive visual aesthetic but rarely produces high-performing content. Once again, placing an emphasis on quality content and relevance, and fostering a connection with the audience, will ultimately generate more positive outcomes than solely prioritizing visually appealing posts. Only after identifying the right performance drivers and mastering performance within a specific format should you consider standardizing elements.

Top-Five Upward Performance Drivers

Now, let's examine the top-five upward performance drivers. Remember, a performance driver represents the elements in a video or combinations of certain elements that specifically influence a video's views, watch time, and positive engagement. It's important to note that these are the most common drivers that my team and I have identified, not a comprehensive list of all performance drivers. This entire system is designed to help you uncover numerous upward performance drivers as you analyze content. However, understanding the ones most frequently observed will assist you in integrating them into your own content and in identifying other influential factors.

1. Cleverness

Cleverness is the interplay between the unexpected and the intelligent. It is demonstrated by creators who connect seemingly unrelated ideas in a way that is both logical and innovative. This often results in novel concepts that captivate attention. A useful formula to remember is: unexpected + smart = clever. Cleverness involves engaging the audience with witty language or ideas, creating memorable experiences that defy expectations, and eliciting the reaction, "Why didn't I think of that?"

Leveraging cleverness effectively often requires a deep understanding of the subject and a creative approach to problem-solving. By coherently and logically linking two unrelated concepts, content creators can grab their audience's attention and prompt them to see a topic in a new light.

For example, consider creators who demonstrate clever process shots while filming commercials for mundane objects. Grace Wells, in her TikTok Spoon commercial, with more than 7.4 million views, orchestrates an aha moment by cleverly combining disparate objects and imagery to produce a witty outcome.

Another instance can be found in Planet Money's approach to making finance entertaining: *It's Not One Big Percent, It's a Bunch of Little Brackets with Their Own Percents*, which garnered more than two million views on TikTok, transforming something as mundane as tax brackets into compelling content.

Musicians are also known to embrace cleverness, turning unexpected sources into catchy tunes. For instance, DanTDM took game sounds from Minecraft and turned them into a catchy song in his video *I Made a Song in Minecraft!*, garnering more than 7.3 million views.

Although cleverness can be challenging to teach or learn, recognizing it often comes naturally. These moments showcase a creator's ingenuity and quick-wittedness in linking diverse images, ideas, or thoughts. This driver almost invariably indicates a positive impact on content performance.

2. Absurdity

Absurdity involves the incorporation of unexpected, ridiculous, or illogical elements to captivate the audience's attention and craft a memorable experience. The novelty of an absurd scenario is highly likely to pique viewers' interest, and the sheer eccentricity of the situation makes it difficult to look away. Additionally, the absurdity of a situation can elicit reactions of disbelief from viewers who lack prior context for the experience. When viewers encounter something so unexpected, it can trigger a range of emotions, fostering a desire in the audience to continue watching in anticipation of its resolution. Particularly in today's oversaturated market, absurd content has the potential to stand out and grab people's attention.

There are two key ways in which absurdity can enhance content. First, the novelty of an absurd situation is likely to pique our interest and encourage us to engage with a new storyline. For example, as mentioned earlier, in Areyoukiddingtv's video titled *Yes, Microwaved Is Acceptable*, with more than 51.7 million views, students are asked to deliver cooked mac-n-cheese, throw a book in the air, and dump apple juice on themselves. The utter weirdness of the situation makes it hard to look away.

Second, the absurdity of a situation can provoke reactions of disbelief in viewers who have no prior context for the experience. In the moments before the person we're observing realizes what's happening, we may witness rare, unfiltered expressions of their core personality. Again, as mentioned earlier, in ThatWasEpic's video titled *Cutting Peoples* [sic] *Earphones, Then Giving Them Airpods*, with more than 53 million views, a prankster cuts a woman's headphone cords. We're treated to the mix of emotions passing over her face as she processes what just happened.

Absurd content offers a literal escape from the mundane, allowing us to see or experience something outside of our day-to-day lives. Whether scrolling on the bus, at work, or before bed, many of us seek such an escape. By providing this kind of experience, absurd content can be a powerful tool for creators seeking to capture and retain audience attention.

3. Perspective Shift

A perspective shift is a powerful revelation or aha moment that challenges viewers' perceptions of the video's topic by debunking misconceptions, presenting new ideas, or highlighting different viewpoints. It enables creators to introduce commonly held beliefs and then present topics in innovative and clever ways. This performance driver prompts a transformative shift in viewers' perspectives, compelling them to reevaluate the topic in a manner that challenges their preconceived beliefs or views.

You can create a perspective shift by debunking misconceptions and subverting expectations, which allowed calltoleap's video *Making $80K at Home* to accumulate more than 3.6 million views. This video demonstrates how to make $80,000 a year with only one hour of work a month, completely going against the idea of the modern nine-to-five workweek.

You can also take your audience's preconceived notions and completely flip them on their head to create a performance they won't forget. For example, in Yes Theory's *Traveling to the Least Visited Country in the World*, which garnered more than 16 million views, they document their travels to the least visited country, playing off our assumptions that the journey will be a disaster. However, to everyone's surprise, their experience turns out to be wildly positive. This unexpected twist leads to a truly dynamic and unforgettable moment.

When creating a perspective shift, your aim is to captivate your audience with a unique and memorable idea that will leave them mesmerized and pondering new perspectives. Your goal is to have them walking away saying, "Wow! That was incredible!" and eagerly anticipating the next opportunity to learn something from you.

4. Viewer Connection

This concept involves forming a personal relationship with viewers and acknowledging their perspectives. This often includes practices such as maintaining eye contact, addressing viewers directly by using the pronoun *you*, framing your content or message from the average viewers' points of view, and predicting what they might think or feel about something you share.

A potent way to create viewer connections is by providing actionable or educational value. This entails offering information that viewers can immediately apply, leaving them thinking, *I'm glad I watched that.*

Another method for establishing a connection with viewers is through educational insight, which involves presenting intriguing information that not only satisfies viewers' curiosity but also imparts new knowledge. It differentiates itself from actionable or practical educational value, which offers information directly applicable to viewers' lives. However, it's important to note that these terms often overlap, depending on the specific interests and experiences of the viewers.

Educational insight frequently appears in science and journalism-style content, where creators delve into the stories behind specific events or scientific concepts. For example, Vox's video titled *Why We All Need Subtitles Now*, with more than 10 million views, tells the interesting story of how subtitles became a common fixture in content consumption, imparting intriguing, though not necessarily practical, information. The same can be said for Veritasium's viral videos, such as *Math's Fundamental Flaw*, with more than 25 million views. To capture and maintain attention, top creators skillfully integrate educational insight into compelling narratives.

Another way to establish a connection with viewers is by introducing implications into the content. Implications refer to the broader or more significant consequences of a message or story. They can help viewers understand why the content is important and how it can impact their lives or the world around them. By highlighting these broader implications, creators can generate a sense of urgency and relevance that goes beyond mere entertainment or curiosity.

Implications can also enhance the appeal of stories for viewers. For example, in Cheddar's video *Why the U.S. Hates Roundabouts*, which has garnered more than 5.6 million views, a seemingly mundane topic such as roundabouts becomes much more interesting when the creators highlight the implications of traditional traffic lights, including the increased incidence of car accidents. By emphasizing the broader consequences of the topic at hand, the creators can make the content more engaging and relevant to their audience.

Additional ways to create a strong viewer connection include:

- **Eye contact:** Establishing virtual eye contact by looking directly into the camera lens can create a more personal and engaging connection with your viewers.
- **Meta elements:** Incorporating self-referential or self-aware elements, such as breaking the fourth wall or acknowledging the medium in which the content is presented, can add a unique and relatable touch to your videos.
- **Formal vs. colloquial language use:** The choice of language and tone plays a crucial role in creating a specific mood and engaging your audience. It's essential to use the natural syntax, slang, and communication patterns of your target audience, avoiding marketing jargon or industry terminology.
- **Head voice:** This refers to using language and expressions that resonate with your audience on a deep, authentic level. Utilizing head voice can have a significant impact on viewer engagement and may lead to increased impressions and interaction.
- **Personal pronouns:** The use of personal pronouns such as *you* helps create a more personal and direct connection with your audience. Remember, you're speaking to an individual on the other side of the screen, so avoid using terms like *All of you* or *Hey, you guys*, which can dilute the personal connection.

All these strategies can help you establish a stronger and more meaningful bond with your audience, ultimately leading to increased viewer engagement and loyalty.

5. Tension Building

Tension building is a technique that compels the viewer to eagerly anticipate what happens next by indicating or creating a problem within the content, generating a strong desire to see a resolution. Tension can be effectively heightened by introducing not only a main problem but also several minor challenges that ultimately lead to the resolution of the initial issue.

A key way to build tension includes "completing the scale," which involves delivering a satisfying resolution to the content's narrative or message, setting up viewers to think, *I absolutely must see what happens next.* The resolution can be dramatic or subtle, manifesting as a visual cue that makes them want to see the next shot or a pivotal shift in the storyline. This effect can be subconscious or obvious. In essence, completing the scale is akin to playing a musical scale on a piano, where the final note brings about a sense of completion. Content creators aim to create a promise and fulfill it in a way that keeps viewers engaged. Failing to complete the scale can leave them feeling unsettled and unsatisfied.

By strategically structuring your content to include a buildup and payoff, you can craft a compelling narrative that holds your audience's attention. The initial setup serves as a hook, generating anticipation and curiosity. This anticipation acts as a driving force, motivating viewers to stay engaged until the resolution is reached.

Many creators and formats rely on a powerful setup and payoff dynamic to maintain audience engagement. For example, highly successful engineering-related creator Mark Rober always begins his videos with a teaser that includes the final scenes of the content. This introduction strongly suggests that he succeeded with his experiment but encountered interesting obstacles along the way. As viewers watch the rest of the video, they have the teaser clip in the back of their minds, trying to figure out how everything will align for the final reveal, which Rober delivers in a satisfying way to complete the scale. You can see a compelling example in his viral video *Glitter Bomb 1.0 vs Porch Pirates*, which has garnered more than 89 million views.

A teaser intro is just one way to set up your audience to anticipate a satisfying resolution. Other creators, such as TwoHotTakes, rely on the controversy of their topics as a setup—the audience absolutely must know how the bizarre stories end. For example, in *What Would You Do If Your MIL Did This?! Part 2 Up!*, with more than 15 million views, the video shares the story of someone whose mother-in-law tampered with her birth control, resulting in her getting pregnant three months postpartum.

Even cute dog videos, like mayapolarbear's *The Moment She Realized It*, with more than 11.8 million views, sets up the question, "When will this dog realize it's being given imaginary treats?" and answers the question as part of the resolution.

Building tension is a powerful tool for content creators to keep their audiences engaged and eagerly awaiting the next chapter of their content. Whether through dramatic cliffhangers, intriguing teasers, or compelling setups, tension building can captivate viewers and leave them hungry for more.

Now that we've explored the elements that drive content performance, let's shift our focus to some other marketing tactics. Let's examine how your marketing strategies can ensure that your messages not only reach, but truly resonate with, your target audience.

Push Marketing vs. Pull Marketing

In the vast realm of marketing strategies, two primary approaches frequently emerge: push marketing and pull marketing. Understanding the distinction between these methods can significantly optimize your marketing efforts, but it's crucial to note that neither approach guarantees a connection with the audience.

Push marketing involves "pushing" your product, service, or message in front of an audience, even if they aren't actively seeking what you're offering. For instance, on social media platforms, businesses run ads that appear on users' feeds, regardless of whether they were actively searching for that content or not.

Pull marketing, on the other hand, attracts customers already looking for a product or service like yours. When someone searches for "best running shoes" and is presented with a list of sponsored product links, that's pull marketing in action.

However, regardless of whether you opt for a push or pull marketing strategy, the ultimate objective should always be genuine communication. Simply broadcasting a message, even if tailored for the specific marketing approach, might not guarantee engagement—hence, the importance of understanding the difference between marketing and communication.

Marketing vs. Communication

To effectively engage your audience, it's essential to prioritize establishing a connection and gaining their trust before diving into sales or promotion. Speak to them in a language they understand, and provide value up front. In Part III of this book, The Communication Algorithm, I'll focus on insights to help you better understand how to communicate most effectively across a wide spectrum of people. Now, our focus shifts to understanding why communication, rather than straightforward marketing, is so important.

Picture this scenario: A plastic surgeon tries to capture your attention with a video that begins, "My goal as a practicing cosmetic and plastic surgeon is to achieve exceptional, natural-looking results while ensuring an excellent patient experience. My office stands out due to its unique attributes, supported by a dedicated team of more than 30 professionals who work with me daily. . . ." Does this content make you want to watch further? Although it may be informative, it lacks engagement and relatability. We recognize it as a hard push marketing effort, and that realization immediately turns us off.

Family medicine practitioner Doctor Mike, known as @doctormike on YouTube, uses a much more engaging approach, as illustrated in the script below, which is inspired by his content:

Person 1: Do your patients call you Dr. Mike?

Dr. Mike: They change it up. What were you about to say?

Person 1: I wanted to ask you, why do I sweat more than the average person? Like right now, my seat is a swamp? No, literally. I've been sitting on this paper town. Look how wet it is!

Dr. Mike: Do you want another paper towel?

Person 1: No, I'm good.

Dr. Mike: The reason people sweat is usually for thermal regulation purposes. But you're probably sweating more now than usual because of your coffee. [Dr. Mike points to Person 1's coffee cup.]

Person 1: I do drink it every day, but everybody drinks coffee.

Dr. Mike: A lot of people do, but just know that after a cup of coffee, you sweat more. Another thing that could be going on—your metabolism makes you run at a slightly different temperature. . . .

In this scenario, we witness a conversation centered around the relatable issue of excessive sweating. This dialogue establishes an immediate connection with the audience that builds intrigue. This connection paves the way for viewers to be more receptive to the information shared, enhancing the overall impact of the message.

It's important to remember that simply marketing and promoting your services without providing value or building a connection instantly puts up a barrier between you and your audience. We seek connection, not overt marketing pitches. Therefore, it's crucial to provide valuable insights before talking about your products and services. By creating a genuine, relatable experience, we can capture our audience's attention and keep them engaged throughout the journey.

Bridge Personal Passions with Popular Topics

Connecting with as many people as possible is pivotal for going viral, and there are many ways to go about it. For instance, Charles Cornell, an internet personality and the founder of Cornell Music Academy, takes the approach of seamlessly weaving popular elements such as anime, cartoons, and video game music into his music-related content. He finds unique ways to link his content to these cultural references, such as commenting on heavy-metal music in a video game from the perspective of a jazz pianist. This interplay of varying interests and genres enables him to resonate with a diverse audience, a strategy that you, too, can adopt to broaden your reach.

Illustrating this principle is Cornell's video *The INSANE Rhythm of Doom Eternal*, which amassed more than 1.1 million views. Here, he explores the musical construction of a song from a popular video game that he's never heard before. By leveraging the existing fan base of the game and combining it with his piano expertise, Cornell crafts content that resonates with both gamers and music enthusiasts, allowing him to tap into new audiences.

The key takeaway is that bridging your personal passions with popular and widely appealing subjects can amplify your reach and draw in new viewers. By exploring the intersection between your passions and broader trends, you can create content that strikes a chord with a diverse range of audiences.

Also, when watching Charles Cornell's *Piano Meme Compilation*, you see multiple storytelling layers. First and foremost, there's the music he performs. Then, his reaction to the meme of the girl speaking in the background of the shot adds another layer of engagement. Finally, the content is transformative in that it takes two familiar elements—music and memes—and combines them in an unexpectedly funny context to create a song.

Analyzing Cornell's content in this manner offers insights into why the video has amassed nearly 10 million views. We learn that he focuses on providing viewers with an immersive experience and finds ways to invite them to enjoy the world he constructs. It's clear that he genuinely enjoys playing music and aims to share his passion with those who may not have felt the same type of passion before. The integration of layers, an immersive experience, and genuine enthusiasm are noteworthy content drivers to use when developing your own social media content.

Noticing Nuances

As mentioned earlier, there are various nuances that play a significant role in how we perceive a video. Now I'll walk you through some of the most essential nuances to consider, including lighting, pacing, cadence, energy, the video's capacity to create a satisfying effect on the viewer, and luck factors. Exploring these nuances in social media content is not about passing judgment on whether they're good or bad, but rather, understanding the strategies and techniques used to achieve desired effects.

Analyzing nuances allows us to gain insights into how different elements—such as composition, storytelling, pacing, and visual design—contribute to the overall impact of a piece of content. This knowledge empowers us to make deliberate decisions when creating our own content, ensuring that it aligns with our intended effect and that it resonates with a wide audience. By learning from successful and unsuccessful social media content, we can enhance our ability to create compelling and engaging content that achieves our desired goals.

For example, the use of lighting can create different atmospheres. Similarly, the composition of your shots can affect the visual dynamics and the focus of attention within the frame. The colors you choose can convey different moods or associations, and sound design can significantly enhance the emotional impact of your content. Although high production value isn't essential, there's a caveat concerning composition and color. It's not about having the best lights or a fancy setup, but it *is* crucial to understand and thoughtfully incorporate these nuances. By aligning them with your intended purpose, you can produce content that resonates more powerfully with your audience.

LIGHTING

Analyzing the lighting choices in your references can provide valuable insights into the impact and effect that different lighting setups can have on the viewer. Although there's no one-size-fits-all approach to lighting, understanding the specific effect you want to create and studying references can guide you in making informed lighting decisions for your content.

Consider the role of lighting in shaping the mood and atmosphere of your videos. Bright and vibrant lighting, for example, can create a cheerful and energetic atmosphere, while dim and moody lighting can evoke a sense of mystery or suspense. Let's delve deeper into how lighting choices can contribute to a viewer's perception.

In James Hoffman's videos, the use of bright, sterile, almost lab-like lighting serves a specific purpose. It aligns with his brand as a coffee scientist, giving his content an analytical and informative feel. This unconventional approach to lighting in coffee-related content, which typically features warm, cozy, and rustic aesthetics, sets him apart and reinforces his unique brand identity. You can see an example of Hoffman's approach in one of his videos titled *Dalgona Coffee—Explained and Upgraded.*

In contrast, if you watch Teddy Baldassarre's video *An Iconic Dress Watch Now in Green*, you'll notice a moody and cinematic lighting setup. This choice enhances the sense of luxury and sophistication associated with the topic of luxury watches. The play of shadows and highlights contributes to a visually appealing and high-end presentation.

By exploring and understanding how lighting can be tailored to your content's theme and your brand identity, you can elevate the visual impact of your videos. So, when considering your lighting choices, think beyond the technical aspects; and consider how they align with the emotions, atmosphere, and brand you wish to convey.

COMPOSITION AND COLOR

Composition and color choices can be intentional and align with the desired effect or message of the content. In DIY videos, for instance, a neutral and bland background allows the focus to be on the main driver of the video, which is the clever and unexpected process being demonstrated. By avoiding distracting and bright colors in the background, the video keeps the viewer's attention on the main point. An example of this approach can be found in HGTV Handmade's video *How to Wrap a Present Perfectly Every*, with 4.6 million views.

In a different context, such as personal finance content on YouTube, the composition and color arrangement of a video may try to evoke a feeling of affluence and accomplishment in the viewer. The selection of a spacious setting, accompanied by a softly blurred background, can foster a sense of ease and credibility. The strategic placement of props such as a piano, an art installation, a money-themed poster, and even an aspirational item like an expensive sports car collectively contributes to the perception that the YouTuber possesses the expertise to guide viewers toward financial success. An example of this strategy can be seen in Graham Stephan's video *I Sold Out*.

PACING

Many people associate the concept of pacing in content creation with the number of cuts or edits that occur within a specific time frame—be it a minute or a few seconds. Yet, this simplified view fails to capture the true essence of pacing. The crucial aspect to consider is not the quantity of cuts, but rather how the information is delivered and the pace at which it unfolds. Pacing is a nuanced interplay between content elements that guide the audience's experience and engagement.

For instance, imagine filming various angles of my face while I recite the same script. If I were to mechanically repeat words without conveying any valuable insights or progressing the narrative, the pacing would feel sluggish. Even if I interspersed the shots with a new angle every second, resulting in 20 different face shots, the overall effect would be lacking. The viewer wouldn't gain anything substantial from the content, and the story wouldn't advance. An example of effective pacing can be observed in Rico Roman's *The Roman Empire Invades Tokyo*, with more than 1.1 million views.

CADENCE

Cadence refers to the rhythm and flow of speech, playing a crucial role in effective content delivery and conveying different effects. Let's examine three examples, highlighting the differences in vocal cadence:

1. In Techquickie's video *Why Is the Start Menu at the Bottom?*, the YouTuber has a playful and energetic vocal cadence. The delivery feels scripted but engages the audience with a lighthearted, conversational tone. The cadence is lively, with a quicker pace and minimal pauses, emphasizing the fun and enjoyable nature of the content.
2. In Mrwhosetheboss' *OnePlus 9 & 9 Pro REVIEW*, the YouTuber takes a more serious and cinematic approach. The vocal cadence includes more pauses, allowing for a deliberate and dramatic effect. The pace is slower, giving

the audience time to absorb the information, and it adds a sense of importance and depth to the content.

3. Unbox Therapy's video *You've NEVER seen a Keyboard Like This . . .* features a more casual and authentic vocal cadence. The YouTuber speaks in a conversational manner, as if having a chat with the viewers. The cadence feels natural and relaxed, with pauses and a more leisurely pace. This style aims to create a personable and relatable connection with the audience.

These variations in vocal cadence contribute to the different effects and atmospheres created in each video. The playful cadence enhances the fun and entertainment value, the dramatic cadence adds depth and seriousness, and the conversational cadence fosters authenticity and relatability. The choice of cadence depends on your desired effect and the tone you wish to convey to your audience.

ENERGY

Dynamics and changes in energy are essential components in creating engaging and captivating content. YouTuber Mark Rober is a master at employing dynamic changes to maintain audience interest. By shifting the energy, visuals, and narrative focus, he effectively captures and holds viewers' attention. Let's look at his video *World Record Domino Robot (100k Dominoes in 24hrs)*, which demonstrates dynamic changes through the following elements:

1. Introduction of the friendly robot named Dom, with a playful and light tone.

2. Transition to a more intense and suspenseful energy, with the music and emphasis on the project's significance and complexity.
3. A shift from a small idea to a big idea by challenging the human expert and attempting to get a Guinness World Record.
4. The use of rhetorical questions to engage viewers and stimulate their curiosity.

By incorporating these dynamic changes, Rober effectively maintains viewer engagement and creates a more interesting and uniquely fascinating experience.

SATISFYING TO WATCH

Satisfying content evokes sensory experiences—whether through audio, visual, or temporal elements—which subconsciously elevate the viewer's sense of enjoyment. It thrives on patterns that generate a sense of completion akin to hearing the last note of a musical scale such as "do" in "do re mi fa so la ti do." As a result, this type of content becomes captivating and engaging for viewers; it taps into our inherent human tendency to seek patterns and derive pleasure from their repetition or satisfying culmination.

Two examples of videos that are satisfying to watch include: NileRed Shorts' *Watch This Superconductor Hover Around in Midair*, which boasts more than 40 million views; and Brainian75's *Monster Magnet Meets Magnetic Fluid*, which garnered more than 13 million views.

LUCK FACTORS

When analyzing content and searching for references, it's wise to steer clear of content that gained traction due to luck or the unique personality traits of a creator. Although some creators may achieve success by possessing an appealing personality or a fascinating way of presenting themselves, these factors aren't easily duplicated. A classic example of a luck-driven (and undeniably adorable) video example is Wild Candy's *Sneezing Baby Panda*, with 6.6 million views.

Instead, it's more effective to focus on creating content that stands out through its structure, concept, and process. By developing clear and compelling concept, implementing an engaging structure, and showcasing a well-defined process, you can create content that drives performance based on its own strengths rather than relying on external factors such as celebrity status or fortunate circumstances.

Analyze Your Own Content for Breakthrough Success

Even when your content achieves remarkable success, it's crucial to analyze it to identify areas for improvement. Your highest-performing content should serve as the new benchmark for your future creations. For instance, let's say you had a video that performed exceptionally well, but you didn't take the time to understand why. In such a case, you might create another video with a similar opening sequence, unaware that the opener was the part that didn't resonate with the audience. Whereas, if you had done a proper analysis, you could have recognized that a slight adjustment in the first few seconds would have significantly improved performance. Paying attention to small details like this can lead to a dramatic increase in views, propelling your content from one million to 20 million in no time. By continually refining and optimizing your content based on thorough analysis, you can unlock even greater success.

Delving deep into the nuances of your content might mean posting less often, but the trade-off can be worth it. Consider top creators such as YouTube icons MrBeast and Mark Rober; for years when they were solo creators without a team, they posted only once a month or even less, yet they ascended to the pinnacle of social media stardom. Although it's true that these creators now have extensive production teams enabling them to produce content more frequently, they've always remained committed to a core principle: it's paramount to create breakthrough content that reaches and deeply engages the masses. In contrast, regularly producing content that garners little attention or repeatedly reaches the same viewers doesn't yield the same impact.

Avoid getting trapped in a routine, such as posting just because it's a particular day of the week. Before sharing any type of content, assess your confidence in its potential to truly stand out. If you're not convinced, it might be wise to hold off on publishing.

When your content pops up in someone's feed, the goal is for them to eagerly anticipate watching it—be it instantly or at some point during their day. Delivering bland content not only risks diminishing their trust in what you offer but can also erode the algorithm's likelihood of promoting your work in the future. Always strive to excite and engage, preserving both viewer and algorithmic trust.

Navigating Content Analysis: Step by Step

FIGURE OUT WHAT'S WORKING

Let's walk through an analysis of musically based reaction content. Even if you're not a musician, this analogy will be valuable in helping you understand the process. This format features reactions to songs or music videos. In the video we will analyze below, the creator plays both the musician(s) and a character who reacts to the music. As the performance improves with each iteration, the character displays funny reactions, which enhances the viewer's perception of the increasing quality of the music.

Our first step is to assess the creator's subscriber or follower count to understand the size of their audience. Then we gauge the expected performance of their videos by looking at average view counts. Although these numbers may vary depending on the format and the creators being analyzed, it's essential to establish a baseline.

For instance, if a creator typically receives 200,000 to 300,000 views per video, you can classify these videos as their Silver Tier videos. Videos achieving significantly higher view counts, such as 800,000, or more than one million views, would qualify as Gold Tier content. Videos with view counts below 100,000 fall into the Bronze Tier, or the category of underperforming videos. It's generally recommended to focus on content that's one to two years old, with a possible stretch to three years, while content older than four or five years is considered too old for analysis.

Once you've gathered this initial information, you're ready to delve into the mechanics of successful videos. Begin by examining the core idea behind the content, often discernible from video titles themselves. As you explore these titles, you're likely to identify patterns or themes. For example, in Charles Cornell's music-related content on YouTube, a pattern emerged where he created five versions of a particular song—think "Happy Birthday" or "Jingle Bells"—each iteration escalating the level of quality, finesse, or complexity. In his videos, songs either progressively become a little jazzier or evolved from a terrible to an amazing version. The birthday-related example can be seen in his video *5 Happy Birthday Versions, Terrible to Amazing*, which garnered 9.6 million views.

The "Levels" concept—where activities, explanations, or ideas are shown in increasing complexity or finesse—is not only used in music. It's been implemented across many content verticals including, food, neuroscience, and skateboarding. When you come across a format concept that works across different channels and content verticals, it indicates that it's a promising approach to consider for your own content creation. Top of FormBottom of Form

A prime example of this concept in a different vertical can be seen in the video *The 21 Levels of Skateboarding with Tony Hawk: Easy to Complex*. Hawk's approach of watching skateboarding footage and providing commentary on the technique and progression creates a fascinating viewing experience. Once you start watching, it's difficult to stop, because you want to witness the performance improve.

The Levels concept also has an intriguing effect on the viewer (EOV). Content creators who incorporate this concept generally find it to be a useful format. It works because it offers viewers a promised effect and a journey at the onset—they're taken through different levels of performance or a skill. This is the type of insight you want to find when conducting your analysis.

IDENTIFY WHAT'S NOT WORKING: A PRACTICAL APPROACH

Once you've analyzed successful content, shift your focus to videos that didn't perform as well. These should be within the same format, whether they are from the same creator or from different creators who use the same format. The goal is to uncover the reasons behind their lackluster performance. To do so, compare a high-performing video (referred to as a Gold video) with a low-performing one (a Bronze video). Look for differences in topic, structure, and storytelling techniques. Comparing these examples side by side—which we recommend for a clearer understanding—will help you understand what makes content succeed or fail, enabling you to fine-tune your own strategies.

With this understanding in mind, let's delve into the practical steps of this analysis:

Step 1: Choose your videos: Start by selecting two videos: one that performed well (a Gold performer), and one that did not (a Bronze performer). For example, let's consider two videos by Charles Cornell:

- High-performing: *How to Train Your Dragon Is a MASTERCLASS in Theme Writing*, which amassed 1.1 million views.
- Low-performing: *Why You Can't Get Lin-Manuel Miranda's Music Out of Your Head*, which has 155,000 views.

Step 2: Analyze differences: Note the differences between the two videos in terms of topic, structure, and presentation. Ask yourself:

- Is the topic engaging?

- Is the headline catchy?
- Is the information well structured?

For example, in the low-performing video *Why You Can't Get Lin-Manuel Miranda's Music Out of Your Head*, Cornell talks about the music from the movie *Moana*. Start your analysis with questions such as: "Is Moana an uninteresting topic for the masses?," "Is the headline too vague?," and "Could the video's structure be improved?"

Step 3: Confirm through comparison: To confirm your initial observations, look at a video from the same creator that performed well and tackles a similar topic, leveraging the same format. For example, *How to Train Your Dragon Is a MASTERCLASS in Theme Writing* is also about an animated film and achieved high viewership. This comparison indicates that the topic of an animated film is engaging enough. The distinction is that, in this high-performing video, Cornell used a more effective headline by including the name of the movie in the title. This choice likely appealed to the masses, compared to the less successful Bronze video, which specifically mentioned composer Lin-Manuel Miranda. Then, move on to analyze the next key difference and continue until you've reviewed all the distinctions between the Gold and Bronze videos.

Step 4: Test your hypotheses: Finally, validate your observations by comparing them against additional low-performing videos to see if your hypotheses hold up. Check to see if the issues you've identified are consistent.

Final Thoughts

By carefully dissecting what sets high-performing videos apart from low-performing ones, you'll be better equipped to create content that resonates with your audience.

EXERCISE: ANALYZING YOUR GSB SHEET WITH NEW AWARENESS

Practice makes perfect! With the insights and understanding you've gained in this chapter, revisit the GSB (Gold, Silver, and Bronze) analysis sheet you made at the end of chapter 2. Or find a new creator or format that inspires you, and follow these steps:

1. **Determine follower size:** Begin by looking at the creator's subscriber or follower count to gauge the size of their audience.
2. **Identify performance baseline:** Observe the expected performance per post. You want to find a baseline for understanding the typical views the creator receives.
3. **Select Silver videos:** Choose at least 5 videos that fall within the typical view count for the creator or account, which can be considered Silver Tier content.
4. **Analyze Gold performers:** Identify at least 5 breakout, top-performing Gold videos that have significantly outperformed typical view counts.
5. **Study Bronze videos:** Choose at least 5 low-performing Bronze videos to analyze. This allows you to draw meaningful insights from both ends of the performance spectrum.

6. **Identify patterns:** Look for patterns or commonalities in the Gold and Bronze videos separately. Are there any noticeable trends or differences in content topic, opening sequences, storytelling techniques, energy levels, lighting, transitions, or other factors?
7. **Formulate hypotheses:** Based on your observations, formulate hypotheses about why the Gold videos outperform the Bronze ones. Pay attention to how the story is being told and the EOV. These factors are often the most influential drivers of success.
8. **Validate hypotheses:** Test your hypotheses about what drives performance in Gold videos by cross-referencing them with the low-performing Bronze videos. If one of your hypotheses about a top performance driver is found in a low-performing video, you need to go back to the drawing board. Otherwise, you can use the insights about the potential success drivers to influence the ideation and creation process, which we will dive into in chapter 4.

By following these steps, you will gain insight into the factors that contribute to content success or failure. This approach identifies effective storytelling, engagement drivers, and resonating elements, helping optimize your content strategy. Each time you practice this exercise, you will get closer to becoming a viral sensation!

AN EXAMPLE OF PERFORMANCE DRIVERS DERIVED FROM A THRIFT VLOGGING ANALYSIS

To guide you in formulating your own hypotheses, I'll share some that my team developed while deeply analyzing thrift vlogging content on platforms such as Instagram and TikTok. Thrift vlogging is a type of video content where creators share their experiences of shopping at thrift stores or secondhand shops. These vlogs often showcase the process of sifting through items, finding unique or valuable pieces, discussing the prices, and sometimes even offering tips on how to shop at thrift stores effectively. After the shopping experience, thrift vloggers may also include a "haul" segment, where they show and discuss all the items they purchased. Example creators in this genre include "deathbythifting" or "peachstatevtg" on TikTok. An example with more than four million views from "peachstatevtg" is *Gotta Love $20 Thrift Hauls.*

Although these performance drivers were identified within the specific niche of thrift vlogging, they offer a broader resonance and serve as universal principles applicable to various content domains:

- **Ensure clarity in communication:** Thrift vloggers emphasize concise information delivery. Regardless of the content domain, it's imperative to ensure that your message is lucid and directly conveyed.
- **Highlight the value proposition:** Showcase the unique benefits or value of what you're presenting—be it a product, idea, or story.
- **Maintain focus:** Avoid excessive camera flipping; stay on topic and eliminate unnecessary distractions.
- **Create a sense of urgency:** Craft your content to feel timely and immediately relevant.

- **Add an interactive element:** Incorporate commentary with dialogue throughout your videos.
- **Ensure relatability:** Be certain that your audience sees themselves and their world in your content.
- **Establish authority and expertise:** Gleaned from vloggers sharing insights about thrifted items, position yourself as a trustworthy source by offering expertise on your subject.
- **Build authentic emotion:** Thrift vloggers express genuine excitement over their finds. Similarly, let your true feelings shine through, whatever your content topic.
- **Insert an educational or value-added component:** As thrift vloggers offer styling tips, always aim to provide added value or educational insights in your content.

By understanding and applying these foundational drivers within this format, content creators in any vertical can significantly boost their social media presence and engagement rates.

CASE STUDY: HOW JOHN MALECKI TURNED A PASSION FOR WOODWORKING INTO A THRIVING BUSINESS

Introduction: John Malecki, a former Pittsburgh Steelers offensive lineman, had a passion for woodworking but faced the challenge of transitioning into this new career. A targeted social media strategy helped him turn his woodworking hobby into a successful business.

Background: Malecki made a significant career transition to pursue his love for woodworking and DIY projects. Despite his expertise, he struggled to effectively communicate his excitement and capture the attention of others. Recognizing Malecki's potential, we stepped in to assist him in developing a robust social media presence to promote his DIY business coaching course, "Craft to Career."

Challenge: The primary challenge Malecki faced was finding ways to engage and captivate a large audience around the niche of woodworking. He needed assistance in standing out among the vast sea of DIY content creators and reaching the masses to promote his coaching course effectively.

Solution: To address Malecki's unique needs, we crafted a social media strategy specifically designed to create content that captivates the masses. Malecki used a Viral Format called "Testing Viral Hacks," and further enhanced his content by layering elements like ASMR. This approach not only showcased his expertise but also transformed each video into an immersive experience. Furthermore, Malecki's "impossible" projects serve as a compelling Hook Point, or concept used to grab the audience's attention quickly and effectively in the shortest amount of time possible. He draws viewers in with the implausible nature of tasks, such as building a bookcase from a single sheet of plywood. This unbelievable premise and Hook Point captivates viewers as he experiments to see if these feats can be accomplished. By focusing on these dynamic projects, he has established a compelling Hook Point that paves the way for a distinctive brand identity.

Three crucial elements were interwoven into his content: absurdity, clever problem-solving, and a dose of his personal struggles and personality. Together, these components served as significant performance drivers. Malecki was set on a path to tackle unexpected challenges, each governed by its unique set of "rules." A pivotal part of this format was its explorative nature, allowing the audience to join Malecki on his journey—witnessing his trials, errors, and innovative solutions.

To heighten the experience further, the importance of drama and cinematic sequences was underscored. Also, some innovative content ideas were proposed, such as crafting a table using only tools from a dollar store, taking on projects with items solely from wish.com, and a playful challenge where Malecki's significant other would construct something by following his guidelines without him touching the tools.

In addition, the application of the Communication Algorithm, detailed in Part III of this book, empowered Malecki to forge a more genuine connection with his target audience.

Results:

Following this strategy led to significant growth on Malecki's social media platforms. His average video views increased dramatically, from 100,000 to over a million, and his collective video view count now exceeds 150 million. Part of his success came from experimenting with various Viral Formats, optimizing thumbnails, and capitalizing on viral TikTok woodworking hacks, all of which allowed him to reach a significantly wider audience.

In his breakout videos, Malecki strategically incorporated ASMR elements, tackled seemingly impossible challenges, and layered absurdity in his storytelling (discussed in chapter 5). These key performance drivers were instrumental in driving the outstanding results he achieved.

EXAMPLES OF BEFORE AND AFTER CONTENT

Before:

ULTIMATE Shop Storage Cabinet Build

135K views • 3 years ago

ULTIMATE Shop Storage Cabinet Build, with 133,000 views is a good example of Malecki's content before implementing the strategies you're learning in this book.

After:

Testing Viral Woodworking TikToks Again...

1.8M views • 1 year ago

The video *Testing Viral Woodworking TikToks Again . . .* , with more than 1.6 million views, is a good example of Malecki's content after implementing the Viral Content Model. Remember, this video and all other videos and references shared throughout the book can be viewed at http://guide.hookpoint.com/.

Conclusion: Malecki's story serves as a reminder that with the right approach, even niche subjects can connect with the masses online. Effective social media strategies can amplify unique skills and attract a larger, more engaged audience.

Recommendations: Companies or individuals facing challenges in reaching a wider audience can learn from Malecki's case. By focusing on finding a Viral Format that resonates and understanding the mechanics of effective communication, it's possible to grow an online presence and monetize expertise.

CHAPTER 4

THE CREATIVITY BLUEPRINT: STRATEGIC IDEATION IN ACTION

After conducting thorough research and identifying a Viral Format that aligns with your brand's or business's needs, the next step is to develop content ideas. It's essential to understand that the strength of a format lies in the quality of the ideas it contains. The real challenge—and opportunity—begins at this stage: generating impactful ideas to use within your chosen format.

The ideation process, which is essentially the generation and development of new ideas, empowers you to prioritize these concepts through evidence-based decision-making. Unlike traditional approaches that may involve latching on to the first idea that comes to mind and investing time, energy, and money only to see it fail, this method is different. Guided by the research and analysis components of the Viral Content Model, it encourages you to explore a wide range of potential concepts. By constructing an expansive catalog of ideas, you can compare, evaluate, and ultimately rank them. This ensures that you invest your time and resources in the most impactful and compelling ideas.

Central to this process is a deceptively simple yet powerful tool: the Ideation Sheet. This resource offers a dedicated space for capturing and evaluating your ideas. By diligently documenting your creativity within this framework, you generate a valuable resource that can be revisited, refined, and expanded over time.

The Ideation Sheet transforms into a canvas for your imagination, anchored by scientific insight. It lets you brainstorm and explore various possibilities—enhanced by your newfound understanding of performance drivers, formats, nuances, and storytelling formats. It encourages you to think outside the box, challenge conventional thinking, and expand your capacity for creating viral content.

Remember, this process is not solely about idea generation; it's also about fostering a culture of continual improvement. By constantly revisiting and refining your ideas, you ensure that each piece of content you produce is infused with breakthrough potential.

The Importance of Chaos in Ideation

During your brainstorming sessions, welcome the chaos, and dive into unconventional ideas, drawing inspiration from diverse industries. Avoid confining yourself to tried-and-true approaches. Instead, push the envelope, even if some ideas initially feel "way too crazy."

Don't fixate on the status quo—reach for the stars! By going beyond traditional boundaries, you open yourself to a reservoir of untapped creativity and innovation. Remember, you can always backtrack and tone down your ideas later on. But venturing into uncharted territories, you may discover hidden gems and groundbreaking concepts.

100 to 1: Generating More Ideas Than Necessary

Embrace the strategy of generating a multitude of ideas. Aim for a high ratio, like generating 100 ideas for every one you'll finalize. This emphasis on quantity allows for a wider exploration of possibilities and increases the chances of discovering unique and innovative concepts.

When you feel like you've exhausted your ideas and reached a point where you "can't think of any more," don't give up. This is often the moment when new patterns and directions emerge. Push through the initial barrier and stretch your creative limits.

It's also important to take a step back and evaluate your ideas critically. Look for patterns and themes that may indicate an overemphasis on a particular direction while neglecting other potentially valuable avenues. A balanced exploration of perspectives and possibilities is essential.

The creative process often requires repeated cycles of ideation and refinement. By continually generating ideas, exploring different directions, and embracing new patterns, you increase your chances of arriving at a truly impactful and original concept. Embrace the journey of exploration, and remain open to the unexpected paths it presents.

Using Hook Points to Amplify Your Ideas

Occasionally, an idea for a video might be decent but lacks a compelling hook to truly shine. It's possible to rejuvenate an overused concept by coming up with an appealing Hook Point. Remember, a Hook Point refers to a concept used to grab the audience's attention quickly and effectively. It's designed to capture interest in the shortest amount of time possible, ensuring that viewers are immediately engaged. This tool is crucial for standing out in a crowded social media landscape, where the ability to draw viewers in from the first glance can determine the success of content. Consider Mindvalley's Vishen Lakhiani and his morning-routine video as an example.

Initially, a morning-routine video sounds generic and overdone. But to amplify its appeal, my team came up with a unique angle. In the video, Lakhiani shares a thought-provoking statement: "Saving 15 hours a week saves 60 hours a month, which is 720 hours a year, or 30 extra days of your life that are given back to you every year." This powerful Hook Point, emphasizing the idea of reclaiming days of one's life, instantly captivates viewers, pulling them into Lakhiani's daily routine.

To capitalize on the Hook Point about saving time, we titled the video *How to Gain Back 15 Hours a Week with These Smart Hacks* (this video and all other videos throughout the book can be viewed at http://guide.hookpoint.com/). This strategy distinguishes it from the multitude of generic morning-routine videos, which often have ineffective titles such as *5 Ways to Be More Productive in Your Workday*. In contrast, the title *How to Gain Back 15 Hours a Week with These Smart Hacks* not only offers a fresh perspective but also provides a compelling reason for viewers to engage with the content.

This example illustrates the power of a well-crafted Hook Point in transforming an overused concept into a video that not only captivates but also resonates with a wide audience. It serves as a reminder of the crucial importance of finding unique angles and hooks to differentiate your content in an overcrowded digital space. For a deeper dive into crafting effective hooks, check out my book *Hook Point: How to Stand Out in a 3-Second World*.

QUICK TIPS FOR IDEA GENERATION

Before we dive into how to use the Ideation Sheet, let's revisit some quick tips for generating great ideas:

1. **Address a fresh audience:** During brainstorming sessions, visualize an audience that doesn't know or care about your subject matter. This mindset helps you craft content that appeals to new potential viewers, rather than relying solely on existing fans. An exercise we practice is "How would you make this video interesting to your mother or grandparent?" We even have some clients that ask their loved ones which video subject or title they would be more likely to watch.
2. **Tap into popular topics:** Anchor your ideas to subjects already in the limelight. Associating your content with current hot topics (such as trending TV shows, movies, common problems people are addressing, renowned celebrities, hit music, etc.) increases the potential of drawing a larger audience. When working with Katie Couric, I would often go to Google News or Google Trends, type in the subject or person we were covering, and see which hooks or stories were trending.
3. **Avoid industry jargon:** When crafting your ideas, steer clear of using industry-specific language. Instead, opt for words and phrases that resonate with the masses, making your content more accessible and appealing to a wider range of viewers.
4. **Seek strong references:** Use the Gold, Silver, and Bronze (GSB) research process to find and base your ideas on

strong references. If you find reference videos that have achieved high performance, it's a great indication of your idea's potential. Drawing inspiration from references, especially as you're learning this process, will greatly increase your chances of producing impactful content.

Filling Out the Ideation Sheet

Let's walk through the process of filling out the Ideation Sheet. Before we get started, look at this example of a filled-out sheet:

	A	B	C	
1	Rank 1-5	IDEA	REFERENCE LINKS	NOTES
2		Generalist principle Potential applicable easy to follow advice Promise of value		
3	1	*Can you eliminate all work related stress from your life? Yes, here's how...*		
4	1.5	Do you want to cure your anxiety once and for all?		
5	1.5	Do you want to eliminate all work related stress from your life?		
6	1.5	Time heals all wounds right? Well actually there is a faster way.		
7	2	Do you want to get along better with your romantic partner?		
8	2	Do you want to not be tired all the time?		
9	2	Do you want to eliminate all stress from your life?		
10	2	Can you eliminate all work related stress from your life?		
11	2	Do you want to fall asleep faster?		
12	2	Want to know the fastest way to be happy, it's not about getting a new job, partner, or moving to a new envioroment. It's about these 3 things	https://www.tiktok.com/@robertcroakofficial/video/7329302256040480046	
13	2.5	Do you want to get better sleep at night?		
14	2.5	Do you want to know the fastest way to heal trauma?		
15	2.5	Time heals all wounds right? Well...		
16	2.5	If you have problems, just move to a new city right? well..		
17	3	Do you want to be free of stress?		
18	3	Do you want to be free of your anxiety?		
19	3	Are you tired all the time?		
20	3	Do you want to beat your depression?		
21	3	Do you want to find work life blance?		
22	3	Do you want to heal your trauma?		
23	3	Do you want to know if your partner is		
24	3	Do you want to stop the voices in your head?		
25	3	Changing jobs is not the fastest way to increase happiness, unless you _____	https://www.tiktok.com/@robertcroakofficial/video/7329302256040480046	

You'll begin with a blank Ideation Sheet:

If you'd like to access a filled-out and a blank Ideation Sheet template, you can do so here: http://guide.hookpoint.com/.

Now, let's walk through filling out each section of the Ideation Sheet:

IDEAS SECTION

This segment captures the overall concept of your video. Aim to come up with at least 20 initial ideas, though you can develop up to 100. When formulating the video concept, strive for conciseness—limit yourself to one or two sentences to create a succinct snapshot that encapsulates the main idea for quick comprehension. You can later elaborate on each concept, adding intricate details as needed.

When generating ideas, it's wise to draw inspiration from high-performing Gold reference videos. For instance, if you analyzed MrBeast's *$1 vs $10,000,000 Yacht!* on your GSB sheet, you can adapt its format by substituting the word *Yacht* with a placeholder: *\$1 vs \$10,000,000 "X"!* This can then be customized to your topic, such as jewelry or art: *\$1 vs \$10,000,000 Ring!* or *\$1 vs \$10,000,000 Painting!*

Similarly, if you encountered *How to Make Homemade Plant Food with Just 2 Ingredients* by Creative Explained, take the core format: *How to Make Homemade Plant Food with Just 2 Ingredients*, remove the topic-specific words, and you're left with a template: *How to Make "X" with "Just X."*

Here's a visual of how this works, with additional examples:

	A	B	C
1	**ORIGINAL FORMAT AND TOPIC**	**SAME FORMAT WITH BLANK TOPIC**	**FILL IN THE BLANKS WITH YOUR TOPIC**
2	**For every rows (2-11) below these instructions:** **2. Watch part of the hyperlinked video under "ORIGINAL FORMAT AND TOPIC" column.** **3. Take a look at the next collum which breaks down the format without the topic.** **4. In the third collumn, fill in the _____ with subjects/items that relate to your business/niche.** ***KEYBOARD SHORTCUTS:*** **ALT-ENTER = Enter to new line**		
3	$1 vs $1,000,000,000 Yacht!	$1 vs $1,000,000,000 _________!	$1 vs $1,000,000,000 House! $1 vs $1,000,000,000 Condo! $1 vs $1,000,000,000 Apartment! $1 vs $1,000,000,000 Real Estate Firm! $1 vs $1,000,000,000 Mortgage Lender!
4	How much do you pay for rent in NYC? Can I take a tour of your apartment?	How much do you pay for ______? Can I take a ____ of your ______?	How much do you pay for mortgage in Austin Texas? Can I take a tour of your house? How much did you pay for your house? Can I take a tour of it?
5	How to make homemade Plant Food with just 2 ingredients	How to make _______ with just _______	How to buy a house with just $1,000 down payment How to buy a house without paying a 20% down payment How to buy a house without a real estate agent How to seell a house with just a real estate agent
6	I Spent 50 Hours Buried Alive	I Spent 50 Hours __________	I Spent 50 Hours Sellling Houses I Spent 50 Hours In a bad house I spent 50 hours prepping a house I spent 50 hours looking through listings I spent 50 hours making cold calls I spent 50 hours at open house I spent 50 hours trying to live in an open house
7	This is why your Biceps aren't Growing	This is why your _____ aren't / isn't ______	This is why your house is falling apart This is why your house isn't selling This is why nobody wants to buy your house This is why you can't get a mortgage This is why you need a home inspection This is why you keep failing your home inspection
8	Are Coach leather bags worth it?	Are/Is _________________ worth it?	Is a house in beverly hills worth it? Is a house in miami beach worth it? Is a 120,000 new townhouse worth it? Is a $5,000 house in detroit worth it? Is a $1 castle in Italy worth it?
9	How to beat evil car dealerships	How to beat _______________	How to beat evil mortgage lenders How to beat the home inspection process
10	How different dog breeds would react to robbers	How different __________ would react to ________	
11	Can you turn my McDonald's gourmet?	Can you/I turn _________ to _________	
12	why Japan's internet is weirdly designed	why ________________________	
13	**5. Repeat the same process with the rows below (14-16) but this time, fill the "SAME FORMAT WITH BLANK TOPIC" yourself.**		
14	Testing Viral Woodworking TikToks Again...	Testing Viral ________	Testing viral real estate hacks
15	If people slide instead of walked		
16	Draw a world made out of pie		
17	**6. Now start from scratch.** **-Grab video examples that feature a strong format, copy the link and paste into "ORIGINAL FORMAT AND TOPIC"** **-Press ctrl/command + k on the link to add a hyperlinked title that summarizes the hook/premise of the video.**		
18	I Make $2.4M/Year With 6 YouTube Channels	I Make X With Y ________	I Make $100k/Year With 3 Rental Properties I Make $272k/Year With 5 Wholesale Real Estate Deals I Make $17k/Month With 4 Real Estate Businesses

The goal is to generate concepts that grab people's attention in the shortest possible amount of time. Remember to integrate core performance drivers identified during your research and analysis. Don't hesitate to think big! Even if an idea seems too ambitious or resource intensive, include it. You can later scale it down to a more manageable version. Let your creativity run wild, and enjoy the brainstorming process!

REFERENCE LINKS SECTION

Having high-performing video references for each concept not only serves as a potent source of inspiration but also provides a structural blueprint that makes the production process much easier. It's crucial to keep these references handy, so consider adding the links directly into your Ideation Sheet. That way, you can quickly revisit them, draw insights, and add unique elements into your content as you create your videos.

NOTES SECTION

Use the notes section to jot down pertinent details. Include insights that remind you of what stands out in a reference or elements you'd like to replicate. For example, you could point out a time stamp in the reference link, a specific moment you want to include, or anything else you feel is important. These notes will offer clarity and direction as you transition into the execution phase.

RANKING AND ASSESSING YOUR IDEAS

In the final stage of the creative process, after coming up with a ton of ideas, it's time to rank and evaluate them using a quick and . . . well, ruthless approach. Follow these steps to effectively assess and prioritize your ideas:

1. **Rate each idea:** Using a scale of 1 to 5, where 1 signifies top-notch and 5 is the least appealing, quickly rate each idea. Rely on your gut feeling, which stems from your knowledge of what works and what doesn't on social media, to assess their potential success. If you're generating ideas based on a format you've researched, also rank them based on the drivers you identified during that research. Treat each idea as a Hook Point (or headline), without diving deep into extensive explanations or attempting to restructure it. Give the idea a 1 if:

    a. It is rich in detail.

    b. It has a good reference from a strong creator (someone with a track record of generating substantial views).

    c. Is easy to visualize with a clear narrative.

    If, on the other hand, it's vague and generic, lacks an interesting Hook Point, and doesn't have a clear narrative structure, give it a 5. Ideas that have potential but are not yet refined score between a 2 and a 4, depending on the tweaks required to strengthen them.

Example:

- "Outfits for travel" would be a 5.
- "Outfits to wear on a five-hour plane ride" might be positioned at a 3.
- "Outfits inspired by *The Little Mermaid*" would claim a 1.

2. **Prioritize your highest-rated ideas:** Focus your attention on the ideas that you ranked as a 1. These represent the concepts with the highest potential for breakthrough performance. When you're just starting out, it's smart to focus on the top-rated ideas that also have strong references. This strategy gives you the option of emulating and learning from proven storytelling techniques and drivers.
3. **Workshop your top pick:** Once you've identified a top-rated idea full of potential, develop it further. Dedicate time to expand upon it. Brainstorm variations, consider different angles, and revisit or broaden your reference pool. Do whatever you need to do to enhance the appeal and impact of the concept.
4. **Embrace the learning journey:** Remember, this ranking and vetting process isn't just about producing great ideas; it's also about evolving as a creator. As you analyze your content's performance, make adjustments, and adapt, you'll sharpen your skills and fine-tune your understanding of what drives an idea's success.
5. **Adapt and refine as you go:** Keep in mind that your initial rankings aren't set in stone. As you gain experience

and gather insights by posting your content, don't hesitate to revisit and adjust some concepts, even those you initially deemed less promising. Always find ways to improve and enhance your ideas.

By following this process, you'll prioritize high-potential ideas, dive deep with research and analysis, and consistently refine your concepts to create impactful content that truly resonates.

SAYING NO (A LOT) TO MEDIOCRE IDEAS

When you treat each piece of content as if your life depends on it, you establish a mindset of continual improvement and a dedication to excellence. To solidify an effective idea-vetting process, consider the following guidelines:

1. **Prioritize research-driven insights:** Base your content decisions on solid research and data, not personal preferences or biases. For instance, if evidence indicates that recognizable characters and well-known brands resonate more with audiences, then opt for making videos where they'll be featured over those lesser-known niche brands. It's essential that every idea you pursue is rooted in objective analysis, ensuring both its relevance and potential for success.
2. **Embrace brutal evaluation:** If you work on a team, avoid the pitfall of team members supporting each other's ideas simply to please one another. Encourage a culture of critical thinking and healthy debate where ideas are thoroughly examined and evaluated based on their merit.

Challenge assumptions, ask probing questions, and be willing to constructively critique ideas to ensure that only the strongest concepts move forward.

3. **Promote insightful feedback:** Instead of simply saying, "I don't like it," articulate specific reasons when expressing reservations about an idea. Phrases like "I don't think this will work because it doesn't promise value for the viewer," or "I don't think this will work due to the lack of opportunity to subvert expectations" are more constructive. By pinpointing specific concerns, or the reasons why an idea may not be viable, you foster a productive environment that leads to stronger decision-making.
4. **Adopt a high-stakes mindset:** Treat each piece of content as if its value is crucial to your reputation and success. Anticipate potential pitfalls and challenges that could arise, and use research and data to vet your ideas thoroughly. This mindset prioritizes excellence and ensures that your content meets the highest standards.
5. **Avoid settling for "good enough":** Especially when you're still building experience, always elevate the quality and impact of your work by leveraging insights from the research and analysis process detailed in this book. Don't wing it.

By adhering to these principles, you create a culture of evidence-based decision-making, critical evaluation, and constructive feedback. This ensures that only the most promising ideas are selected and developed, increasing the likelihood of success in creating viral content.

Creating Addictive Content

Creating addictive content is crucial for building a loyal and engaged audience. The aim should always be to produce videos that audiences will binge-watch, building viewers' trust that each release will be both compelling and enjoyable.

To maintain this trust, it's essential to avoid releasing videos that are, frankly, dull. Ideally, each video should be addicting, leaving viewers eagerly awaiting the next. The ultimate compliment from your audience is: "I love every one of your videos."

When brainstorming content ideas, it's essential to balance what excites you with concepts that appeal to a wide audience. Brands such as Yes Theory serve as a prime example, consistently delivering captivating content. Their strategy often revolves around the theme of stepping outside of one's comfort zone, regardless of the video's specific topic. Whether it's about *Traveling to the Least Visited Country in the World*, *Asking a Stranger to Go on a Date across the World*, or an *Abandoned City In America with No Laws*, what captivates their audience is an engaging narrative style, not just the subject itself.

Building trust and creating addictive content can be likened to being a renowned chef. If customers love a chef's signature style, they'll anticipate excellence in every dish, even if the menu changes weekly. In the same vein, strive to be a sought-after content creator online, consistently delivering content that delights and meets viewer expectations.

When ideating and creating, ensure that each concept has the potential to be breakthrough content. If an idea feels mediocre or lacks the spark to captivate an audience, invest more time in refining it. It's better to postpone a release to ensure quality rather than rush . . . and risk diminishing your brand's value.

In the end, the objective is to build a dedicated and enthusiastic following that trusts your storytelling approach and consistently returns for more. Concentrating on creating addicting content that resonates with a wide audience will leave a lasting impact in the world of digital media.

Set Plays vs. Triangle (aka Structured Consistency vs. Adaptive Strategy)

The difference between Set Plays and the Triangle in basketball serves as a great metaphor for the ideation and decision-making processes. Set Plays can be likened to a golfer's systematic routine—waking up early, getting dressed, eating breakfast, driving to the golf course, and then playing golf—regardless of external factors. This structured approach works well when the situation is predictable and a consistent outcome is expected.

On the other hand, the Triangle approach, inspired by basketball coach Phil Jackson's offense strategy, embodies adaptability and situational awareness. It involves considering multiple factors before deciding. For example, before playing golf, golfers may scan the weather—assessing if it's sunny, cloudy, or windy—prior to deciding whether or not to play. This flexible approach allows them to make informed decisions based on ever-changing variables.

In ideation, the Triangle philosophy tends to be more fruitful. Rather than being fixated on a specific idea from the start, it's essential to consider various factors and potential challenges before committing to a particular concept. Just as you wouldn't play golf when it's windy and rainy, you may need to shift focus from an initial idea if it doesn't align well with the current circumstances or possesses significant challenges.

An evaluation of ideas should go beyond mere acceptability. It's essential to strive for excellence and consider concepts that have greater potential and fewer obstacles. Although an idea may be appealing or your favorite, if another concept performs better and checks more boxes, it's wise to channel your energy into the more promising option.

Embracing the Triangle approach to ideation ensures that you remain adaptable and make informed decisions. This mindset allows for more flexibility and creative problem-solving, leading to the development of breakthrough content that resonates deeply with your audience.

EXERCISE: FILL OUT YOUR OWN IDEATION SHEET

In this hands-on assignment, you're going to create your very own Ideation Sheet. This is your space to document, organize, and classify your content concepts. The purpose of this exercise is to:

1. Catalog ideas over time.
2. Fine-tune your knack for prioritizing ideas and efficiently using your time and resources.
3. Provide a systematic approach for selecting from a myriad of ideas.
4. Improve your ability to generate strong ideas.

STEPS TO FOLLOW

1. **Accessing and copying the Ideation Sheet template**
    a. Visit the Ideation Sheet template: http://guide.hookpoint.com/. Note that the template is read-only to preserve the original data and formatting.

b. To make a personal copy that you can edit:
   - Go to File in the menu.
   - Select Make a Copy.
   - Save the new copy to your desired location.
   - Begin editing your copy as necessary.

2. **Navigating the Ideation Sheet**
   a. For guidance on each column in the Ideation sheet, refer to the Read Me tab at the bottom of the page.
   b. A completed example can be viewed on the Sample Ideation tab.
3. **IDEA column:** In this column, briefly summarize your idea within one or two sentences. If your idea already incorporates a specific Hook Point, detail it here.
4. **REFERENCE and NOTES columns:** Use these columns to jot down any pertinent notes that will help you quickly understand your ideas when you revisit the sheet in the future.
   a. REFERENCE: Use this column to provide additional context to your idea. This could include links to videos or creators that embody the style or concept you're aiming for; or a brief description of the intended look, feel, or structure of your content.
   b. NOTES: This column is for deep-diving into the essence of your idea. Capture key aspects like a significant moment from a reference link, particular scenes you want to re-create, or other critical details. Although you

don't need to write an exhaustive description, offering a rich understanding here will aid in the eventual scripting and production. As you refine your ideas, remember to integrate performance drivers that can amplify their appeal and success.

5. **Idea generation:** Aim to fill your sheet with at least 20 compelling ideas, each accompanied by its reference.

GOLDEN NUGGETS TO REMEMBER ABOUT REFERENCES

- **Gold-level content:** Choose references that are standout successes, either in their formats or for their creators. Although you may appreciate content that isn't objectively successful, focus on ideas backed by evidence of wide appeal.
- **Adaptation:** Consider how to adapt any reference idea to your field. Even if seems like a long shot, there's probably a way.
- **The more the merrier:** Don't stifle yourself: include all of your ideas. You can always take them off the list later on.

CASE STUDY: REFINING MINDVALLEY'S SOCIAL MEDIA STRATEGY WITH HOOK POINT'S MASTERY IN VIRAL CONTENT

Introduction: Mindvalley, a pioneer in educational technology, observed that their online engagement had plateaued despite a significant following on social media platforms such as Instagram and Facebook. The Mindvalley team, including founder Vishen Lakhiani and former CMO Alessio Pieroni, aimed to revitalize their online interactions by pivoting their strategy to leverage viral content.

Background: Aiming to unite top educators on a single platform, Mindvalley had established a solid online presence; yet their brand promotional content was not achieving the desired viral effect. As Pieroni shared, "For a long time, we wanted to do great things on social media, but when it came to creating viral content consistently, we didn't know where to start."

Challenge: The challenge for Mindvalley was to transition from traditional marketing to a model that could predictably engineer viral content, meeting the evolving demands of the social media landscape.

Solution: Recognizing the need for a radical change, Mindvalley sought innovative strategies to revamp their social media content strategy. Their partnership with Hook Point provided guidance, yet it was Mindvalley's commitment to redefining their approach that drove the transformation. The new goal was to shift from traditional brand-centric content to storytelling that resonated with a larger audience, thus optimizing for virality.

Action plan: To achieve this goal, the Mindvalley team underwent a comprehensive training program in key aspects of virality:

- **Training in the Viral Content Model and Hook Points:** The social media team learned to craft compelling narratives to captivate viewers.
- **Streamlining an internal communications strategy:** Mindvalley realigned their internal communications strategies for improved comprehension and performance across departments.

- **Innovating content development:** They brainstormed innovative viral content formats and scripts.
- **Engaging influencer strategies:** Mindvalley started collaborations with influencers to expand their reach.

Reflecting on the partnership, Pieroni said, "It was a master class in virality. We felt a sense of co-evolution with Hook Point, ready to discover and implement new and cool together."

Results: The strategic pivot led to a significant increase in Mindvalley's online visibility. Within six months, Instagram and Facebook follower numbers surged from about 70,000 to 900,000. Additionally, Lakhiani's personal Facebook following grew from 300,000 to 2.3 million. These platforms collectively amassed more than 150 million views in the first few months, proving the content's appeal and the team's ability to engage and grow their audience.

Today: Encouraged by this success, Mindvalley continues its partnership with Hook Point, extending their efforts to platforms like YouTube, and ensuring the continuation of their impressive engagement and growth.

Conclusion: Mindvalley's shift from traditional, ad-centric content to a narrative-driven approach has significantly boosted user engagement and expanded their reach. This strategy—focusing on storytelling and value-driven content over branding—has distinguished them in the market and fostered a dynamic, growing online community. With new strategies and insights, Mindvalley has a sustainable model for continued success.

Recommendations: Organizations aspiring to Mindvalley's transformative success should adopt a storytelling-driven content strategy that engages audiences beyond traditional marketing techniques. This approach can create a self-sustaining momentum of virality, engagement, and substantial results. Mindvalley's experience showcases the impact of strategic content innovation in building a robust social media presence.

CHAPTER 5

THE ART OF STORYTELLING: CAPTURING AND KEEPING AUDIENCE ATTENTION

Now that you've brainstormed some promising ideas, the next phase involves refining them for effective execution using first-rate storytelling techniques. Our minds are naturally drawn to stories. This chapter will guide you in developing compelling storylines that hook your audience from the beginning and keep them engaged till the end. The aim is to offer genuine value—whether through informative insights or entertainment.

Imagine typical viewers scrolling through their social media feeds. Your content should capture their attention instantly with a uniquely interesting introduction and a rewarding payoff. Ultimately, you want to leave your audience feeling satisfied, reflecting, *I'm glad I watched that.*

Effective Communication Hierarchy

To capture your audience's attention, keep your message clear and concise. Rather than bombarding them with an overload of information, present only what's essential. For instance, if using captions or title cards, it's crucial to select a readable font size and style. Give your viewers time to absorb the information, and avoid overwhelming them with too much or boring them with too little.

A visual hierarchy is equally crucial. It ensures clarity in your message, leaving no essential detail unnoticed. To achieve this aim, steer clear of cluttered backgrounds or distracting colors. In your videos, emphasize the primary subjects—whether they're people, objects, or actions—to highlight them and make them easily visible.

Since your video will encompass various elements, it's crucial to prioritize them. Determine which aspects should be emphasized (and at what moments) and which can be made less significant. By doing so, you allow the most important elements to take center stage.

Communication Design

The best designers disappear—not in a literal sense, of course, but in their approach to designing content. When someone watches your video, their attention should be on the content's essence, not on the details of how it was created. The aim is for the visual design to blend with the content's intention so seamlessly that it seems almost nonexistent.

Consider the subtlety of a film score. If a movie's music stands out to the point that viewers say, "Wow! That's beautiful music," it distracts them from the intended emotional impact of the scene and defeats the music's purpose. Although as creators, we want our work to be recognized, it shouldn't be at the expense of overshadowing the narrative or message.

In essence, the goal is to achieve a harmonious balance: Design elements support and enhance the content's purpose without demanding unwarranted spotlight. By focusing on creating resonant, impactful content, you ensure that your work is appreciated for its intended effect.

Here are some top tips for communication design:

EMPHASIZE LINEAR COMMUNICATION

Focus on conveying one message at a time to ensure clarity. Your visuals and audio should work together cohesively, just like in a gym setting. Imagine having a trainer guide you: for an effective workout, you'd want to focus on one exercise at a time. If the trainer started explaining the next three exercises while you were still on the first, it would be overwhelming and confusing. A common mistake among new social media creators is overloading their videos with captions, title cards, movement, and dialogue simultaneously. This sensory overload can disorient viewers—they don't know where to focus and feel left behind—making them more likely to scroll past.

START WITH YOUR INTENDED EFFECT

Begin with the emotional reaction you want to elicit from your audience, and reverse-engineer from there. Instead of beginning with your message and trying to make it fit, zero in on the emotions you want to invoke in your viewers. Bear in mind that sometimes your intended message might need a tweak if research suggests it won't resonate as expected.

BE GOOD, NOT DIFFERENT

Drawing a parallel between "being different" and "being good" is similar to differentiating between art and design. Art thrives on personal expression, a realm where there's no concrete right or wrong. Whether it manifests as a distinctive brushstroke on canvas or a bold fashion choice, art celebrates individual vision and creativity.

Conversely, design is anchored in solving specific problems. When designing something like a landing page, the overriding concern is functionality, leading to questions such as, "How can I streamline the purchasing process for users?" Identifying these issues paves the way for innovative solutions.

When it comes to content creation, the approach leans more toward design than art. Although there's room for personal flavor, the heart of content creation revolves around problem-solving. While everyone has different tastes, good content sticks to certain principles to achieve its goals.

MAKE UNSAID PROMISES AND CAPTURE ATTENTION

To effectively create content, it's crucial to grab your audience's attention right off the bat. Many newcomers on social platforms begin videos with bland introductions such as, "Hi, my name is X, and today we'll talk about fabric softeners." This can come across as dull and disengaging and risks losing viewer interest.

To truly engage, the initial seconds of a video must captivate viewers. It's all about promising entertainment up front and then consistently delivering on it. Take MrBeast's video previews as an example. Ever since YouTube rolled out mini preview trailers that appear as you scroll over a thumbnail, MrBeast and his team have dedicated countless hours to crafting these previews. Their aim? To immediately hook viewers, compelling them to watch the entire video. I'd suggest checking out a few of his mini previews on YouTube for inspiration.

I-You vs. You-All

In the digital age, content consumption is primarily a solitary experience. One of the most impactful things I learned from working with Taylor Swift is that behind every screen, there's usually just one individual watching your content, not a collective audience. Whether on smartphones, computers, or other devices, most people consume digital content alone.

This solitary consumption pattern makes the "I" to "you" communication approach most effective. Addressing the audience as "you" establishes a personalized and direct connection with the viewer. It feels as if you're having a one-on-one conversation, eliminating the barrier of the screen between the two of you.

Steer clear of generic phrases like "Hello, everyone" or "Hey, guys." These can lessen the personal feel you're aiming for. Instead, use language that feels natural and conversational, as though you're having a casual dialogue with a friend. This not only enhances viewer engagement but also builds a stronger bond with your audience.

By directly addressing the individuals behind the screen, you convey appreciation for their time and engagement. It communicates that you're speaking directly to them and care about their experience, which makes them more likely to resonate deeply with your content.

Don't Listen to Your Audience

"If I had asked them what they wanted, they would have said faster horses." — Henry Ford

As content creators, we must find a balance between valuing our audience's feedback and understanding that they don't always know their true preferences. Our role is to make people care and offer appealing experiences, drawing both from data and our own instincts. Those without a grasp of social media research or algorithm nuances may not provide helpful insights.

Audience feedback—even if loud and insistent—can be misleading. This is because the primary objective of many viewers is to voice their opinions, rather than elevate the content's quality. For example, consider the case of Alex Stemp, a renowned street and portrait photographer known for approaching random strangers on the street and offering them professional photo shoots. Stemp creates engaging videos detailing captivating stories behind his chance encounters, strategically withholding the final shots until the end. Stemp shared with me that, despite numerous viewer requests to unveil the photos early on, his videos continue to rake in millions of views. Interestingly, when Stemp *did* comply with these demands, showcasing the photographs from the outset, those videos underperformed. The suspense generated by postponing the photo reveal is a crucial element driving the success of his series. As such, when navigating feedback on your content, approach comments with caution, and discern which ones align with your vision rather than accommodating each request.

Additionally, creating a page filled with compelling content that explores unconventional topics can still lead to success. Consider the engaging videos by Tom Scott, in which he explores unique topics such as the practical uses of monorails or the volume of helium necessary to lift a person. These aren't trending topics that the average person thinks about daily, nor are they ones commonly requested by viewers. Yet it is precisely because they move beyond conventional thinking that they work.

This isn't an advocacy for disregarding audience feedback entirely, but a reminder that as creators, our role is to lead, innovate, and sometimes challenge expectations. Continue to conduct thorough research, and utilize the Viral Content Model to craft outstanding content. Present stories that are intriguing, foster trust, and are compelling. Invite your viewers to go on an enticing adventure with you, as that's the key to generating intrigue and building a dedicated following.

When inviting them, the pitch isn't "Here's what you asked for," but "Would you like to discover something captivating with me?"

Remember, your audience consists of consumers, not professional content creators. They know how to care, but they don't necessarily know how to make *others* care. Trust your instincts and expertise in content creation, as that is *your* area of specialization, not theirs. Besides, if you seek growth, marketing solely to your existing audience isn't the most effective strategy for driving consistent virality. Expand your horizons, venture into the unexplored, and reach out to a wider audience, transcending the confines of your current following.

Think Like Your Audience

Thinking like your audience is a powerful strategy for effective communication and marketing. To connect with your audience on a deep level, it's essential to speak in the language that resonates with them, and not merely stick to traditional marketing jargon. This means balancing formal language with colloquial language, echoing the voice they naturally hear in their own thoughts.

To avoid being tone-deaf and to truly connect with your audience, immerse yourself in their world and learn their language. Familiarize yourself with their unique phrases, expressions, and thought processes. Approach content from their perspective so you can create content that feels genuine, authentic, and personal.

One technique is to add a touch of commentary into your messaging. Instead of crafting overly polished and logical marketing copy, infuse your content with the logic you'd use in your own head. Avoid sounding like a traditional marketer who follows a script. Instead, speak and write in a way that feels natural and conversational, as if you're sharing a casual internal monologue.

A perfect example of this approach is showcased in The Food Theorists' video titled *Food Theory: Don't Order These Chicken Sandwiches!* The video dissects the marketing tactics of Popeyes and Chick-fil-A concerning their chicken sandwiches. In August of 2019, Popeyes launched their take on the chicken sandwich. Chick-fil-A tweeted a seemingly harmless but slightly passive-aggressive, corporate-sounding jab at Popeyes, which read: "Bun plus chicken plus pickles, equals all the love for the original." While it's well written and checks all the traditional marketing boxes, it was detrimental to business. In a stroke of brilliance, Popeyes retorted with a familiar Southern expression: "Y'all good?" This didn't sound like an ad; it echoed the colloquial thoughts of a Southerner. Garnering 20 billion impressions, this tweet was valued at approximately $220 million. Consequently, Popeyes' chicken sandwich sales skyrocketed, and they even ran out of chicken sandwich supplies. Upon restocking in November, sales were off the charts. In turn, Chick-fil-A suddenly found itself, for the first time ever, in second position for chicken sandwich sales.

The lesson here is clear: To connect with your audience, use language and tones that mirror your audience's internal dialogue. Speak as though you're in a face-to-face chat, facilitating deeper connection and brand engagement. Popeyes' social media triumph teaches the power of authenticity over the traditional marketing playbook. Such genuine and relatable communication strategies can amplify marketing success.

Additionally, to gain a deeper understanding of the language used on platforms such as Facebook, TikTok, Instagram, and YouTube, observe top-performing creators. By understanding how these platforms function, you can better align your content with their ecosystems, positioning you as an insider instead of just another marketer trying to break in.

Start with the Desired Effect

In content creation, the key is to prioritize the subconscious reaction over conscious understanding. Viewers feel the emotional impact of a piece first and process the experience in words later on. The true power of the story is elicited by the emotional response it generates.

Rather than starting with a message and then figuring out how to present it in an interesting fashion, reverse-engineer the process: Decide on the emotions you want viewers to experience—whether it's awe, surprise, or wonder. Aim for reactions such as, "Oh my God, that is so cool!," "Why didn't I think of that?," "I can't believe that's possible," or "I've never seen it that way . . . wow!"

If you can't identify the precise emotional effect you want to produce in your audience, it's best not to proceed with its creation. Begin with the end in mind: the desired impact. Then, craft the content to steer the audience toward that feeling.

Consider the process of songwriting: To create a dance hit, you'd want to start with the desired outcome of making people dance. The goal is to get people moving, and the music is made to match this intention. This approach is much more effective than writing a song first and then attempting to make it danceable.

Similarly, if you were creating a horror movie, the primary objective would be to instill fear. This choice then informs subsequent decisions, such as moody lighting and casting actors skilled in portraying fear. By focusing on the emotional outcome first, the rest of the production decisions naturally fall into place.

These principles apply to the content you create. Start by asking yourself how to infuse drama or heightened impact into your content. This not only provides a clear road map but also ensures that you include the necessary drivers to make your content go viral. Starting with the desired effect gives you a clearer vision of what to do to make your content resonate effectively with your audience.

MetLife: Storytelling That Resonates

When it comes to evoking strong emotional reactions, the MetLife video *My Dad Is a Liar* is a testament to the power of storytelling that leads with intended effect. Instead of relying on traditional advertising methods, MetLife focused on the emotional impact they aimed to achieve.

The video immediately captures viewer attention with a touching portrayal of the bond between a father and his daughter. Then, the narrative takes an unexpected turn when the daughter dubs her father a liar, generating intrigue and piquing viewer curiosity. The audience becomes invested in the emotional story, wanting to understand the reason behind the daughter's claim. This heartfelt narrative is the reason why a video that ultimately delivers information about an insurance company could amass millions of views.

Even after repeated viewings, the narrative continues to evoke emotional responses. The brilliance behind this piece is rooted in the marketing team's approach: they focused on the effect they wanted to have on their audience rather than on a logical message about their products or services.

This strategic shift in focus from selling a product to connecting emotionally with an audience resulted in a narrative that doesn't just promote insurance but shares universal truths about love, sacrifice, and familial bonds. By starting with the effect, MetLife not only captured audience attention but also created genuine affection for its brand.

METLIFE EXERCISE

Watch MetLife's heartwarming video *My Dad Is a Liar* here: http://guide.hookpoint.com/, where, again, you can also watch all the other videos in this chapter. One of the driving forces behind the success of this video is the twist—a pivotal moment when the daughter reveals, "He lies." This unexpected turn creates intrigue and hooks the viewer's attention.

Can you identify other reasons for this video's standout performance? What hypotheses can you make about the potential performance drivers that engage viewers and make them care?

ABC: Always Be Clever: Harnessing the Power of Cleverness in Social Media Videos

Cleverness, defined by the equation "Unexpected + Smart = Cleverness," is one of the best-kept secrets to achieving virality in social media. It represents the capacity to discover innovative solutions or insights in unexpected ways, combined with the ability to perceive and connect seemingly unrelated elements. This results in unique perspectives or solutions that others might overlook. Cleverness thrives on the element of surprise, presenting a fresh angle or an innovative twist to familiar scenarios.

Many top-performing content pieces across various formats showcase this trait. By integrating clever elements throughout each aspect of your content—from visuals and perspectives to processes and concepts—you can elevate your videos to make them stand out in the crowded digital landscape. While the ideal goal is to combine both a clever concept and clever production, mastering even one can set you apart.

An excellent example of the impact of being clever can be seen in Prince Ea's *Dear Future Generations: Sorry (2023)*. Although the theme of saving the planet might appear routine and potentially boring, Prince Ea's approach illustrates that with cleverness, even commonplace topics can captivate viewers. Through innovative delivery and visual interpretation, as well as smooth editing, he transforms an ordinary idea into an extraordinary call to action.

In his video, Prince Ea presents himself as a representative apologizing to future generations for the state of the planet that the current generation has left behind. By using poetry and rhyme, he mourns the lost beauty of the Amazon rainforest and emphasizes the crucial value of trees in sustaining life on Earth. By cleverly wrapping his message in this unexpected format, he breathes new life into a familiar topic, challenging viewers to rethink their viewpoints.

True cleverness extends beyond mere intelligence or information sharing; it thrives on the element of surprise by being unexpectedly intelligent, witty, and insightful. This is precisely what Prince Ea achieves, attracting more than 30 million views for his video. By delivering an unanticipated interpretation on a seemingly simple concept, he leaves a lasting impression that sparks conversation.

Implementing cleverness in social media videos is a compelling strategy to captivate and connect with viewers. Whether through clever ideas, unexpected interpretations, or innovative visuals, the surprise factor leaves a memorable impact. As you craft content, let the phrase "Always be clever" be your guide to lasting viewership.

The Golden Triangle Technique: A Powerful Approach to Effective Communication

The Golden Triangle Technique is a potent tool for conveying a message succinctly and compellingly, using three essential elements:

1. **Personal touch:** Share a personal story or anecdote. This helps establish an emotional connection with the audience by tapping into relatability and authenticity.
2. **Evidence and facts:** Strengthen your narrative with hard facts—be it data, research, or concrete examples. This

provides credibility to your message and supports its validity.

3. **Timeless wisdom:** Weave in philosophical insights or carefully researched information. This adds depth, grounding your message in universal truths and connecting it with time-honored principles.

When these three elements come together, they present a persuasive narrative that's not only emotionally resonant but is also backed by evidence and deep insight. This approach allows you to communicate effectively and leave a lasting impact on your audience.

My team discovered the Golden Triangle Technique by analyzing content created by Jay Shetty—a renowned author, coach, former monk, and influential content creator. He skillfully applies this method in many of his content pieces. A standout example is his video *You Can't Love Someone You Don't Know.* Here, Shetty shares a beautiful Indian tale about a musk deer searching for a fragrance, only to realize that it emanates from a gland within its own body. The story serves as a metaphor highlighting the fact that oftentimes we search for external validation and love when real joy emerges from within, through self-awareness and self-love. Throughout the video, Shetty seamlessly integrates relevant data, personal experiences, and philosophical insights to deliver his profound message.

When crafting content, some pieces may benefit from the Golden Triangle Technique: interweaving personal stories with data and facts to lend undeniable credibility, then anchoring them in time-tested wisdom for a universal touch. Such a holistic approach deepens the resonance of your content, making it both impactful and memorable.

The Jenga Theory: Crafting Engaging Narratives through Tension and Anticipation

Inspired by the game of Jenga, where players meticulously pull blocks, balancing tension with anticipation, the Jenga Theory of storytelling relies on similar principles, effectively engaging audiences. Although the collapse of a Jenga tower is predictable, it's the buildup—the small stories each block tells—that captivates players. Similarly, Jenga Theory storytelling excels in crafting narratives with interconnected elements, keeping the audience on the edge of their seats, eager for the next development.

STRUCTURE AND MECHANICS OF JENGA THEORY IN STORYTELLING

1. **Set the stage with a primary concept:** Start by introducing the central idea, giving a teaser about the broader narrative.
2. **Introduce smaller questions and challenges:** These act as the individual blocks in the Jenga tower. Instead of a linear path, introduce smaller, interconnected segments or questions that need answering.
3. **Layered revelation:** As one layer of tension (or one question) is resolved, introduce a new one, maintaining the tension and anticipation.

MARK ROBER AND THE ART OF JENGA THEORY STORYTELLING

As mentioned earlier, Mark Rober, a renowned content creator boasting more than 50 million YouTube subscribers and often garnering over 30 million views per video, is an expert at using the Jenga Theory. While he predominantly focuses on engineering—a subject not traditionally associated with mass appeal—Rober's skillful storytelling captivates and retains his audience's attention. His videos frequently kick off with a primary objective—be it resolving a problem, answering a pivotal question, or breaking a record. However, instead of a linear narrative, Rober intersperses his journey with mini subsidiary questions, challenges, and obstacles, all of which he must overcome to get to the final resolution. Each of these elements heightens the suspense, keeping the story fresh. By the end, much like a teetering Jenga tower on its last leg, the climax delivers an amplified viewer anticipation and pay off.

In his video *Testing If Sharks Can Smell a Drop of Blood*, which has garnered more than 108 million views, Rober masterfully employs the Jenga Theory. Rather than diving directly into the main experiment, he begins by posing a smaller question: "Do sharks prefer blood over other scents?" Before revealing the results of the experiment, he explains the methodology. It becomes evident that sharks prefer the scent of blood. Then he delves into another question: "How much blood attracts a shark?" Again, before commencing the experiment, he explains the procedure. Surprisingly, during this experiment, the viewer learns that sharks show no interest in human blood. Last, Rober introduces a final experiment: Could he re-create the iconic effect from *The Matrix* where time appears to stand still and the camera moves around a subject in slow motion, known as the "Matrix bullet time effect," while diving with sharks? This layered approach ensures sustained audience engagement throughout the entirety of the video.

VERITASIUM'S MASTERY OF JENGA THEORY

Veritasium, a YouTube channel with more than 14.3 million subscribers that creates content primarily about science and education, also uses the Jenga Theory in many of its videos. For example, in the video *Why Are 96,000,000 Black Balls on This Reservoir?*, which has amassed more than 96 million views, the narrative doesn't simply explain the phenomenon. Within the first 20 seconds, Veritasium states that these shade balls are commonly believed to reduce evaporation. However, they quickly debunk this misconception and pose the question: "What are they really for?" This inquiry sets up the framework for the Jenga-style narrative. The astonishing sight of 96 million balls on water is emphasized, leading to more questions around the one-minute mark: "Why are the balls black?," "Are they safe for drinking water?," "How much do they cost?," "Do they reduce evaporation?," and "What is their real purpose?" The video then shifts to answering these questions one by one, with each answered question paving the way for another, culminating in heightened anticipation and curiosity about the true purpose of the balls, which is revealed at the very end.

* * *

The Jenga Theory, with its intertwining layers of tension and anticipation, crafts appealing narratives. By harnessing this method, creators can produce content that resonates and keeps millions of viewers hooked.

Visualizing Complex Topics in a Simple and Unexpected Way

Transforming complex subjects into clear, engaging visuals is a powerful driver for audience engagement. This performance driver allows content creators to catch viewers off guard, turning seemingly dry or mundane topics into memorable and engaging content.

An excellent example of this approach is demonstrated in Vox's video *How Tax Brackets Actually Work*. To many, tax brackets might come across as a snooze-fest. Yet, Vox's clever use of physical objects, such as paper cutouts, illustrates the idea in a way that adds a whole new layer of intrigue and makes it more accessible. Instead of leading with the plain facts, the approach of starting with an engaging effect and then unraveling the logic behind it proves effective, as it drew in nearly two million views. Although most of us would rather avoid topics such as death and taxes, Vox's innovative visual storytelling brings the topic to life. A clever interpretation, backed with the right props, can simplify concepts, making them more memorable.

In a similar vein, creator Jack Corbett, who joined NPR as the Tiny Desk Intern and is a videographer and producer for Planet Money, known as planetmoney on TikTok, tackles this topic in the video *It's Not One Big Percent, It's a Bunch of Little Brackets with Their Own Percents*. Instead of using paper cutouts, Corbett puts animated visuals directly on his body. This playful, unique approach turns a potentially stale subject into something amusing and fun.

When ideating content, content creators can consider this approach and work backward to craft engaging stories about almost any subject. By embracing creative and unexpected visual techniques, you can breathe life into dry topics, leaving a lasting impact on viewers.

Analogies: Bridging the Known to the New

Analogies act as bridges, connecting what your audience *already* understands to the new ideas you *wish* to introduce. These bridges are powerful drivers both in ideation and execution, which create a profound impact on viewers. In Wired's video with over 5.2 million views, *Neuroscientist Explains One Concept in 5 Levels of Difficulty*, the use of analogies is brilliantly demonstrated. Here, a neuroscientist explains the complex concept of the connectome—the intricate network of neural pathways in our brains and nervous systems—to individuals of varying ages and expertise.

The video opens with the neuroscientist talking to a five-year-old about the connectome. The child's shocked and amazed reaction to learning that our brains have more cells than the visible stars in the sky mirrors the effect that well-crafted analogies have on viewers. Such comparisons can blow our minds and change our perspectives.

Ernest Lupinacci, a seasoned creative director, also introduced my team to the potent "You know how . . . ?" phrase, a tool to uncover impactful analogies and memorable Hook Points for brands, products, or services. When relaunching the Dasani brand, Lupinacci shifted the focus from the health aspects of bottled water to taste—a more universal preference. Using the "You know how . . . ?" framework, he devised an engaging narrative:

> You know how there are 75,000 water brands in the market, and we're supposed to drink eight glasses of water a day? "Yeah, I do know that. I hear it all the time. People repeat that to me. There's one of those giant water coolers in my office. Water, water, water, water." Well, you know how you can't figure out if one is better than the other? "Yeah." Well, you know how at the end of the day, whatever you drink or eat still needs to appeal to you? It's got to

> taste good; otherwise, it's medicine, right? "Yeah, I do know that." Well, you should try some Dasani. Dasani is the water that makes your mouth water.

By using the "You know how . . . ?" methodology, you can gauge the effectiveness of your ideas and their resonance with your audience. This structure helps you identify analogies that genuinely strike a chord, making your content and stories more compelling and engaging.

One More Layer

In content creation, depth is often the difference between a fleeting engagement and a memorable experience. Single-dimensional storytelling can fall flat unless it's extremely appealing, which is why introducing multiple layers to your narrative is helpful.

An excellent example is Wired's video *Neuroscientist Explains One Concept in 5 Levels of Difficulty*, which I mentioned in the previous section. Again, at its core, the video presents the idea of the connectome—an intriguing concept but not necessarily one with mass appeal. Yet, the additional layer of presenting the concept in five levels of difficulty (to a five-year-old, a teenager, a high school student, a graduate student, and an industry professional) adds depth and intrigue, resulting in more than 5.2 million views.

One of the driving factors behind the success of these multilayered videos is adaptability. Explaining a complex concept to varied audiences requires adjusting the delivery for a child, a teenager, and an expert. These different layers of interactions and reactions make the concept even more fascinating and relatable to a wider audience.

Another creative iteration of this approach is seen in Brian Mendoza's video *Horrible Singer Uses Magic Water & This Happened.*

This video provides an intriguing example of adding layers to music content. Layer one revolves around his musical performance, which is engaging but not extraordinary. Layer two comes into play when he decides to play his music to strangers on the internet. At first, Mendoza meets their expectations, as he deliberately sings poorly while the strangers try to be polite. Then, layer three is introduced when he takes a sip of "magic water," resulting in a sudden improvement in his singing. This captivating gimmick not only hooks viewers but also leaves them pleasantly astonished.

The combination of these layers—music performance, virtual interactions, and the gimmick—elevates the video into an immersive experience. As viewers witness the strangers' genuine amazement on-screen, they can't help but be drawn into the shared experience. The story of his transformation from a bad singer to a skilled one becomes a powerful hook that carries them through the entire journey and helped Mendoza garner more than 3.7 million views. Without these layers in his storytelling, his music and videos wouldn't attract this much attention.

You can apply the concept of adding multiple layers to *any* content vertical. Recognizing the impact of these layers and their ability to captivate an audience can be a game-changer in creating content that doesn't just get watched but is also remembered and shared.

Harnessing Absurdity

Absurdity can be a magnet for attention in a content-saturated world. Consider The Food Theorists' video *Food Theory: The Candy Commercials That HAUNT Your Brain!* Here, they unpack the history of a peculiar starburst commercial, "Berries and Cream." Although the ad first went viral in 2007, it's unexpected resurgence in 2022 on TikTok demonstrates the staying power of absurd content.

The key takeaway from the video is that breaking the mold, straying from convention, and embracing the unexpected not only grabs attention but retains it. The secret lies in adding a twist to familiar events so they become a little unexpected and absurd. This approach resonates with viewers, leaving a lasting impression and making memories that stick with them for a lifetime.

Per Sederberg, a psychology professor at The Ohio State University, explains that memorable experiences often arise from intertwining the familiar with the unexpected. While we build memories on the foundation of known experiences, it's the unexpected twist that surprises us and firmly imprints the event in our memory.

The power of absurdity lies in its ability to be just strange enough to make people stay and keep watching. It doesn't need to veer into the realm of the utterly bizarre; even a subtle twist is often enough to leave a lasting impact on an audience. By infusing content with elements of absurdity, you can create a distinct, engrossing viewer experience. This not only keeps viewers hooked but also encourages them to share the content, increasing its reach and influence.

The Audience Is Yours to Lose

Once someone starts watching your video, the challenge is to *maintain* their attention. Viewers typically drop off as videos progress, making it essential to hook them from the outset and keep them engaged throughout. Every moment in your video needs deliberate thought and attention. From the opening scene to the closing shot, ensure that you're crafting content based on thorough research and that incorporates relevant data. Even a slight oversight can dramatically impact your video's success.

It's important to remember that viewers have countless other options readily available. If the intro of your video doesn't captivate them, many might click away before reaching the content's peak moments. This drives home the importance of structured, immediate engagement. Seize your audience's attention from the beginning, and sustain their interest through to the end. By blending strategic planning with compelling storytelling and data-driven insights, you heighten the chances of retaining your viewers and maximizing your content's reach.

EXERCISE:
EVALUATING YOUR VIDEO SIDE BY SIDE WITH YOUR REFERENCE: BRINGING YOUR BEST IDEA TO LIFE

After identifying your standout idea—one that's rooted in research, is powered by compelling performance drivers, features an effective hook, applies engaging storytelling techniques, and is supported by an outstanding reference—it's time to bring it to life in video form. Refer to your Ideation Sheet and craft your video, keeping in mind all the insights you've gathered thus far.

Before posting your video, it's beneficial to compare it side by side with your Gold reference video. Applying the insights from this book during this pre-posting analysis will help you discern how well you've integrated the nuances and key performance drivers, and also pinpoint what could be improved. This step is crucial for refining your skills and progressively enhancing your content. Also, if a video doesn't perform as expected after posting, this comparative exercise can provide valuable insights into why it may have fallen short, guiding your strategy for future content. Remember, each video you create and analyze is a learning opportunity, taking you one step closer to mastering the art of resonating with the masses.

Follow this step-by step guide to conducting a detailed analysis of your video alongside its benchmark Gold reference:

STEP 1: SIDE-BY-SIDE VIEWING

Open two separate windows on your computer, and place them side by side for easy comparison. As you watch, break down each element and performance driver's contribution to the reference video's success (as noted in your Ideation Sheet), and assess whether your video achieves the same impact. Focus specifically on qualitative elements such as transitions, visuals, audio, pacing, and the overall storytelling structure. Try not to get drawn into the content itself, but rather, the way it's presented. Reflect on the emotions elicited by each video, and consider how the benchmark Gold video maintains viewer engagement.

STEP 2: IDENTIFY OPPORTUNITIES FOR IMPROVEMENT

During the analysis, identify areas in your video that may require improvement. Does the Gold reference video have certain elements that outshine yours? Consider how you can enhance your content to match or outperform the benchmark video.

STEP 3: REFINE YOUR VIDEO

If you notice that parts of your video fall flat, make the necessary edits to refine the storytelling, and include the performance drivers from the Gold reference. Make adjustments in order to mirror what makes the Gold reference video stand out. Keep refining until you're sure your video nails the correct elements.

STEP 4: FINAL REVIEW

After adjustments, conduct a final review. Keep polishing your video until it impeccably integrates the sought-after performance drivers and subtleties.

Remember, video content creation is a journey of continual learning. By regularly analyzing and adjusting based on top-performing benchmarks, you're setting yourself up for success. Happy creating!

RATIOS VS. ABSOLUTES

When you begin posting content and seek to analyze its metrics, understanding the difference between ratios and absolutes is crucial. Metrics like reach or impressions might appear impressive, but they don't delve deep enough to reveal genuine viewer engagement. Reach merely signifies that content appeared on someone's timeline, without confirming whether they actually viewed the video.

Rather than focusing solely on broad metrics such as reach or impressions, delving into ratios can offer more meaningful insights into viewer engagement. It's essential, however, to note that the availability and specificity of these metrics can differ across various social media platforms. The following examples act as guidelines, drawing from metrics frequently available across platforms.

A key metric, available on many platforms, is the **view rate**. This measures the proportion of individuals who viewed at least three seconds of the video, in relation to its reach. For instance, if you have a 40 percent view rate, it means that 40 out of 100 people viewed at least three seconds of your video. This ratio sheds light on how effectively the video's initial moments hold viewers' attention. Platforms such as Facebook and Instagram offer insights about viewers who've watched at least three seconds of videos. A low view rate on these platforms suggests enhancing the beginning of the video to better captivate the audience.

Platforms such as YouTube, Instagram, Facebook, and TikTok offer another metric: the **retention graph**. This metric depicts the percentage of viewers who continue watching the video as it progresses. Typically, this graph starts at 100 percent and gradually tapers off as viewers stop watching. Analyzing the retention graph allows you to identify specific segments in the video where viewers lose interest or engagement drops. Recognizing these dips in retention is crucial, as it guides content creators to refine their strategies and video content accordingly.

It's important to familiarize yourself with the analytics tools or dashboards specific to your chosen platform. Each platform brings its unique metrics and insights to the table, tailored to its user behavior and content type. Recognizing and adapting to these subtleties can significantly enhance your content strategy.

Overall, the primary advantage of focusing on ratios and actionable data lies in their power to drive purposeful action. Instead of being satisfied with high reach or impressions, you can proactively analyze the view rate and retention graph to optimize your content and elevate viewer engagement. By leveraging this actionable data, you can make informed decisions and continually improve the effectiveness of your social media content.

CASE STUDY: DEAN SHEREMET'S CULINARY CONTENT REVOLUTION WITH HOOK POINT

Introduction: Dean Sheremet, a nationally recognized chef, TV personality, and author, recognized the potential of social media to broaden his culinary influence. Despite his substantial experience in upscale cuisine and a natural talent for performing, Sheremet struggled to stand out in the crowded digital landscape. Eager to stand out on social media, he partnered with Hook Point to unlock the power of viral content.

Background: Transitioning his focus from a successful career in the kitchen to the realm of digital content creation was a daunting task for Sheremet. Motivated by a desire to share his culinary expertise and establish a unique digital identity, he encountered obstacles in producing content that resonated on a broad scale. His initial efforts featured basic videos that lacked the strategic foundation necessary for viral success.

Challenge: Sheremet's main challenge was identifying the elements needed to transform his content from merely informative to widely engaging and worthy of going viral. He sought a reliable strategy to amplify his reach beyond the typical confines of food-related content.

Solution: Partnering with Hook Point, Sheremet embarked on a comprehensive journey to overhaul his content strategy. The collaboration involved deep dives into audience engagement through Hook Point's Communication Algorithm, leading to several strategic developments:

- **Strategic Content Development:** Sheremet created content with engaging hooks and formats tailored to his strengths and the interests of his audience, all supported by analytical insights. He used hooks like "4 Microwave Hacks You Will Actually Use" and implemented various Viral Formats such as "Cooking Hacks," "Clever Recipes," and "Reaction Videos." Among these, "Cooking Hacks" emerged as the most successful format in connecting with the masses.
- **Messaging and Language Refinement:** Sheremet refined his communication style to genuinely connect with a wider audience. He applied the five rules of the Communication Algorithm, detailed in Part III of this book, to each of his videos.
- **Repeatable Storytelling Framework:** A consistent, data-informed content creation process was established, making every piece impactful and engaging.

- **Virality Optimization:** The strategy emphasized creating compelling visuals and narratives, enriched with actionable culinary advice, to enhance engagement and shareability.

This multifaceted approach empowered Sheremet to share his culinary insights in a format primed for viral success.

Results: Sheremet's revised strategy led to impressive results, establishing him as a digital force in the culinary world:

- **Viral Engagement**: His videos achieved viral success, garnering over 1.9 million likes and 50 million views across TikTok and Instagram. Standout videos include:

    1. *4 Microwave Hacks You Will Actually Use*, where he shares four microwave hacks that chefs use for preserving fresh herbs, juicing citrus, steaming vegetables, and peeling garlic, which attracted over 13.8 million views.

    2. *Sweet Potato Mochi Balls*, showcasing the process of making a sweet potato snack, which received over three million views.

    (You can watch these videos, and all the rest of the videos in this book, at: http://guide.hookpoint.com.)

- **Brand Development:** Improved content quality and increased visibility attracted significant brand partnerships, elevating Sheremet's culinary brand. Partners include Vuori Clothing, Breville/polyscience, AG-1, the Propane Education & Research Council, Horl Knife Sharpeners, and more.

- **Audience Growth**: In just six months, Sheremet's audience expanded fourfold, leading to a surge in traffic and engagement across his social media platforms. His followings on TikTok, and Instagram all experienced significant growth. On Instagram alone he went from 100,000 to 375,000 followers. Bottom of Form

- **Return on Investment**: This growth in audience and engagement not only validated the effectiveness of the Viral Content Model but also resulted in returns far exceeding the initial investment in Hook Point.

Reflection Sheremet: He views his partnership with Hook Point as a transformative educational experience, akin to a rigorous academic course in social engineering, complete with extensive preparation and strategic planning. He opted for a focused approach, prioritizing the creation of a few high-quality content pieces over a higher volume of average content. This strategy not only enhanced the quality of his content but also led to massive exposure; he expects to continue learning and growing his following.

Conclusion: Sheremet's newfound digital influence marks a significant shift in his career, from a chef navigating the digital landscape to becoming a celebrated social media influencer. His experience highlights the impact of a strategic, goal-oriented approach to social media, proving that with commitment and the right strategies, achieving widespread success is possible.

Recommendations: Sheremet's success is rooted not just in his engaging content but also in his strategic approach and execution. Content creators seeking similar achievements should embrace the strategic planning and steps that are found using Hook Point's tools such as the Viral Content Model, Viral Formats, and the Communication Algorithm. Committing to continuous learning, removing ego from content assessment, and staying true to finding the right storytelling framework are crucial. By combining strategic content creation with a growth mindset, creators can set themselves on the path to becoming viral sensations in their respective domains.

AMAZON REVIEW REQUEST

People who help others, expecting nothing in return, often experience higher levels of fulfilment, enjoy longer lives, and achieve greater financial success. I aim to extend this value to you through your reading or listening journey. To this end, I have a simple question:

Would you help someone you've never met if it cost you nothing and you received no recognition for it?

If your answer is yes, I'd like to make a request on behalf of someone unknown to you, and whom you likely will never meet. They are much like you, or perhaps how you were a few years ago: less experienced, eager to share their products or services with the world, and searching for information but unsure of where to find it. This is where you come into play.

At Hook Point, our core mission is to equip entrepreneurs, influencers, and businesses with the strategies they need to stand out and succeed. This mission thrives on community support—yours included.

If this book has offered you valuable insights, I kindly ask you to consider leaving an honest review on Amazon. Your feedback not only helps us refine our approach but also guides others in their quest for success. Think of it as extending a hand to a fellow traveler on their journey, a gesture that takes less than a minute but can have a profound impact.

For those who've listened on Audible: Simply tap the triple-dots icon in the upper right corner, select "Rate and Review," and share your thoughts along with a star rating.

For Kindle or e-reader enthusiasts: Upon reaching the end, swipe up, and you should see a prompt to leave a review.

Have you encountered a challenge during the review process? No problem. Head over to the book's Amazon page (or wherever you made your purchase), and post your review there.

Should you have any feedback or wish to share your thoughts directly, please feel free to reach out to us by going to http://guide.hookpoint.com/. Your insights are invaluable to us.

P.S. To all who root for the underdog and believe in the power of giving, you are why we do what we do. Your support inspires us to keep pushing the boundaries of what's possible.

P.P.S. Remember, sharing knowledge is one of the most powerful forms of generosity. If you found this book helpful, consider passing it on to another entrepreneur or friend. You might just spark a transformation.

Thank you for your time, your support, and for being a part of this journey. Together, let's continue to make a difference.

My gratitude knows no bounds. Let's jump back into the action.

With appreciation,

Brendan,

Your number-one supporter

PART II

VIRAL FORMATS

FORMAT STRATEGIES—SECTION 1

THE BEAUTY OF A VIRAL FRAMEWORK

Having mastered research, analysis, ideation, and the art of storytelling, you're now better equipped to understand more of the intricacies of Viral Formats. Remember, a Viral Format is a storytelling structure that can adapt to any type of subject matter and remains relevant for extended periods of time—even years. This is different from a trend, which is fleeting. A format dictates the way in which a story unfolds, and how information is presented in a social media video. Mastering a single successful format can dramatically increase your odds of consistently going viral.

Top creators across the globe frequently choose a specific format and consistently use it to craft their stories. By mastering a chosen format, they see improved performance metrics and achieve greater success by understanding its nuances.

As you might now realize, becoming a consistent and lasting viral sensation rarely occurs from producing a massive amount of content, adopting trendy hashtags, or chasing fleeting trends. Instead, it's about investing your time, energy, and resources to excel in a single top-performing format.

There are countless formats to choose from for your content. In fact, to date, Hook Point has conducted in-depth research on more than 200 different formats. However, identifying one that consistently yields the best outcomes is just the beginning. It's crucial to thoroughly analyze and understand every aspect of this successful format. As outlined in the research section of this book, such detailed examination is key to replicating and enhancing successful outcomes. By fully understanding the components and nuances of the format you select, you can strategically execute it and fully capitalize on its potential in your social media strategy.

Renowned content creators have proven that success comes from concentrating on, and excelling in, a single top-performing format. The success stories of Dr. Julie Smith, Hunter Prosper, Dylan Page, Alex Stemp, Vox, Dylan Page, and Danielle Labelle attest to the power of focusing on one content format. These content creators and media companies have consistently used a specific storytelling structure that resonates with their viewers, driving significant growth and engagement.

Alex Stemp's consistent use of the "Man on the Street" format has allowed him to reach a massive following of 20 million. His approach, which involves offering professional photo shoots to random strangers within this format has proven to be compelling.

Media powerhouses such as Vox and Veritasium have also recognized the value of mastering a single format. Their commitment to refining their chosen storytelling structures has established their status as reliable sources of engaging and informative content, securing them a loyal audience and widespread recognition.

Formats: The Three-Act Structure of the Digital Age

As mentioned earlier, Viral Formats are video storytelling structures that serve as frameworks into which creators can strategically insert their own brands, identities, stories, or ideas. These structured templates provide a consistent narrative framework, guiding the presentation of content in a way that connects with the masses. Top formats offer a versatile canvas for creators to insert their messages and creativity.

Although some might express concerns about potential creative constraints, it's essential to recognize that just as most movies follow the three-act structure, social media content similarly thrives when aligned with platform-specific formats. The three-act framework is a storytelling technique that segments a narrative into three distinct phases, often termed the Introduction, the Challenge, and the Climax. This method gained traction through Syd Field's 1979 book, *Screenplay: The Foundations of Screenwriting.*

The Introduction (Act I):

- Presents the central characters, their environment, and the initial dilemma.
- Sets the scene and identifies what's at risk.
- Concludes with a pivotal event that drives the protagonist into the story's core conflict.

The Challenge (Act II):

- Is central to the narrative and delves deeper into the story's complications and character developments.
- The point where the protagonist faces multiple obstacles, often leading to a critical turning point.

The Climax (Act III):

- Resolves the central conflict, drawing the narrative to its conclusion.
- Provides a resolution for the protagonist and other key characters.

Take a legendary filmmaker such as Steven Spielberg as an example: His unparalleled success stems from his commitment to understanding and using the time-tested three-act structure in cinema. He has won three Academy Awards and nine Golden Globes by adhering to this tried-and-true storytelling method. Spielberg has never compromised his creativity, but rather, has mastered the art of translating his vision within this structure. If he tried to reinvent the three-act structure (aka the format) each time he created a film, he wouldn't be a world-class storyteller. It's too complicated and wastes valuable time. Instead, he strengthens his use of this structure to tell the stories he's passionate about.

The beauty of the three-act structure is its adaptability. Despite being a staple across diverse genres—be it drama, comedy, horror, action, or sci-fi—it never diminishes the distinctive charm of each film. Similarly, even when multiple creators use the same format, each video emerges with its own distinct flavor. It's in this spirit that I urge you to identify a format using the research model detailed in this book—one that truly resonates with you—and commit wholeheartedly to mastering it.

My team has identified and analyzed hundreds of top-performing formats using the model outlined within these pages, gleaning insights into the nuances behind structures that consistently yield impressive outcomes. The analysis of formats in this section serves as a testament to how the Viral Content Model operates, as well as my team's dedicated research and analysis.

While we journey through a few standout Viral Formats, it's essential to understand that these are merely examples of how we break down and understand their mechanics. If the formats showcased here don't align with your brand or business goals, don't be discouraged. You can always utilize our research model to identify other formats that suit your needs. Remember, these are not the only formats you can use to achieve success, but they provide insight into the kind of analysis that can lead to such success.

Note: Content formats span both short- and long-form narratives. Short-form formats, typically ranging from 10 seconds to three minutes, are popular on platforms such as TikTok, Facebook, YouTube shorts, and Instagram Reels. Meanwhile, long-form formats, usually eight or more minutes, and occasionally extending into hours, are featured on YouTube, enabling creators to dig deep into a subject—even mini documentaries. In this chapter, our primary focus will be on short-form formats, with one long-form example. If you're interested in delving deeper into long-form formats, the model in this book offers guidance for conducting your own research. (Additionally, my team and I collaborate with clients to carry out research and craft strategies tailored to their needs. To explore the possibility of working together, feel free to contact us at: http://guide.hookpoint.com.)

FORMAT STRATEGIES—SECTION 2

THE VISUAL METAPHOR VIRAL FORMAT (SHORT FORM)

Have you ever felt that your product or service is too mature for TikTok? Have you assumed that the platform was just for lighthearted dance routines and the like? Well, you're in good company. Many content creators—especially those who are serious professionals, such as physicians, therapists, and financial advisers—hesitate to engage on TikTok, worrying that their profound insights may fall on deaf ears. Yet, innovative creators are shattering the misconception that TikTok is "too young" for their messages, effectively harnessing the platform's power by learning to speak its language.

Introducing the Visual Metaphor Viral Format

Thanks to the Viral Content Model's meticulous research and analysis, we've successfully analyzed this Viral Format. It stands as a powerful tool that makes abstract or complex topics digestible and, believe it or not, primed for virality. Let's dive into its mechanics:

1. **An abstract or complex topic:** The core subject or idea.
2. **A visual representation:** Using physical objects to represent the topic visually.
3. **A verbal explanation:** Articulating the topic for clarity.

Notable content creators, such as psychologist Julie Smith, who has over 4.7 million followers on TikTok and more than 1.9 million on Instagram, break down complex subjects like PTSD, panic attacks, and stress. Take, for instance, her video titled *Want to Be Happy? Don't Make This Mistake,* which can be viewed at http://guide.hookpoint.com/, along with all the other videos in this book and chapter. This video, which has amassed more than 20 million views, features Smith using a rubber fish and a fish tank to illustrate the toxicity in our environments and how it impacts our well-being, drawing parallels to real-life scenarios.

The video script is as follows:

> *Don't make this mistake when you are working on your own happiness. Imagine this is you* [she holds up a rubber fish] *and this is your life* [points to a fish tank]. *But like most people's lives, there are problems that can make it toxic* [she drops some brown colored dye into the water]. *If a fish is living in a toxic environment, eventually it gets sick. So you take her out of the dirty water and put her in a new tank for a while* [puts fish in a clean tank of water], *kind of like how you take a break—you go on holiday for a few weeks into a new environment and it helps, everything gets better and feels great for a while until you return and go right back to that toxic situation again* [puts

> the fish back in the dirty tank]. *It doesn't matter how clean the water was on your break or how refreshed you feel, eventually you will get sick again. If you want to thrive in the long term* [drops fish back in the clean tank of water], *you have to focus on cleaning up the environment that is affecting you every day. I'm a psychologist. Follow for more.*

Although this video stands out as one of Smith's top-performing pieces, not every one of her visual metaphors reaches the same level of success. So, what differentiates the Gold (high performing) from the Silver (baseline) and the Bronze (underperforming)?

Based on my team's analysis, the primary drivers influencing the virality of content within this format are:

4. **Active metaphor:** Use an object as an active participant in the narrative, which visually demonstrates concepts and effectively complements verbal storytelling.
5. **Tension:** Build anticipation or suspense to engage viewers.
6. **Potential energy:** Engage the viewer's attention from the start by suggesting that the story or object possesses potential and kinetic energy that is on the verge of being released.
7. **Perspective shift:** Present a familiar idea or circumstance; then reframe it in a way that viewers have likely never experienced before.
8. **Cleverness:** Depict the topic visually in an unexpected and smart way.
9. **Immediately applicable:** Offer advice that not only presents a new way of thinking but that can also be applied instantly by the viewer.

Now, let's delve deeper into each of these performance drivers.

ACTIVE METAPHOR

The high-performing Gold videos feature dynamic visual metaphors, where objects are active participants in the story and explanation. These visual elements embody the concept being explained, reducing the viewer's dependence on the verbal explanation. This combination of visual and auditory storytelling enhances understanding and captures the viewer's attention effectively.

Top of FormConsider Smith's *Crumpled Paper Trauma,* which has gotten more than 12 million views on TikTok. She goes beyond verbal explanation and physically manipulates props to demonstrate the experience of trauma and its therapeutic management. The video begins with a basket filled with crumpled paper—a visual metaphor for the overwhelming sense of stress or trauma. By the end, the paper is neatly folded at the bottom, creating space in the basket, which visually represents relief and therapeutic process.

As emphasized in Part I of this book, the performance drivers for Gold video formats are more apparent when cross-analyzed with the lower-performing Bronze category videos. Smith's *Cars in Traffic,* which garnered a modest 128,900 views on TikTok, fails to maximize the potential of the objects. The props are static, and viewers are asked to imagine the concept rather than see it demonstrated. The lack of movement and interaction prevents the props from effectively symbolizing the narrative, making the video less engaging and more difficult to follow.

TENSION

Building tension is a crucial component of visual metaphors. It creates a sense of a looming problem that needs resolution, compelling viewers to keep watching. This engagement is beneficial, as it signals to platform algorithms that the content retains viewer interest.

For example, in the high-performing Gold video *Burnout*, which has amassed more than 3.6 million views, Smith introduces tension by lighting a match at the beginning and holding it as the video progresses. The flame inches closer to her fingers as she speaks, which makes it obvious that if she doesn't put out the fire, she's going to burn her fingers. This growing tension not only symbolizes the mental strain that occurs as one nears burnout, but also strengthens the verbal message with a compelling visual narrative.

In contrast, the low-performing Bronze video *Confidence Check-In*, which only garnered 61,400 views, fails to incorporate tension in its visual metaphor. Although Smith points to different colors in a rainbow to represent different levels of confidence, there's no visual indication of a problem that needs addressing. Without this element of tension, the visual metaphor lacks urgency and fails to engage viewers as effectively.

POTENTIAL ENERGY

Openers in videos are crucial. In the Visual Metaphor Viral Format, the high-performing Gold videos subtly hint to the viewer that the story or object possesses potential and kinetic energy, signaling that this energy is about to be unleashed.

In Smith's video *Kintsugi*, which has gained 854,600 views on TikTok, the very first frame shows Smith holding a plate in one hand

and a hatchet in the other, immediately setting the stage for potential action. This visual creates a strong sense of potential energy. However, the video could have been more effective if she had delayed smashing the plate to build up tension for a longer period of time.

On the other hand, Smith's *Improvements and Setbacks*, with 108,600 views on TikTok, demonstrates lower potential energy in its introduction. Initially, it's unclear what Smith is holding. Only when she removes the cap does it become apparent that it's a marker. Since viewers cannot immediately identify the object, they are less likely to form subconscious expectations about any visible release of energy.

CLEVERNESS

Top-performing Gold videos in this format often distinguish themselves through their cleverness, which my team and I define as being *unexpectedly smart*. Although many videos showcase smart ideas or unexpected elements, the top ones combine these aspects to create something that fits this description. The goal is to present content that makes viewers think, *Why didn't I think of it like that?*

In Smith's *Grief Circle Painting*, which has more than 4.5 million views on TikTok, the cleverness is evident. The video uses a black spot to symbolize grief. For most of it, the secondary camera focuses on this black spot as colorful circles are painted around it, making the spot appear large and dominant. However, in the end, it's revealed that the black spot is quite small in the context of the surrounding colors. This symbolic representation of grief is clever because it draws an unexpected parallel between seemingly unrelated elements.

Conversely, Smith's *Anxiety Rainbow*, with 73,700 views on TikTok, displays less cleverness in its visual metaphor. The video uses layers of a rainbow to represent different levels of coping with anxiety.

As each layer is removed, symbolizing how anxiety erodes various aspects of a person's life, the metaphor becomes predictable. When the final layer is removed, it's fairly obvious that the layers will be reapplied. Although the metaphor is smart, its predictability detracts from its cleverness.

IMMEDIATELY APPLICABLE

A key element for creating high-performing Gold videos is to provide advice that can be immediately put into practice. Suggestions that introduce fresh perspectives and are universally applicable tend to engage audiences more effectively and yield better performance. Conversely, content that presents recommendations not readily actionable tends to fall short in viewer retention.

For example, Smith's *Toxic Environment* , with more than 12 million views on TikTok, offers universally applicable advice. It guides viewers on assessing how their everyday environments impact their mental health. This advice is actionable right away, as viewers can always reflect on their surroundings.

In contrast, goodwisequotes' *Four Top Psychology Tips,* which has garnered 13,800 views on TikTok, offers multiple pieces of advice but is lacking in terms of immediate applicability. An example from this video suggests that if viewers suspect someone is staring at them, they should look at the ceiling; if the other person looks up as well, it likely means they were indeed staring. This scenario is not commonly encountered by most people, meaning that viewers might have to wait an indefinite amount of time before they can apply this suggestion. Such a delay in applicability can make the advice less impactful and relevant.

YOUR FREE BONUS: INCORPORATING MARGINAL GAINS

Dive into the intricacies of viral content with our exclusive video tutorial, *Test Your Knowledge on the Visual Metaphor Viral Format*. Now that you've learned to distinguish Gold-level (high-performing) content from Bronze-level (low-performing) content, it's time to put your knowledge to the test! Watch the video and see if you can identify the standout post.

Access Your Tutorial Easily. Visit online: Go to http://guide.hookpoint.com/ to access *Test Your Knowledge: Visual Metaphor Viral Format*. This concise tutorial is designed to enhance your understanding and make the analysis process straightforward.

Scan for Quick Access. Prefer to skip typing? Scan the QR code below for instant access.

I offer this resource as a complimentary token of my commitment to enriching your learning experience. Absorb the insights and elevate your content to the Gold standard!

FORMAT STRATEGIES—SECTION 3

THE "TWO CHARACTERS, ONE LIGHTBULB" VIRAL FORMAT (SHORT FORM)

Urban legends and modern myths captivate us all; yet, at times, an enlightening "lightbulb" moment reframes our misconceptions. This format gives creators an innovative way to address and debunk such misconceptions. A standout example of this format is *Are You Eating Puppy Portions?* by Creator @EmilyHackettFitness. This video, along with all other videos in this chapter, can be found at http://guide.hookpoint.com/) and has garnered more than seven million views.

In these videos, the creator often plays two roles: expert and novice. The novice, unaware of their misconception, is enlightened by the expert during a short exchange. This revelation, or lightbulb moment, leads to actionable advice from the expert.

Top creators who use this format excel in highlighting the differences between novice and expert roles, building compelling tension. They use this tension to position their channel or expertise as the solution to common misconceptions. This versatile format spans various domains such as fitness, law, real estate, and finance, where creators debunk myths and showcase how they can guide their audience toward clarity and understanding. By skillfully using this format, creators produce content that entertains, educates, challenges norms, and promotes personal growth.

Top-performing Gold videos in this format are fun and informative. By using contrasting elements, they shift perspectives and drive home their messages. Their wide appeal stems from debunking common misconceptions and offering solutions that resonate with a diverse audience.

The hypotheses that my team and I have developed regarding the performance drivers that contribute to virality in this format include:

1. Contrast
2. Breaking misconceptions
3. Digestible, actionable Information
4. Effective pacing
5. Leave viewers wanting more
6. Let's explore each of these in depth.

CONTRAST

Contrast plays a pivotal role in Gold-performing videos in the Two Characters, One Lightbulb format. It highlights the stark differences between the two characters. Creators cleverly incorporate contrast through various means such as delivery, visual elements, or the script, establishing tension between the characters. This tension crafts a compelling narrative that juxtaposes two viewpoints on a single subject. The exaggerated differences often elicit humor, which engages and entertains the audience. Through this dynamic, creators position themselves, or their services, as the catalyst for the novice's perspective shift.

A Gold-standard example of contrast can be seen in calltoleap's video *Making $80k at Home*, which amassed 3.6 million views. In the video, the novice character's arrogant demeanor starkly contrasts with the expert's composed manner. Intriguingly, both characters earn $80,000 a year; yet the novice is tied to a conventional nine-to-five grind, which is much less appealing than the expert's enviable 15-minute workweek.

On the other hand, a Bronze-standard example of contrast is showcased in *Insurance for Your Stocks*, which only captured 130,000 views. Although there's a subtle difference in the personalities of the characters, the primary topic lacks the sharp contrast observed in the Gold-standard video. Instead of building tension between the characters, it merely presents information. There's no significant aha moment, and the novice character doesn't appear to conflict with or oppose the expert in any manner.

The effective utilization of contrast enables creators to craft content with humor, anticipation, and dynamic flow. It paves the way for building tension, which provides an opportunity to introduce a creator's service as the solution. Contrast can be infused into every aspect of content creation—be it the delivery, visuals, or story structure.

By exaggerating contrasts, creators infuse humor, captivating their audience.

So, to maximize the impact of contrast, try to incorporate prevalent industry misconceptions into your content. This strategy produces relatable videos that resonate with viewers.

BREAKING MISCONCEPTIONS

The Two Characters, One Lightbulb format gains viral traction when it effectively clarifies or challenges common misconceptions, leading to a shift in the audience's perspective. Gold content in this format defies expectations by presenting alternative and innovative ways to consider familiar topics.

A prime example of breaking misconceptions is showcased in the *Making $80k at Home* video. As touched on above in the "Contrast" section, it challenges the notion of a standard workweek by showing how someone can make $80,000 a year while working only 15 minutes a week, challenging conventional beliefs.

Conversely, the Bronze example *Car Insurance*, with only 150,000 views, fails to effectively address misconceptions. It lacks contrast and doesn't offer valuable insights to truly engage its audience.

Gold videos in this format give the viewer a perspective shift and completely change what they think is possible. This equips the audience with valuable insights and triggers enlightening aha moments.

DIGESTIBLE, ACTIONABLE INFORMATION

Gold videos in the Two Characters, One Lightbulb format deliver practical advice on seemingly complex tasks, such as buying a home, making them appear straightforward and attainable. Creators present this advice concisely, ensuring that viewers aren't overwhelmed with technicalities. As a result, viewers leave with invaluable takeaways.

A Gold example of incorporating digestible, actionable information in the Two Characters, One Lightbulb format is *Mortgages Explained* by @ecommjess. This video, which garnered 1.9 million views, takes the monumental task of buying a house and makes the process feel achievable by explaining the loan options available to first-time buyers.

Conversely, the Bronze example *Roth IRA*, has only 20,000 views, failing to achieve a standout performance. It opens using inaccessible jargon, which disconnects and overwhelms viewers. From the outset, they feel left behind, pondering the definition of a Roth IRA. This lack of clarity about the topic causes viewers to tune out immediately.

To make your content compelling and engaging, it's essential that information is both actionable and widely comprehensible. Top performers in this format captivate viewers by addressing common and relatable topics—from buying a house to fitness routines. Attracting a wider audience—even those not inherently interested in a subject—amplifies engagement. Before attempting to shift perspectives, ensure that viewers grasp the subject at hand. Bombarding them with technical terms will only deter engagement, as viewers pay attention to creators who take a complex topic and make it approachable.

EFFECTIVE PACING

Pacing in videos refers to the rhythm at which ideas and stories are presented, focusing less on the quantity of shots and more on the speed at which the narrative progresses. Effective pacing highlights key information while swiftly moving through repetitive details, ensuring that the audience remains engaged. In Gold videos, creators master the art of pacing, getting straight to the point and propelling the story forward with precision. The script and delivery provide just the right dose of background information to spark viewers' interest, maintaining a pace that keeps them engaged without being overwhelmed. The seamless flow of content elements leaves no room for boredom or loss of interest. In Bronze videos, there are often random jokes thrown in that slow down the pacing of the video.

Earning the Gold for effective pacing, with 1.2 million views, is EmilyHackettFitness' *Bored of Your Diet*. This video is fun, engaging, and effectively highlights the contrast between different diets without resorting to over-the-top acting or silliness. It shows one character eating delicious protein pancakes for breakfast, while the other character is having rice crackers, broccoli, and chicken. The character eating the pancakes explains that she's still following a diet that helps her lose fat. This video's fast pace keeps viewers engaged, stays on the subject, and continually propels the story forward with each line the characters say.

In contrast, the Bronze example *TALKING TO HEALTH INSURANCE PT. 1*, by @ecommjess, with a modest 28,000 views, falls short in pacing due to a drawn-out story that prompts viewers to click away before the message lands. The entire narrative involving the pizza, counting money, and the interaction with the woman's boss takes up too much time before introducing the truly important element: the pharmacy.

To create compelling content, it's crucial to find the right balance in the pace. Getting to the heart of the matter quickly and maintaining an engaging tempo will keep your audience interested and invested in the story. Avoiding excessive theatrics and unnecessary prolongation helps enhance message delivery, creating a lasting impression. It's tempting to pack content with multiple points and an abundance of jokes. However, the key to truly resonating with your audience lies in crafting one major aha moment or a significant shift in perspective. This singular, powerful insight is what truly captivates viewers. People aren't looking for an exhaustive rundown of every detail or step. They crave that *one* transformative insight that fundamentally alters their thinking.

Gold videos in this format drive the story forward with rhythmic pacing that grabs viewers' attention. These videos always move forward, and the tempo never slows or stalls. That way, when the creator begins providing advice, the transition feels like an organic and obvious next step. Although subjects such as "Roth IRA" or "mortgage" might not inherently spark excitement, the right pacing can inject energy into these otherwise mundane topics.

Although videos in this format are typically short, length is secondary to viewer experience. Focus on maintaining engagement, rather than on meeting some arbitrary time limit. Experiment with your content. If you hold your audience's attention, they'll keep watching—whether it's for 30 seconds or 30 minutes.

LEAVE VIEWERS WANTING MORE

The best content in this format paves a clear pathway for viewers to learn more about a topic. Top creators give us just enough information to entice us without overwhelming us, demystifying seemingly difficult subjects and encouraging us to follow along. This gives the creator the opportunity to insert a clear call to action (CTA), which is an instruction to the audience designed to provoke an immediate response, typically using an imperative verb such as "Follow," "Find out more," or "Visit a store today." This CTA encourages the audience to take the next logical step, whether it's following the creator or watching a second video.

When these CTAs emerge organically, after delivering valuable insights, they don't feel petty or insincere. The audience appreciates that the creator didn't leave them hanging, and they are gratified rather than teased. Viewers feel smarter for having watched the video and are motivated to learn more.

Earning the Gold in CTA with 5.9 million views is *Creatine Explained* by @noeldeyzel_bodybuilder on TikTok. In this video, he simplifies the complex debate of being natural versus using performance-enhancing drugs in bodybuilding. He clarifies that taking creatine, a legal sports supplement, does not make a bodybuilder "unnatural." He explains that only those who use anabolic hormones or performance-enhancing substances fall into the unnatural category. After watching this video, viewers feel informed and empowered, gaining confidence in the benefits of following his advice, and they are compelled to check out the Ryse creatine being promoted.

On the flip side, the Bronze in CTA for the Two Characters, One Lightbulb format goes to *I Will Never Be Able to Buy a House* by @ ecommjess. With only 11,000 views, the video presents a jargon-heavy introduction, delving into topics related to real estate investment trusts. It necessitates an understanding of terms such as *dividends*, *trusts*, and *Roth IRAs*. The content's complexity tends to deter viewer engagement and interest in learning more about real estate investment trusts (REITs).

A well-executed CTA can motivate your audience to become more involved with your brand, either by becoming a follower or even a client. A misplaced or impromptu CTA can seem artificial. So, try to build up a question or interest in your audience (by presenting contrasting elements, for example), and then present the CTA as a natural resolution to this question. By serving value up front and directing viewers toward the next step, you can foster a sense of trust and credibility, making them more likely to engage with your brand and content in the future.

UNLOCK YOUR FREE BONUS: MASTERING THE TWO CHARACTERS, ONE LIGHTBULB VIRAL FORMAT

Immerse yourself in the intricacies of viral content with our exclusive video tutorial, *Test Your Knowledge on the Two Characters, One Lightbulb Viral Format.* Having acquired the skills to distinguish the Gold-level (high-performing) content from Bronze-level (low-performing) content, it's time to translate knowledge into action! Watch the video and see if you can identify the standout post.

Access Your Tutorial Easily. Visit online: Go to http://guide.hookpoint.com/to access *Test Your Knowledge: Two Characters, One Lightbulb Viral Format.* This short tutorial will deepen your grasp of content quality.

Scan for Quick Access. Prefer to skip typing? Scan the QR code below for instant access.

This resource is free of charge as a testament to my promise to enhance your learning curve. Harness these insights and scale your content to the Gold standard!

FORMAT STRATEGIES—SECTION 4

THE UNTOLD STORIES VIRAL FORMAT (SHORT FORM)

Daniel Wall is a master of the Untold Stories Viral Format. With a behind-the-scenes lens, he delves into the intricate, often unexplored narratives of the entertainment industry. Just when viewers believe they're following one story, Wall takes them on a journey into uncharted territory, evoking an exhilarating "Oh wait, what?!" response.

"Daniel's Wall," the name of his channel on YouTube and TikTok, cleverly reflects Wall's ability to pull back the curtain to expose untold captivating stories hidden behind the walls of the entertainment world. He immerses viewers into these narratives, spotlighting the intriguing stories that go beyond superficial tropes. The content focuses on the underappreciated "deep cuts" of the industry, offering a fresh perspective on familiar subjects. Although Wall uses this format primarily to break down stories in the entertainment industry, it is versatile enough to be applied to a wide range of subjects and industries.

Wall's consistency as a creator is evident; his videos consistently surpass a million views. Yet, it's in his standout videos—those garnering three million views or more—where we see key nuances that contribute to his success.

The hypotheses my team and I developed regarding the performance drivers for virality in this format include:

1. Strong hooks with the promise of a story.
2. Introducing the deep cut.
3. Highlighting narratives centered on overcoming obstacles with high stakes.
4. Resolving tension by delivering impactful conclusions for characters or intriguing insights for the audience.

Strong Hooks with the Promise of a Story

Strong hooks that promise an intriguing story have an effect on the viewer that captures attention and builds expectations immediately. They give viewers an initial reason to invest their time in watching the entire video. The Untold Stories format uses one-liner hooks that make viewers pause to give the video a chance. They particularly excel at offering the promise of hidden insights, fostering a sense of discovery that piques viewer interest.

As Wall gradually provides context about the hook through additional information, he starts to craft a narrative that heightens audience expectations. This increased curiosity urges viewers to stick around and discover what happens next so they can either confirm or challenge initial assumptions.

In his most successful Gold videos, Wall captures the audience's attention right from the start by employing hooks that are interesting and hint at the general framework for a narrative. In his top videos, Wall relies on a reasonable assumption—that the viewers are familiar with viral entertainment content. By framing his hooks around popular subjects, he provides viewers with sufficient context to grasp the narrative direction, and the promise of an undiscovered story or insight, thereby elevating their expectations.

For instance, in his viral video *It's Corn: Have You Heard This Viral Song*, which has amassed six million views and can be viewed at http://guide.hookpoint.com/, along with all the other videos and references in this book, Wall captivates his audience by featuring the well-known TikTok song trend "It's Corn!" He then piques viewer interest by hinting at a deeper story: "But the people who made this song . . . have also made the biggest songs on the internet. . . ." This Hook Point, a concept designed to capture the audience's attention as quickly as possible, inspires the audience's curiosity about the song creators, prompting them to eagerly learn more and continue watching.

In contrast, Wall's underperforming Bronze content often features unclear hooks or introductions that fail to establish a clear narrative direction. In these instances, he sometimes wrongly assumes that the audience shares specific background knowledge.

A case in point is the follow-up video to *It's Corn: Have You Heard This Viral Song*. The follow-up video, *It's Corn: Have You Heard This Viral Song Part 2,* only brought in 256,000 views. This video underperformed because Wall assumed that viewers had seen the first video about the song "It's Corn." As a result, he didn't invest enough in creating a compelling introduction, leading to a lack of viewer interest in learning more about the creators of the song.

Take *The Biggest Series Debut HBO's Ever Had*, which only has 146,000 views as another example. This content primarily attracted a niche audience, as most people lack a strong emotional connection to HBO's streaming service itself, unlike the bond they might have with a specific song or show. Also, the visual presentation is overwhelming, displaying numerous intellectual properties (IPs) simultaneously. As the camera swiftly pans across the screen while Wall speaks, it becomes difficult for the audience to absorb all the details, resulting in a lack of one central focal point.

To maximize viewer engagement, aim to craft a Hook Point that can attract the masses within the first three seconds of your video and that promises to unearth an untold story or new revelation. Make sure your Hook Point builds sufficient context and sets a clear narrative direction. This approach will raise audience expectations and increase the likelihood they'll watch your content to the end. For a deeper dive into Hook Points, explore my book, *Hook Point*, which you can find at http://guide.hookpoint.com/.

Introducing the Deep Cut

Introducing the deep cut, or lesser-known stories, into your narrative builds tension and makes viewers feel like insiders. These stories captivate viewers because they trigger an "Oh, wait, what?!" reaction, keeping the audience engaged. Wall masterfully achieves this effect by gradually unveiling unexpected insights, with each revelation serving as a stepping stone toward that next surprise. This builds layers of tension that hook viewers, keeping them invested in an unpredictable narrative journey that gives viewers access to exclusive information.

In his top-performing Gold videos, Wall excels at creating those unexpected "Oh, wait, what?!" moments. Starting with stories that initially appear predictable or familiar, he delves deeper to uncover hidden layers, revealing often overlooked or underappreciated deep cuts that significantly impact the narrative. One frequent technique that Wall uses is exploring the origins of a song, artist, or group, which usually leads him to interesting side narratives. Each new layer adds to accumulating tension that keeps the audience engaged. This continual unveiling of hidden insights—like being let in on a secret—fulfills the viewer's craving for surprise and discovery.

For example, in the mega-viral video *Pogo—Forget (Slowed Down)*, which has garnered more than 21 million views, Wall delves into the viral trend behind this video and reveals lesser-known stories behind the trend's origins. The viral trend of using the song "Pogo—Forget (Slowed Down)" in a TikTok dance where a partner dodges a stick held by the other partner (reminiscent of scenes from *The Matrix*) has an intriguing backstory. Many people believe that the user shiro_snake not only sparked the trend with a video that garnered nearly 40 million views but also created this song. Yet, Wall's research revealed something different: he found that another user, opppleeen, had posted a similar video with the stick-duet dance two months earlier, attracting more than 15 million views. Further digging showed that the song, available on YouTube for over three years before the trend-setting video, is actually a slowed-down version of a track from seven years prior. Intriguingly, this original track was composed of chopped-up samples from various Disney movies. This discovery sheds light on the complex and often-unknown histories behind a viral sensation that many enjoy.

In *Coco*, which garnered 3.7 million views, Wall immediately grabs attention with one of his signature hooks. This time, he delves into the behind-the-scenes challenges faced by the creators of the beloved Pixar film *Coco*. He then dives into the story, focusing on the unexpected journey of the main singer and voice actor for Miguel, the young protagonist of *Coco*. Interestingly, we discover that he was initially rejected for the part and was only intended to do scratch vocals while they looked for the official voice actor for the character.

In contrast, Wall's less successful Bronze videos miss the mark by failing to explore untapped layers or by skimping on research. Although he may introduce central tension, he doesn't incorporate additional micro-tensions within the narrative, focusing solely on one story thread. Unfortunately, this single thread often fizzles out, failing to build adequate anticipation. Instead of layering multiple compelling stories, Wall tends to elongate a single, moderately interesting narrative beyond its natural conclusion.

For example, in *The Biggest Series Debut HBO's Ever Had*, which only generated 146,000 views, Wall explores the success of HBO's show *House of Dragons* and its relationship to the massively popular series *Game of Thrones*. Although many viewers naturally assume that *House of Dragons* drew inspiration from its predecessor's triumph, Wall's discussion doesn't offer much more than mildly interesting statistics comparing the audience sizes of the two shows. The video falls short in exploring additional layers of the narrative, such as the creative challenges faced during production or the strategic decisions that led to the new show's success or failure.

In *Lizzo* which received only 260,000 views, Wall covers the initial lack of success of one of Lizzo's hit singles, "About Damn Time." Given that the song eventually became a hit, and the audience is already familiar with its ultimate rise to popularity, the video fails to offer any new or unexpected insights. The narrative falls short in delivering the "Oh, wait, what?!" moments that are a hallmark of Wall and the Untold Stories format. It fails to delve into the less-explored nuances of the story, missing an opportunity to uncover deeper insights. As a result, the video doesn't hold the same level of intrigue or tension, compared to his more successful pieces that unravel lesser-known narratives.

Some ways to uncover deep cuts and explore lesser-known or overlooked aspects within familiar stories in your field or niche involve doing the following:

1. Research nuances, side narratives, or hidden details to provide fresh insights and captivate your audience. (For example, one of Wall's most common research themes involves the Origin Stories of hit creations, artists, or groups.)
2. Reframe a linear, logical story in a less obvious manner. Consider what the standard way to tell a story is, and then craft scripts that deviate from that norm.
3. Share unexpected revelations or exclusive information to which you may have access.

Additionally, don't overlook the importance of stacking tension. Instead of fixating on a single story, weave in multiple micro-tensions within your narrative. This could involve exploring different angles, perspectives, or subplots that contribute to the larger resolution.

Overcoming Obstacles with High Stakes

Focusing on narratives that showcase overcoming high-stakes obstacles creates underdog stories that are both relatable and tension building. These narratives tap into the universal human desire to witness triumph in the face of adversity, resonating with viewers who identify with the struggle. The heightened stakes add a layer of suspense, as the characters' lives or careers depend on overcoming these challenges.

As a result, viewers are more likely to stay engaged, eagerly anticipating the potential for a life-altering victory or a heartbreaking setback.

In his Gold Videos, Wall focuses on individuals who defy the odds as underdogs, achieving unexpected success. With a keen eye for detail, he selects stories that naturally embody the underdog narrative or reframe a seemingly successful character who had to overcome hidden challenges. By skillfully emphasizing the significant stakes involved, Wall not only builds anticipation but also sets the stage for transformative outcomes that can make or break the artists' careers.

For example, in *Have You Heard This Viral Song, Mr. Telephone Man*, with 7.7 million views, Wall follows a child who went viral for covering a song from the '80s. This viral video led to a string of successes for the young artist, including a starring role in a Broadway play.

In another video, *Let's Talk about the Problem Every Artist Has*, which garnered more than 9.3 million views, Wall presents Elton John as an underdog fighting the notion that older artists can't recapture their past glory. This unconventional angle shows the struggles even superstars face against societal pressures.

In contrast, the less successful Bronze videos lack the essential elements of transformation and stakes. They fail to mention what's on the line, and as a result, don't inspire viewers or position them for a satisfying payoff.

For example, in *How Artists Got Their Name*, with just 88,000 views, Wall discusses how the British rock group Coldplay chose their name. However, he fails to explore the name's impact on their success, leaving the narrative feeling emotionally flat.

To craft videos that resonate deeply, look for stories that naturally embody or can be reframed to showcase the underdog narrative.

Remember, the underdog story is just one example; other compelling themes might include coming-of-age, self-discovery, perseverance, love and relationships, and overcoming fear. Importantly, make sure to emphasize the stakes involved, and clearly articulate the way in which they can set up your audience for a satisfying emotional payoff.

Delivering Impactful Conclusions for Characters

The power of content often lies in its conclusion. A well-crafted ending that resolves tension with impactful conclusions for characters or intriguing insights for the audience leaves viewers feeling impressed, and inspired to share the content. The act of sharing plays a crucial role in a video's virality, as it helps extend its reach and capture the attention of algorithms.

Simply maintaining viewers' attention until the end may not inspire them to click "Share," though. They need to perceive value in the content—something they believe will also enrich the lives of their friends and family. In this context, sharing isn't a one-way street. Although it certainly amplifies Wall's reach, it also allows viewers to feel good about sending valuable content to their social network.

Wall excels at providing value in two principal ways: First, he offers meaningful entertainment through engaging stories. These narratives resonate with viewers, evoking emotions and connecting them to the experiences of the characters. Second, he delivers insider insights that make viewers feel both special and privileged. By sharing exclusive information or unique perspectives, he taps into their desire for knowledge while creating a sense of exclusivity.

In both scenarios, Wall skillfully resolves the narrative tension, leaving viewers with a satisfying payoff, which is amplified by the journey they've just taken.

All of Wall's Gold videos in this storytelling framework either delve into unexplored nuances of traditional stories or feature characters who confront significant obstacles, leading to an insightful or impactful resolution.

Let's look at the Gold Videos within these two main categories:

1. **The underdog videos:** Wall showcases stories of performers and entertainers who face daunting challenges, revealing how overcoming these obstacles leads to transformative decisions with significant impact. The implications feel life-changing for the individuals involved. Throughout the story, Wall subtly hints at the life-changing consequences but only confirms these implications at the very end. For example, in his video *The Biggest Song Was Meant to Fail*, which boasts more than 3.3 million views, Wall narrates the unexpected success story of OneRepublic's song "I Ain't Worried," featured in the film *Top Gun: Maverick*. Interestingly, the song wasn't intended to be the movie's hit, initially overshadowed by Lady Gaga's "Hold My Hand." However, "I Ain't Worried" gained viral popularity due to its association with a TikTok video showcasing a clip from the movie that features actor Miles Teller's abs. Wall also explores OneRepublic's tumultuous journey through the music industry. The band was dropped by Columbia Records just two months before their first album's release. Unfazed, the lead singer used MySpace to release the band's music, leading to their rise as the number-one unsigned act on the platform. This success eventually led to a deal with

Timbaland's label, marking the start of OneRepublic's journey in creating numerous hits.

Additionally, in *Let's Talk about the Problem Every Artist Has*, which has amassed more than 9.3 million views, Wall discusses the challenges musicians face as they age, particularly noting their difficulty in replicating the success they achieved in their youth. He highlights how Elton John successfully navigated this challenge by sampling four of his own songs to create a new hit, "Cold Heart," with Dua Lipa, earning him his first top-10 hit in more than 25 years. Wall also explains how Elton John repeated this successful formula by sampling three of his songs in collaboration with Britney Spears on "Hold Me Closer," which also provided her with an opportunity for a comeback.

2. **The origin-story videos:** These offer a unique and rewarding experience, delving into behind-the-scenes insider stories of popular hits and artists. This content climaxes with intriguing revelations, gifting viewers with exclusive insights. For example, the video *Pogo—Forget (Slowed Down)*, which has garnered more than 21 million views, uncovers the background story of a song released seven years prior that unexpectedly became a viral trend. Another notable video in this series, *Netflix-Wednesday?*, with more than 11 million views, explores the TikTok trend of using Lady Gaga's "Bloody Mary" in relation to the Netflix program *Wednesday*. Interestingly, the song isn't featured in the show. Wall reveals how actress Jenna Ortega

choreographed her dance scene in *Wednesday* to a different song, "Goo Goo Muck" by The Cramps, which is more than 40 years old and also went viral due to the show's popularity. These revelations in both videos affirm the audience's belief that their time spent watching was worthwhile.

In contrast, Wall's low-performing Bronze videos lack both impactful insights and compelling narratives. They don't have the depth or the intrigue that sets his Gold videos apart. Often, these videos follow overused or predictable storylines that lack tension, resulting in unsatisfying endings. For example, *The Biggest Series Debut HBOs Ever Had* with a modest 126,000 views, fails to offer any intriguing details about the origin of *House of the Dragon* beyond the fact that it's a *Game of Thrones* spin-off and performed well despite backlash against the latter's final season. Another example is *How Artists Got Their Name*, which garnered only 88,000 views. It underperformed because it stops short of explaining how Coldplay transitioned from its original name, Starfish, leaving viewers somewhat disappointed.

YOUR EXCLUSIVE BONUS: MASTERING THE UNTOLD STORIES VIRAL FORMAT

Delve deeper into the world of viral content with our special video tutorial, *Test Your Knowledge on the Untold Stories Viral Format*. Now that you've honed your ability to differentiate between Gold-level (high-performing) content and Bronze-level (low-performing) content, let's move from concept to execution! Review the video and determine which post really stands out.

Access Your Tutorial Easily. Visit online: Go to http://guide.hookpoint.com/ to access *Test Your Knowledge: Untold Stories Viral Format*. This brief tutorial will solidify your understanding of what makes content resonate.

Scan for Quick Access. Want immediate access? Scan the QR Code below and jump straight in.

Offered at no cost, this resource reflects my commitment to elevating your educational journey. Leverage this knowledge and raise your content to the heights of the Gold standard!

FORMAT STRATEGIES—SECTION 5

THE 30-DAY-CHALLENGE VIRAL FORMAT (LONG FORM)

The success of the 30-Day-Challenge format is attributed to its balance between personal experience and universal appeal. Matt d'Avella, a well-known YouTuber and documentary filmmaker with more than 3.4 million subscribers and 300 million views, serves as an excellent example of someone who has adeptly mastered this format. He's undertaken various self-improvement challenges, demonstrating his commitment to pursuing a meaningful life through small steps, simple habits, and gradual growth. His content serves as a prime example of how to chronicle self-improvement journeys in a way that informs and inspires audiences.

Among the challenges d'Avella has undertaken include quitting sugar for 30 days and taking only cold showers for a month. These challenges are designed to push his boundaries and encourage personal growth. By documenting his experiences and sharing them with his audience, he offers valuable insights into his journey while also encouraging others to take on their own paths of self-improvement.

In addition to quitting sugar and taking cold showers, d'Avella has also undertaken a variety of other challenges, such as adopting a vegan diet for a month and reading 30 books in 30 days. Each challenge comes with a unique set of obstacles and lessons. His authentic and candid style in his videos resonates deeply with viewers.

The performance-driver hypotheses my team and I have developed with respect to what leads to virality in this format include:

1. Accessible, actionable, and novel topics
2. External research
3. Lighting and composition
4. Storytelling and the Jenga effect
5. Dynamic energy

ACCESSIBLE, ACTIONABLE, AND NOVEL TOPICS

One of the keys to mastering the 30-Day-Challenge format is selecting an accessible, actionable, and novel topic. Viral content within this format features challenges that are achievable for anyone with enough willpower and interest, without requiring special skills or costly equipment. In top-performing Gold videos, the duration of the challenge is carefully aligned with the task's difficulty, ensuring that it's challenging but achievable. For example, a 30-Day Challenge to quit sugar or take cold showers is tough but doable. In contrast, attempting to free dive in deep water without the proper training can lead to drowning, shallow-water blackouts, or decompression sickness, making it extremely unsafe and difficult for most people to accomplish.

The top-performing content also inspires viewers to attempt new challenges they might not have thought of otherwise. Although challenges focusing on well-known paths of self-improvement may fail to grab attention, novel challenges such as taking cold showers have the opposite effect. These intriguing topics naturally spark curiosity about the potential benefits of such challenges, prompting viewers to explore the content further and perhaps even take up these tasks themselves.

EXTERNAL RESEARCH

Gold creators enhance the credibility of their challenges by integrating expert interviews, charts, graphs, and supporting statistics. Many of the videos adopt a documentary-style approach and feature expert content, enriching the audience's learning experience.

Including expert interviews provides viewers with authoritative insights and perspectives, adding depth and credibility to the challenge. These experts contribute valuable tips and advice, enhancing the challenge's legitimacy.

The use of charts, graphs, and supporting statistics strengthens the challenge's validity and its potential benefits. This data driven approach appeals to the viewer's logical side, increasing their trust in the information and their willingness to undertake the task.

Documentary-style narratives offer a compelling storytelling experience that engages the audience emotionally while presenting the challenge in a well-structured and informative manner. This format allows for a more immersive and educational viewing experience.

By incorporating these tactics, Gold creators not only make their challenges more convincing but also increase the educational value of the content, making it more effective in connecting with the masses.

LIGHTING AND COMPOSITION

In Gold content, lighting and composition play a crucial role in creating a visually engaging experience. Talented creators pay attention to detail, ensuring that each shot offers three-dimensional depth with a sharp foreground, a softer midground, and a background. This careful arrangement mimics our natural, real-life perspectives and contributes to a comfortable viewing experience.

These lighting and composition techniques allow top creators to enhance the viewing experience without the need for an elaborate production team or a large budget. The sharp foreground draws the viewer's attention to the main subject or challenge, while the slightly blurred midground and background add depth and dimension, enhancing the storytelling aspect.

The result feels like an intimate conversation with a friend. The visual depth and composition create an authentic atmosphere that fosters a sense of connection between the viewers and creators. It feels as though we're right there, engaging in a discussion about the bold idea of undertaking a weeklong fast with them.

This thoughtful use of lighting and composition not only enhances the overall viewing experience but also keeps the audience engaged from start to finish. This attention to visual detail plays a key role in the content's success, drawing viewers in and sustaining their interest throughout the video.

STORYTELLING AND THE JENGA EFFECT

The Jenga Effect is a powerful storytelling strategy (explained in depth in Part I), for building suspense and engagement in viewers. Like pulling blocks from a Jenga tower, this technique involves progressively introducing new elements and challenges to build tension and anticipation.

As each new twist or obstacle is added, viewers become more invested in the subject's journey. The unexpected elements keep the audience engaged, as they want to know how the challenges will be navigated or resolved.

Creators strategically manage tension and release throughout the video, creating a roller-coaster-like experience for the viewers. Each introduced obstacle heightens tension, drawing viewers into the story and leaving them eager for the resolution.

Using the Jenga Effect, creators maintain a dynamic, exciting, engaging narrative that keeps viewers hooked. As the suspense builds, viewers become increasingly connected to the subject's journey, eager to watch until the end to see how it all unfolds.

DYNAMIC ENERGY

Top-performing Gold creators use a diverse range of shots, captions, images, and segments to create dynamic shifts in energy that captivate and sustain viewer attention. Instead of presenting their content chronologically, viral creators structure their videos around specific obstacles they encounter during their challenges. This creates a more immersive experience that makes the viewer feel like an active participant rather than a passive observer.

The dynamic approach not only keeps audiences engaged but also builds empathy for the creators' struggles and triumphs. By showcasing the highs and lows of their self-improvement journeys, they invite us into their world and keep us emotionally invested in their progress.

The use of appealing visuals—such as meticulously framed shots and eye-catching images—enhances the storytelling and adds visual allure to the content. Cleverly placed captions and segments further elevate the entertainment value, making the viewing experience both informative and engaging.

This format's focus on specific obstacles rather than a linear chronology gives the videos a dynamic, suspenseful quality. This makes viewers eager to see how each obstacle will be overcome, which builds anticipation and maintains engagement throughout the entire video.

By sharing their journeys in this compelling manner, Gold creators not only entertain and inspire but also create a sense of community among their audience. Viewers become emotionally invested in the creators' progress and are often encouraged to undertake their own self-improvement challenges.

30-Day-Challenge Gold Content

I Quit Sugar for 30 Days, which can be watched at http://guide.hookpoint.com/, along with all the other videos in this book, is a challenging feat that few would willingly tackle. Yet for the vast majority, it's an attainable goal. In this compelling video, d'Avella, with 3.4 million subscribers, guides us through his sugar-free month, providing meticulous detail that immerses viewers in his physical and emotional journey.

To enhance the credibility of his message and add value to the video, d'Avella includes an interview with an expert nutritionist who explains the significant health benefits involved in reducing one's sugar intake. These well-informed insights add a layer of authenticity, making viewers feel as if they're gaining valuable knowledge from the video.

Visually, the video utilizes lighting and composition to create engaging depth that captivates the audience. Close-ups of d'Avella's face communicate the reality of his struggle without the need for many words. The inclusion of supportive graphics reinforces viewer retention and comprehension, making the information more accessible and digestible.

The video's storytelling is driven by dynamic shifts in energy to chart the highs and lows of d'Avella's experience, maintaining viewer engagement and a strong connection between the creator and the audience. The 30-day duration of the sugar-free challenge strikes a well-calculated balance: it's long enough to potentially produce noticeable physical changes while remaining approachable for a general audience.

I Took Cold Showers for 30 Days, which has garnered more than 6.3 million views, was based on research from the book *The Flinch* by *New York Times* bestselling author Julien Smith. This research-backed health improvement plan elevates the challenge beyond a simple stunt, adding value and appeal for the viewers.

The video showcases d'Avella's skillful use of visual composition, even during scenes of cold showers, enhancing the overall viewing experience. The inclusion of B-roll footage—which is supplemental or alternative footage intercut with the main shot, featuring topic experts—further enhances the dynamics of the video by providing additional insights and expertise.

The 30-day time frame aligns well with the difficulty of taking cold showers daily. It allows adequate time to experience the potential benefits and changes without becoming excessively long or overwhelming for participants.

In *What Happens If You Don't Eat for 10 Days?* which has garnered 3.3 million views, the creator narrates his experience with a 10-day fast. The skillful use of the Jenga Effect builds tension and anticipation throughout the video, drawing viewers deeper into the unfolding narrative. This successful storytelling technique not only keeps the audience engaged but also boosts retention rates, as viewers are eager to see the challenge's resolution.

Also, the solid visual execution, including compelling shots and compositions, enhances its overall impact. The 10-day time frame of the fast is short enough to maintain interest while emphasizing the challenge's difficulty, elevating the content to Gold-level status and making a lasting impression on the audience.

30-Day-Challenge Bronze Content

The low-performing Bronze content in this format lacks dynamic storytelling, research, visual depth, and interesting or accessible challenge types. For example, Goal Guy's *Cold Weather Workouts*, with 107,000 views, presents an intriguing challenge but limits its appeal to viewers living in cold climates or those who are already physically fit. Additionally, many residents of such climates might already engage in cold-weather activities and view them as regular parts of their routine, not as novel challenges. Thus, the content may not seem particularly interesting or unique to them. Also, although the video mentions research, it misses the opportunity to include visual aids such as charts and graphs, which negatively affect viewer engagement.

Harshibar's *I Quit Social Media*, with only 15,000 views, structures its narrative chronologically rather than around specific obstacles. This approach lacks the suspense-building quality achieved by techniques like the Jenga Effect.

Nathaniel Drew's *30 Days No Alcohol* with 144,000 views, falls short in the visual depth department. The primary shots appear flat and two-dimensional, lacking the appropriate distance between the subject and the camera. Also, the subject's face occupies less than half of the screen's vertical height, missing the effectiveness of a tightly framed shot.

The Unlazy Ways' challenge video, *30 Books in 30 Days*, which has garnered 61,000 views, presents an impossibly short time frame that may be unrealistic for the average viewer. On the other hand, their *I Ditched Coffee for 100 Days,* with 96,000 views, features a significantly longer challenge duration. This extended time frame might discourage viewers from even considering giving up their favorite beverage, potentially making the challenge less appealing.

UNLOCK YOUR BONUS:
MASTERING THE 30-DAY-CHALLENGE FORMAT

Explore the dynamics of viral success with our exclusive video tutorial, *Test Your Knowledge on the 30-Day-Challenge Format.* After mastering the distinction between Gold-level (high-performing) content and Bronze-level (low-performing) content, it's time to apply your insights! Watch the video and pinpoint the post that truly stands out.

Access Your Tutorial Easily. Visit online: Go to http://guide.hookpoint.com/ to access *Test Your Knowledge: 30-Day-Challenge Format*. This concise tutorial is designed to enhance your grasp on creating compelling content.

Scan for Quick Access: For quick access, simply scan the QR code below and dive right in.

This resource is provided at no cost as part of my dedication to your continuous learning journey. Utilize this knowledge to elevate your content creation to the prestigious Gold standard!

FORMAT STRATEGIES—SECTION 6

FROM THEORY TO ACTION: PUTTING YOUR CONTENT TO THE TEST

Congratulations on completing another section of this book! Knowledge is only half of the equation, though; application is what truly makes the difference. By continually comparing your work to Gold-level content, you will effectively reinforce the principles that make it highly successful and shareable. Let's dive into another round of benchmarking to keep refining your skills. Here's how to do just that:

1. **Create another video:** Develop a piece of content using a strong reference video that uses a clear Viral Format. You can choose one from this section of the book or select a reference that you find on your own. If you choose your own, ensure that you conduct thorough research to fully understand the key performance drivers and their nuances before attempting to replicate the format.

2. **Compare your completed video with your Gold reference before you post it:** Open up your video next to your high-performing Gold reference video.
3. **Run the checklist:** Go through a performance driver checklist. While doing so, remember that although certain elements are common across various content formats, each one possesses a unique combination of these features. When comparing your video, be conscious of which format you've selected, and focus on identifying the questions that are relevant to your chosen format.

If you chose the Visual Metaphor format, for example, compare your video with one of Dr. Julie Smith's high-performing Gold-tier videos. Assess how effectively you've incorporated the key performance drivers. These include: the impact of the First 3 Seconds, the use of an Active Metaphor, the creation of Tension, the use of Potential Energy, the introduction of a Perspective Shift, incorporating Cleverness, and the inclusion of Immediately Applicable Insights.

Side-by-Side Comparison

Once you have your first video, watch it alongside your reference and evaluate how closely you're executing on the performance drivers.

Comparison Video: Trauma Bin

Evaluation Tool:

Performance Driver	Your Content's Score	Gold Standard Score
First 3 Seconds		5/5
Active Metaphor		5/5
Tension		4/5
Potential Energy		4/5
Perspective Shift		5/5
Cleverness		5/5
Immediately Applicable		4/5

Remember, the performance drivers listed below are specific to the Visual Metaphor format. If you've chosen a different format, you'll need to identify and focus on a distinct set of performance drivers. My team and I have compiled a general list of elements to consider below, but remember, not every element may apply to your chosen format. Use the research and evaluation skills you've learned so far to accurately assess your content and create a format-specific list of criteria. As you complete this exercise, be constructively critical, find room for improvement, and also give yourself credit for the aspects you've handled well. Here are some performance drivers to consider:

1. **The First 3 Seconds:** Does your video start with a hook that immediately grabs the viewer's attention and establishes the context for what's to come?
2. **Generalist Principle:** Have you intentionally incorporated universal themes or common human experiences in

your content to appeal to the masses? Are you approaching your audience as if they have no prior knowledge of your subject matter? Are you selecting broad and relatable topics as focal points? Are you steering clear of intricate terminology or jargon, and ensuring that any new terms are clearly defined for the audience? Are you framing your topics as stories, with conflicts and obstacles, to draw viewers into the narrative?

3. **Perspective Shift:** Does your video offer a powerful revelation or aha moment that challenges viewers' perceptions? Evaluate if it debunks misconceptions, presents new ideas, or highlights different viewpoints. Ensure that it prompts a transformative shift in viewers' perspectives, compelling them to reevaluate the topic in a way that challenges their preconceived beliefs or views.
4. **Viewer Connection:** Does your video establish a personal connection with viewers, acknowledging their perspectives? This includes:
    - Maintaining eye contact.
    - Addressing the viewer directly using *you*. Keep in mind that you're talking to *one* person on the other side of the screen.
    - Framing your content or message from an average viewer's point of view.
    - Predicting what the viewer might think or feel about something you share. Anticipate the viewer's internal monologue, and try to speak to it.

- Providing actionable value, leaving the viewer thinking, *I'm glad I watched that.*
- Offering educational insights that impart new knowledge and satisfies the viewer's curiosity.

5. **Tension Building:** Does your video effectively build tension, compelling viewers to anticipate what will happen next? Be sure that it introduces not only a main problem but also minor problems leading to the resolution of the initial issue. Can you incorporate a Completing the Scale effect, delivering a satisfying resolution to the narrative or message? This can include visual cues that make viewers eager to see the next shot, pivotal shifts in the storyline, and a compelling narrative with a buildup and payoff that holds the audience's attention. Confirm that the initial setup serves as a hook, generating anticipation and curiosity and motivating viewers to stay engaged until the resolution is reached.
6. **Incorporating Cleverness:** Have you infused your content with cleverness? Assess if it includes ideas that are both unexpected and smart, potentially by logically linking two unrelated concepts. Consider whether you engage the audience with witty language or ideas, creating memorable experiences that subvert expectations and elicit the reaction, *Why didn't I think of that?*
7. **Element of Absurdity:** Does your content include elements of absurdity? Experiment with incorporating aspects that are unexpected, ridiculous, or illogical to captivate the audience's attention and create a memorable

experience. Although not all formats utilize absurdity, this technique is particularly effective when used correctly and in conjunction with cleverness.

8. **Effect on the Viewer (EOV):** Prior to utilizing any tactic, did you consider the effect it will have on viewers? Think about the emotions and thoughts you want to evoke after they've watched your content. Begin with the desired outcome and plan backward, strategizing how to achieve this effect.

Continual Improvement

Once you've gone through the checklist, note what's missing or could be improved in your video. Use this feedback for immediate refinements, or incorporate it into your next project. Repeat this process until your video checks all the boxes and stands up to a Gold-level comparison.

By putting your content to this rigorous test, you'll ensure that it not only meets but potentially exceeds the standards of what makes a video go viral. If you keep honing your craft and iterating based on these principles, you'll be well on your way to creating content that not only resonates with viewers but also leaves a lasting impact.

PART III

THE COMMUNICATION ALGORITHM

The Power of the Communication Algorithm

Now that you've learned how to analyze, research, and identify viral videos, I'm excited to introduce another pillar in our method for achieving Viral success: the Communication Algorithm. This tool, deeply rooted in the principles of the Process Communication Model (PCM), offers a pathway to impactful, large-scale communication for every piece of content you write, create, and speak. Developed by Dr. Taibi Kahler, a renowned psychologist and author, the algorithm draws insights gathered from over 1.6 million individuals globally. Its, effectiveness is evidenced by its adoption across leading organizations—NASA, Bill Clinton, Coca-Cola, BMW, IKEA, L'Oréal, and Pixar—to fulfill ambitious communication and business objectives.

In this section, we delve into mastering communication at scale. At Hook Point, our mission is to guide our diverse clientele in integrating the PCM into their social media content effectively, broadening the resonance of their messages. A common challenge in communication is the inclination to convey messages in a manner that resonates personally, rather than universally, often leading to reduced audience reach due to personal biases in language and structure.

The Communication Algorithm is instrumental in refining our vocabulary, sentence structure, and body language, significantly enhancing our ability to connect with a larger portion of the population. With many content creators struggling to engage more than 30 percent of their audience on social media, this algorithm serves as a transformative solution. It not only identifies the language and messaging that truly engages a wide audience, but magnifies the impact of their communication efforts. By leveraging this innovative approach, businesses can forge meaningful and lasting connections, far beyond mere reach.

This section seeks to enhance your understanding of communication preferences by presenting the Five Rules of the Communication Algorithm for effective communication at scale. These guidelines aim to reveal potential blind spots that could limit your ability to connect with the masses. Recognizing that individuals express themselves through various styles—such as facts, opinions, feelings, imagination, fun, or actions—is crucial. Notably, prioritizing Feelings, Facts, and Fun, while steering clear of Values-Based and Autocratic communication styles, is key to engaging with up to 85 percent of the population.

By adopting the Communication Algorithm and its core principles, you'll be well-equipped to navigate the intricacies of large-scale communication, ensuring your messages not only reach but truly resonate with a vast and diverse audience.

THE FIVE RULES—SECTION 1

HOW PEOPLE PERCEIVE THE WORLD

Individuals communicate using six distinct methods, each with a vocabulary preference that operates on both conscious and subconscious levels. We naturally gravitate toward our preferred mode of communication. The six communication styles are as follows:

1. Feelings
2. Facts
3. Fun
4. Opinions
5. Imagination
6. Actions

It's crucial to recognize that while we possess the capacity to utilize all six styles, we typically favor *one*. This preferred style not only influences our decision-making but also serves as our primary means of connection and comfort. It guides us as content creators in our expression and engagement strategies, and it influences how the audience connects with and responds to our content.

Below you can see that 75 percent of the population wants their content delivered with feelings, facts, and fun.

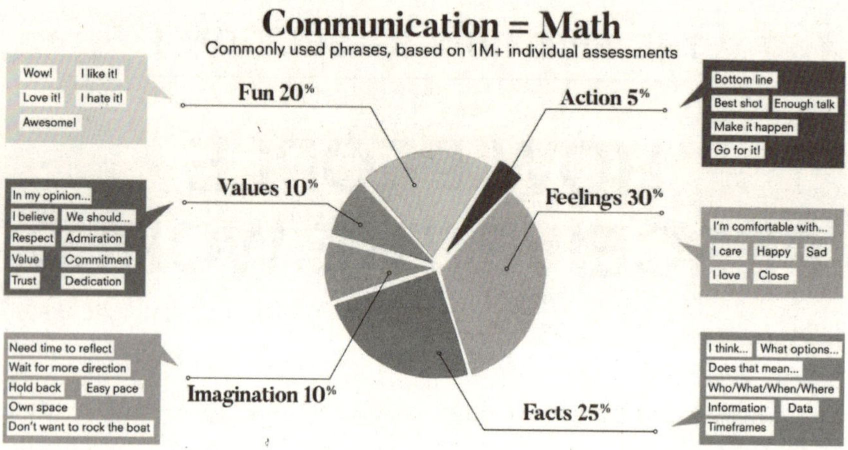

THE BIG THREE: THE LARGEST PERCENTAGE OF THE POPULATION

Feeling-based communicators make up the largest subset of the population, at 30 percent. They are emotion-based and connect with brands and content through feelings, making purchasing decisions based on emotional connections. Phrases that resonate with them include "I'm comfortable with," "I feel," "I care," "I love," "I'm happy," "I'm sad," and "We are close."

Fact-based communicators make up the second-largest group, at 25 percent of the population. This group highly values data and concrete information. They appreciate language such as "I think," "Which options," "Time frames," "details," "Does that mean . . . ," "Who . . . ,"

"What . . . ," "When . . . ," "Where . . . ," ". . . facts" ". . . information," and "data."

Fun-based communicators are the third-largest subset, making up 20 percent of the population. They are motivated by fun and excitement and are drawn to content that elicits reactions. They highly value humor, spontaneity, and creativity. They express their opinions readily, using phrases such as "I love it!" "I hate it!" "Wow . . . ," "I like . . . ," "I don't like . . . ," "I don't want . . . ," "I feel like," "I don't feel like," or "This is awesome!"

These three personality types—Feeling, Facts, and Fun—*are pivotal to engage with if you aim to make your content go viral, as they represent 75 percent of the population.* The key to satisfying all three lies in incorporating a blend of facts, feeling, and fun in your content.

THE LITTLE THREE: THE SMALLER PERCENTAGE OF THE POPULATION

Opinion-based communicators make up 10 percent of the population and are values focused. Their decisions are deeply rooted in trust toward individuals and content, and they evaluate people and situations through their opinions and belief systems. Loyalty and commitment are paramount to them. Opinion-based communicators often ask questions such as, "Can I trust this brand?" and "Do they share my values?" Their language frequently includes phrases such as "In my opinion . . . ," "I believe . . . ," "We should/must/need to . . . ," ". . . respect," ". . . admiration," ". . . commitment," and ". . . dedication."

Imagination-based communicators, who also make up 10 percent of the population, are introspective individuals who often engage in reflection. Unlike other groups, they tend to internalize rather than overtly react, mulling over their thoughts and feelings as they visualize interactions with products or services. They value privacy and personal space and appreciate specific guidance and clear directions before taking their next steps. Their language often includes phrases such as "need time to reflect," "need more direction," "hold back," "visualizing options," "Imagine the possibilities," "Envision," "easy pace," "my own space . . . ," and "don't want to rock the boat . . . ."

Action-based communicators make up 5 percent of population and are action-oriented individuals. They are goal driven and favor quick results, responding positively to directives that lead to immediate decision-making. Preferring action over prolonged discussions, they value initiative, adaptability, persuasion, charm, and self-sufficiency. The language that this group uses is firm and direct and includes phrases such as "Go for it!" "Bottom line," "Best shot," "Enough talk," and "Make it happen."

THE FIVE RULES—SECTION 2

THE FIVE RULES OF THE COMMUNICATION ALGORITHM

Welcome to this detailed guide on the Five Rules of the Communication Algorithm. Mastering these rules equips you to connect with 85 percent of the population, paving the way for extensive engagement. If you're curious why the five rules don't reach 100 percent of the population, it's because communicating in the style of imagination, opinions, and action alienates the other 75 percent of the population. Similarly, adopting a communication style focused on opinions and values can disengage 90 percent of people. Therefore, we use the five rules to engage 85 percent of the audience, which is the highest achievable percentage.

The first three rules address the Big Three communication preferences—Feelings, Facts, and Fun—resonating with 75 percent of the population. This foundation allows content creators to engage a broad and diverse audience. By also embracing the principles of Non-Values-Based and Non-Autocratic Communication, as detailed in the final two rules, your reach expands to an impressive 85 percent of the population.

Data from over 1.6 million communication assessments collected globally validate the effectiveness and ease of applying these five rules. Often, you can implement multiple rules within seconds, significantly enhancing your message and audience reach. However, neglecting Rules 4 and 5 might restrict your audience, as 85 percent of people resist imposed values or directives. Nonetheless, selectively incorporating autocratic elements—contrary to Rule 5—can be effective, particularly when balanced with the other four rules. While ideally all five rules would be applied, using three to four of them still ensures meaningful engagement.

Remember, while this section provides numerous tips, not all advice will apply universally. Your strategy should be influenced by various factors, such as the nature of your content, subject matter, video length, and other considerations. We offer a range of strategies to suit different communication styles, allowing you to choose those that best fit your unique approach, target audience, and personal preferences in expression and presentation.

Rule 1: Create Content for Feelings-Based Individuals

Approximately 30 percent of the global population uses a feeling-based communication style which is why Rule 1 is to create with this group in mind. Feeling-based individuals engage with people, places, and content based on the emotions they evoke. They possess a deep sense of compassion, sensitivity, and warmth, and prioritize meaningful connections and relationships. Feeling-based individuals are drawn to content that delves into the human experience, nurtures emotional connections, and supports authentic self-expression. They seek to establish a relationship with the content creator or experience deep emotional resonance through the content.

TIPS FOR INTEGRATION INTO YOUR CONTENT

- **Share relatable stories and experiences:** Utilize personal anecdotes, real-life examples, and genuine narratives to forge a connection and embark on a shared emotional journey.
- **Build meaningful connections:** Showcase relationships through personal stories, human connection, or the impact of relationships on life to engage feelings-based individuals.

TIPS FOR VOCABULARY AND TONE

Craft your verbal cues to communicate emotional sentiment, evoke a sense of belonging, and foster meaningful relationships.

Do's:

1. Use vocabulary that communicates emotion, such as:
    - "I feel . . ."
    - "I'm comfortable with . . ."
    - "I care about . . ."
    - "I'm sad/happy . . ."
    - "I love . . ."
    - "I appreciate . . ."

2. Use gentle tones that convey empathy rather than indifference.

Don'ts:

1. Avoid dismissive language that belittles emotions and experiences. Acknowledge and validate others' feelings.
    - Instead of "It's not a big deal; don't worry about it," say, "I understand this may be difficult—let's address it together."
2. Avoid judging or criticizing people's emotions.
    - Instead of "Those people should not be reacting that way," say, "I understand that this situation can affect everyone differently."

TIPS FOR BODY LANGUAGE, GESTURES, AND FACIAL EXPRESSIONS

Nonverbal cues that convey warmth, empathy, and acceptance are key.

Do's:

1. Maintain an open, relaxed posture that signals approachability. Extend forward slightly, with palms up in a welcoming gesture.
2. Use relaxed, accepting facial expressions. Soft, genuine smiles and open eyes create comfort. Keep your forehead neutral to avoid appearing judgmental.

3. Maintain eye contact to create a personal connection. Be warm and inviting, shifting your gaze naturally to show active listening and connection.

Don'ts:

1. Avoid closed-off body language, such as crossed arms or slouching, which conveys disinterest.
2. Avoid rigid facial expressions that can seem unengaged. Try not to frown or sport a blank expression.
3. Refrain from aggressive or confrontational body language.

Rule 2: Create Content for Fact-Based Individuals

Approximately 25 percent of the global population communicates in a fact-based style, which is why creating content that appeals to them is Rule 2.

Fact-based individuals are responsible, organized, and logical. When engaging with this group, integrate facts, logic, and ideas into your content. These individuals appreciate content that offers practical information and insights and that satisfies their curiosity with educational material.

TIPS FOR INTEGRATION INTO YOUR CONTENT

- **Show credibility:** Use references, data, and statistics to support your claims and establish believability.
- **Encourage information processing:** Adopt a democratic communication style, providing sufficient background for audiences to form their own conclusions.

- **Present multiple perspectives:** Explore different viewpoints in a logical, unbiased manner to stimulate critical thinking and allow audiences to reach their conclusions.

TIPS FOR VOCABULARY AND TONE

Your language should convey data and information, empowering the audience to make informed decisions.

Do's:

Use vocabulary that facilitates questioning and informed evaluations, such as:

1. "I think . . ."
2. "Does that mean . . . ?"
3. "Who, what, where, when?"
4. "Based on . . ."
5. "The time frame is . . ."
6. "This data/information shows . . ."

Adopt a neutral, natural tone, speaking clearly without implying any action.

Don'ts:

1. Avoid language that prompts impulsive action.
2. Refrain from starting sentences with *You*, which can burden the listener.
3. Rephrase sentences to position *you* at the middle or end.

4. Avoid subjective language. Use facts over opinions, and steer clear of buzzwords or generalizations.

TIPS FOR BODY LANGUAGE, GESTURES, FACIAL EXPRESSIONS

Do's:

1. Maintain a composed demeanor.
2. Adopt a steady, erect posture, conveying confidence and attentiveness.
3. Keep a neutral facial expression.
4. Employ natural body language that is aligned with the content and message you're conveying.

Don'ts:

1. Avoid excessive or exaggerated gestures that can seem insincere or distracting.

Rule 3: Create Content for Fun-Based Individuals

Around 20 percent of the global population prefers a fun-based communication style. So Rule 3 (you guessed it) is creating content that appeals to them.

Fun-based individuals are spontaneous, energetic, playful, and creative. These people are drawn to content that offers lighthearted and enjoyable experiences. They value playfulness, amusement, spontaneous moments, and genuine reactions.

TIPS FOR INTEGRATION INTO YOUR CONTENT

- **Natural reactions:** Fun-loving individuals value shared experiences. Showcase genuine reactions in your content—marked by energy, dynamic tone variations, full-body engagement (movement) when speaking, and the use of slang—to draw them closer.
- **Spontaneous movement in videos:** Keep your audience entertained with high-energy experiences such as energetic camera transitions, action-oriented scenes, engaging visuals, or spontaneous interactions.
- **Light and enjoyable content:** Even when discussing serious topics, infuse fun into the atmosphere with humor, anecdotes, or playful elements.

TIPS FOR VOCABULARY AND TONE

Choose vibrant, expressive language that invites reactions. Infuse your tone with playfulness and spontaneity.

Do's:

1. Use vocabulary that elicits reactions such as "Wow!," "I love/hate . . . ," "I'm so excited to share this with you!," "Awesome!," or "Great!"
2. Use fun, current slang, ensuring that it feels relevant and lively. Examples include:
    - » "Get ready to have a blast, y'all!"
    - » "This is going to be epic!"

- » "SO cool!"

3. Speak in upbeat, enthusiastic tones, using exclamation marks and expressive tones.

Don'ts:

1. Avoid indecisive or apathetic vocabulary such as:
   - » "Need time to reflect . . ."
   - » "Let's take it slow and steady."
   - » "Wait for more direction . . ."
   - » "Easy there, don't want to overdo it."
   - » "Don't want to rock the boat . . ."
   - » "Not sure . . ."
2. Steer clear of monotones or dull expressions.
3. Refrain from starting sentences with *You* to avoid placing undue responsibility on the listener. An effective solution is to rephrase the sentence by positioning *you* in the middle or toward the end.
   - » Instead of saying, "You should try this new productivity app!" you might rephrase it as, "Yo, this new productivity app has been a total game-changer for me—you wanna check it out?" or "I'd love to show you this helpful productivity app that's streamlined my day. Are you interested in seeing it?"

TIPS FOR BODY LANGUAGE, GESTURES, AND FACIAL EXPRESSIONS

Use nonverbal cues that convey excitement, spontaneity, and playfulness.

Do's:

1. Utilize animated, dynamic gestures that express your excitement and passion.
2. Maintain an open, fluid posture. Show your enthusiasm by leaning in and moving around.
3. Use authentic facial expressions to reveal your true emotions, such as joy, sadness, surprise, or any other genuine feeling.
4. Incorporate spontaneous movement into your video content.

Don'ts:

1. Avoid rigid or stiff body language that appears disengaged.
2. Try not to sport tense or blank facial expressions that lack enthusiasm or warmth.
3. Steer clear of static camera shots or monotonous talking-head presentations.

Rule 4: The Rule of Non-Values-Based Communication

Rule 4 advises against using values-based communication. This style centers on personal beliefs and opinions, as seen in statements like "Our supplement is the best on the market" or "Meditating with our app makes you a better person." Such communication appeals to merely 10 percent of the population, finding resonance mainly among those who share similar viewpoints. Yet, it struggles to connect with the overwhelming majority—90 percent—of people, as it can alienate listeners by presenting potential areas of disagreement. For example, emphasizing environmental conservation as a top priority could repel someone who prioritizes economic growth, thus significantly narrowing the communicator's potential audience.

CHALLENGES OF VALUES-BASED COMMUNICATION

The key reasons why values-based communication is not the most effective approach include:

- **Limited appeal:** It resonates with a very small segment of the population, limiting its effectiveness.
- **Risk of opposition:** By nature, it invites counterarguments, fostering division rather than connection.

These challenges show the importance of adopting more inclusive communication strategies. Such strategies steer clear of polarizing values and opinions, aiming instead to unite and engage with the masses.

FROM VALUES-BASED TO INCLUSIVE COMMUNICATION: EXAMPLES

Transforming values-based statements into more inclusive communication can help engage the masses. The objective is to transition from values-based communication to methods that embrace Feelings, Facts, or Fun. These styles promote more inclusive and engaging interactions.

Many brands and influencers, often without realizing it, employ values-based language on their landing pages and social media platforms. The table below presents examples and suggests alternative phrasings that uses Feelings, Facts, or Fun.

Values-Based	Alternative
"Something needs to be done about climate change."	"I'm worried about the changing climate." (Feelings) "Do you want to know the latest info on climate change?" (Facts) "This climate change thing is freaking CRAZY!" (Fun)
"The first-gen version of this hard drive is better because of the sturdy case, even though the new one has better specs."	"I love the first-gen version of this hard drive." (Feelings) "The first-gen version of this hard drive has a hard-shell external casing that gives you protection that the new product doesn't offer." (Facts) "The first gen version of this hard drive is off the hook amazing!" (Fun)

"Our supplement is the best on the market."	"We have a supplement product just for you." (Feelings) "Per 'X' research done on our supplement, we have data to prove we have more vitamins and nutrients than our competitors' products." (Facts) "More nutrients is just what the doc ordered . . . just sayin'!" (Fun)
"If you want to be a better person, you have to meditate."	"Quiet, comfortable, and soothing meditation may help you." (Feelings) "Meditation has been shown by 'X' research to benefit many people's lives. Here is a link to that research . . ." (Facts) "Meditation, dude. Love it or hate it . . . it might just help ya out!" (Fun)

"To become a good content creator, you have to work with Hook Point."	"Hook Point would love to help you go viral." (Feelings) "Hook Point has helped 'X' creators go viral. Here's a link to those creators . . ." (Facts) "Wanna get your viral content exploding . . . Hook Point!" (Fun)
"You shouldn't be eating that."	"We have a healthy eating plan tailored just for you." (Feelings) "Do you want information on how to eat better?" (Facts) "Yo, that stuff is bad for you, dawg." (Fun)

Adopting a non-values-based approach in communication allows for a broader and more inclusive engagement, reducing the potential for alienation and fostering a more open dialogue. This strategy is crucial for connecting with a wider audience, particularly in contexts where building a consensus or mass appeal is essential.

Rule 5: The Rule of Non-Autocratic Communication

Autocratic communication involves directing someone explicitly, often seen in online sales pitches like "Buy now or miss out on this incredible offer!" This style is characterized by directives that allow little room for others' input, thus restricting dialogue and the exchange of ideas. In today's global context, an overwhelming 85 percent of the population resists this direct approach, preferring not to be explicitly told what to do. This significant preference underscores the importance of Rule 5.

One can easily visualize this rule by imagining a parent instructing their children to come to dinner in 15 minutes, only to find them still preoccupied later. This common scenario mirrors a broader truth: a considerable number of individuals, both young and old, instinctively resist being told what to do, a sentiment that goes beyond personal interactions to the digital realm.

ALTERNATIVE COMMUNICATION STYLES

Instead of relying on Autocratic Communication, consider one of these three preferred styles—Benevolent, Democratic, and Laissez-faire Communication—each offering a unique approach to engaging with others:

- **Democratic Communication:** This style involves asking and consulting with the other party, promoting a sense of participation and respect for their opinion. It values the listener's input and decision-making process, encouraging open dialogue for a mutual exchange of ideas and opinions. Preferred by 35 percent of the population.

- **Benevolent Communication:** Conveys warmth, care, and acceptance, focusing on a nurturing and empathetic tone that considers the listener's feelings and needs. Favored by 30 percent of the population.
- **Laissez-faire Communication:** Emphasizes creative, spontaneous, and playful language. It's laid-back and engaging, presenting the receiver with a relaxed and informal manner. Appreciated by 20 percent of the population.

SELLING A LOBSTER EXAMPLE

Consider using content creation to market lobsters. Instead of employing Autocratic Communication with directives like "Buy this lobster" or "Purchase this lobster for a discount," opt for Benevolent, Democratic, or Laissez-faire Communication styles. For instance:

- Democratic Communication might ask: "Would you like to purchase this lobster?"
- Benevolent Communication could express: "We're excited to offer you this special lobster deal."
- Laissez-faire Communication might casually suggest: "Hey, we've got some amazing deals on lobsters!"

FROM AUTOCRATIC TO ALTERNATIVE: EXAMPLES

Our goal is to shift from autocratic language to approaches that incorporate democratic, benevolent, or laissez-faire styles, which foster more inclusive and engaging interactions.Many brands and influencers, often unknowingly, use autocratic language on their landing pages and social media platforms. In the following sections, you'll find examples, along with alternative ways to convey the same message Democratically, Benevolently, or in a Laissez-faire manner.

A common effective approach involves reframing statements into questions. This invites readers to engage with the idea, subtly conveying the content creator's intention to provide value and interact with their audience:

Autocratic	Alternative
"Buy now or miss out on this incredible offer!"	"We have an offer for you." (Benevolent) "Do you want to check out our best offer yet?" (Democratic) "Our offers are the bomb right now!!!" (Laissez-faire)
"Act fast and secure your spot!"	"We want you to secure your spot." (Benevolent) "Would you like to take advantage of our limited-time offer?" (Democratic) "Spots are disappearing like MySpace." (Laissez-faire)

"Don't think twice; click here for instant access!"	"We dropped the prices this weekend just for YOU." (Benevolent) "Do you want to save money this weekend?" (Democratic) "Dropping that price for a sizzling weekend!" (Laissez-faire)
"Sign up now!"	"We would love it if you signed up now." (Benevolent) "Do you want to sign up?" (Democratic) "Gotta sign up to show up!" (Laissez-faire)
"Subscribe to our newsletter or miss out on the latest updates!"	"Our newsletter is created to help you." (Benevolent) "Do you want to stay updated with the latest news?" (Democratic) "Click! Sign! Bang! . . . you got the newsletter." (Laissez-faire)

"Get our product now and start experiencing the difference!"	"We have a new experience just for you!" (Benevolent) "Do you want our new product?" (Democratic) "New experience! New product . . .what, what!!!" (Laissez-faire)
"Upgrade to our premier package!"	"We want you to sign up for our premier package." (Benevolent) "Do you want to unlock our top-tier resources?" (Democratic) "Upgrading is like driving your dream car . . ." (Laissez-faire)

Direct commands often act as a disincentive in communication, a sentiment echoed by the vast majority. By avoiding Autocratic Communication and embracing Benevolent, Democratic, and Laissez-faire Communication styles, you can align more closely with the preferences of 85 percent of the population. Learning to adapt to diverse communication preferences is crucial when trying to go viral online.

THE FIVE RULES—SECTION 3

APPLYING THE COMMUNICATION ALGORITHM TO YOUR CONTENT AND MARKETING PLANS

Understanding your own communication styles, as well as those of your team members and your customers, is invaluable. It provides a foundation for enhanced engagement with your core audience. Consider a situation where your marketing director and your primary customer share similar demographics:

Imagine this scenario:

Your Marketing Director	Your Customer
Female	Female
30-35 years old	30-35 years old
High Income	High Income
Macy's Shopper	Macy's Shopper
Has Children	Has Children
Married	Married
University Educated	University Educated

They look the same on paper...

Although they look the same on paper, their communication styles are totally different:

...but these are their communication styles:

Your Marketing Director **Your Customer**

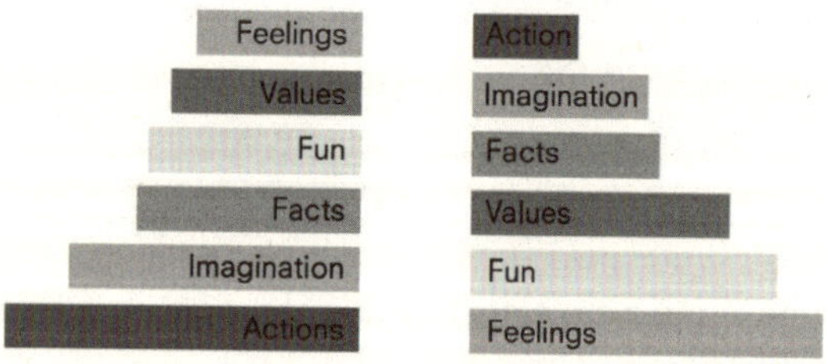

See the problem?

The bars in the graphics above indicate the level of energy each individual possesses for each communication style. A longer bar represents more energy, which translates to their communication strengths and the predominant language they're likely to use. Conversely, a shorter bar signifies less energy, highlighting their communication weaknesses and the language they're less likely to use.

Even though everyone has access to all six communication styles, each person has distinct strengths and weaknesses in various styles, and we tend to predominantly use our strongest ones. If your marketing director excels in action-based communication but struggles with feelings-based communication, while your core customer is strong in feelings-based communication but weaker in action-based communication, a disconnect arises. The marketing director might create content that emphasizes urgency and calls for immediate action, which will not resonate with a core customer seeking an emotional connection.

In this scenario, the marketing director's content might look like: "This is the best. You need to act now or you're going to miss out," which fails to connect with the feelings-based core customer, who desires emotional engagement. Such a disconnect can be problematic. In this example, the marketing director's natural communication style could potentially alienate up to 95 percent of the brand's core target audience because action-based communication typically resonates with only 5 percent of the population: the Promoters. This gap represents lost opportunities and revenue. Importantly, this isn't a critique of the marketing director's skills but rather, highlights the need to be cognizant of varying communication styles and to adapt content to reach the widest audience effectively.

Or imagine a scenario where your marketing director is a values-based communicator and crafts marketing copy from that perspective, they also risk alienating 90 percent of the population. This is because the vast majority do not appreciate content filled with beliefs or heavy opinion-based words like "need," "should," and "ought," as these do not allow them the choice or opportunity to decide for themselves. It's too forceful for them. Statistically, what people desire is to feel good about the content, to find it logical, or to perceive the advertisement or copy as hip, cool, and awesome—essentially the antithesis of "should," "ought," "need," and "we believe."

Consider the direct sales posts on the internet or social media as an illustrative example. This content often appears on our screens with a bold, hard-sell approach, using language that commands immediate action, such as "Buy now!" or "Limited offer—click to purchase!" While this strategy may generate quick sales from a segment of people who respond to urgency, it often fails to appeal to a wider audience that prefers a more nuanced and interactive experience. The direct, hard-sell approach can be off-putting to many and may alienate those looking for authentic engagement and informative content. Adopting this forceful tactic without considering the diverse preferences of the masses could inadvertently narrow your brand's reach, capturing only a small portion of the potential market.

The issue is not the content per se, but rather, the language used, which fails to address Fun, Facts, Feelings, and the Benevolent, Democratic, and Laissez-faire communication styles that resonate with the masses. By understanding The Five Rules of the Communication Algorithm and leveraging the most desired communication styles, you can better engage your audience, thereby maximizing your impact and success. Remember, *how* we say something is often more important than *what* we say.

Selling a House Analogy

To illustrate the importance of diverse communication styles, consider the process of selling a house: Typically, Realtors list properties by just stating facts: a "4BR/3BA home, 2,300 square feet, located at [address], offered at [price]." But this approach only appeals to people who interact primarily through facts and overlooks a broader audience.

By adding to the description so it incorporates all five of the communication algorithm rules, the listing becomes more effective:

- 4BR/3BA home, 2,300 square feet, located at [address], offered at [price] **(Facts)**
- We would love to show this comfy cozy home. **(Benevolent)**
- A home with warmth, and a coziness that feels like you never want to leave.
- **(Feelings)**
- There's a pool out back where you can host the most amazing parties! (**Fun**)
- Do you want to live near excellent local schools? Here's a link with the data about the schools in this neighborhood. **(Democratic)**
- This hip spot won't last long . . . let me know when you wanna check it out. **(Laissez-faire)**

By incorporating elements that cater to Facts, Feelings, and Fun, and by using Benevolent, Democratic, and Laissez-faire communication styles that avoid values-based and autocratic approaches, the advertisement is likely to resonate with at least 85 percent of the population, reaching beyond just the fact-driven individuals. This strategy follows the principle that language, when thoughtfully applied, can broaden appeal and inclusivity, thereby amplifying impact and success.

THE 5 RULES—SECTION 4

THE COMMUNICATION ALGORITHM BREAKDOWN: HOW DR. JULIE SMITH MASTERS TIKTOK WITH VIRAL MENTAL HEALTH CONTENT

In a world where social media platforms are flooded with dance videos and lighthearted content, making serious and informative topics go viral can appear daunting. Yet, Dr. Julie Smith, the clinical psychologist and author mentioned earlier in this book, has challenged this idea. She skillfully uses The Five Rules of the Communication Algorithm to blend Feelings, Facts, and Fun, avoiding value-based and autocratic language to create viral mental health content on TikTok.

With millions of followers, Smith reaches a wide audience with her empowering messages about mental health.

Her video on trauma therapy, *Trauma*, which can be viewed at http://guide.hookpoint.com/, along with all the other videos and references mentioned in this book, has already garnered more than 10.5 million views. In it, she uses crumpled paper and a wastebasket to symbolize how therapy can help individuals process traumatic experiences.

Smith skillfully captivates the 20 percent of her audience drawn to entertaining and dynamic content. She does this with subtlety and finesse rather than silliness and exaggerated antics, but she incorporates fun elements with engaging aesthetics, such as a vibrant, rainbow-themed backdrop that exudes warmth and creates an inviting atmosphere. Avoiding over-the-top gestures, she opts for creative props and playful movements that are both charming and relatable. Through her interactions with the props mentioned above, she evokes tactile sensations that allow viewers to almost feel the experience themselves. The satisfying sound of paper crinkling as she smooths out the pieces, along with the visual of neatly folded paper being placed back into the wastebasket, enriches the sensory experience. This nuanced approach shows that connecting with the segment of the population that enjoys a fun communication style can be gracefully achieved without leaning on humor.

Adding to the video's effectiveness, Smith also incorporates valuable facts and insights, resonating with the 25 percent of viewers who value logical, fact-based content. Her skillful use of framing (the placement and positioning of subjects in a particular camera shot)—leaning into the camera and maintaining eye contact—enhances the video's emotional impact. This strategic framing creates an intimate, one-on-one conversational atmosphere, strengthening her connection with the

30 percent of her audience who appreciates feelings-based communication. Additionally, Smith's warm facial expressions and emotionally resonant content further appeal to this emotionally responsive segment of the audience.

By adeptly combining these elements, Smith succeeds in resonating with 75 percent of her audience, each in their preferred mode of communication. It's important to note that these elements are blended subtly; they don't need to be over the top or exaggerated to be effective. Clients often think that separate videos are necessary to appeal to each personality type. Smith demonstrates, however, that Feelings, Facts, and Fun can be used together with finesse, significantly contributing to a video's viral success.

In another example, Smith's *Stress Bucket* video, which has garnered more than 1.2 million views, uses a vivid visual metaphor: a bucket filled with water to symbolize stress levels. As she outlines various ways to manage and alleviate stress, she uses a drill to release water from the bucket. This imaginative visual metaphor not only drives home the concept of stress management but also offers viewers an unforgettable takeaway.

The video's physical movement and prop interaction engage the 20 percent of the population that responds to fun and playful content. The satisfying sound of the drill and the comical spilling out of the water amplify the entertainment value. Simultaneously, Smith's warm and open facial expressions connect with the 30 percent of viewers who are more responsive to emotional communication. Once again, she subtly yet effectively addresses both fun and feeling in this video.

Additionally, she provides logical, useful, and informative content, appealing to the 25 percent of the audience who value fact-based communication. By skillfully incorporating Feelings, Facts, and Fun, Smith crafts yet another hit video that resonates with 75 percent of her audience.

In both videos, she avoids using value-based language such as "should," "ought," and "need," steering clear of imposing conditions on what one must do to be of value. Rather than preaching, she opts for explaining (appealing to fact-based communicators), describing (catering to feelings-based communicators), and demonstrating (engaging fun-based communicators).

Also, she steers away from autocratic language that dictates actions to her viewers. Instead, she uses a mix of Benevolent, Democratic, And Laissez-faire language, exemplified by sentences like "Let me introduce you to the stress bucket" (Benevolent); "So, what can we do about that?" (Democratic); "Sometimes that stress might be a little trickle, but other times it is thick and fast!" (Laissez-faire). This approach is crucial, as 85 percent of the global population does not want to be told what to do but prefers an invitation to make their own decisions.

Smith's remarkable success on TikTok stands as proof that any topic can resonate with the masses. For content creators, the Communication Algorithm serves as an invaluable tool for building authentic, meaningful connections with viewers. So go ahead—have Fun . . . and Facts and Feelings . . . to captivate and inspire your audience!

THE FIVE RULES—SECTION 5

THE COMMUNICATION ALGORITHM EXERCISES

EXERCISE 1
THE COMMUNICATION ALGORITHM VIDEO ANALYSIS: ANALYZING THE EFFECT OF VIDEOS

Please watch the following videos at least three times. They are available at http://guide.hookpoint.com/.

1. Itslennnie's *Asking for Help Does Not Make You Weak!*
2. Dylan Page's *What an Insane Year!*
3. Hunter Proper's *What's Something You Wish You Would Have Said?*

After viewing, reflect on these questions:

- Did the video entertain you or provide value?
- Was the content compassionate, sensitive, and warm?

- Did it achieve any other notable effect?
- Was there any use of autocratic language?
- Was there any use of values-based language?
- Was the person soapboxing? (In other words, were they preaching in a manner that disregarded other possible viewpoints, assuming their perspective was the only valid one?)
- Bonus: What tactics do you think the creator employed to elicit your response?

EXERCISE 2
TRIPLE F BOOST: ENHANCE YOUR VIDEO WITH FEELING, FACTS, AND FUN

Take a video you've recently created and try to enhance it with more Feeling, Facts, and Fun. You can achieve this by making small adjustments in your choice of:

- Content ideas
- Words
- Tone
- Facial expressions
- Body language
- Posture
- Gestures

(Refer to the section "Feeling, Facts, and Fun 2: The Five Rules of the Communication Algorithm" for specific tips related to content ideas, vocabulary, tone, body language, gestures, and facial expressions.)

ENHANCE YOUR COMMUNICATION STRATEGY WITH OUR EXPERT SUPPORT

Are you eager to uncover the strengths and weaknesses of your communication style? Take our Communication Algorithm Assessment and begin a journey toward social media mastery.

This assessment is more than just an evaluation—it's a critical step in boosting your content's performance. By understanding the subtleties of your communication style, you can significantly enhance engagement and connect more authentically with your audience.

Embarking on this path also opens the door to exclusive, advanced training with the Hook Point team, designed to refine and elevate your communication skills for greater impact.

Ready to transform your communication strategy? Get started here: http://guide.hookpoint.com/.

CONCLUSION

THE FINAL ACT: MASTERING THE VIRAL GAME

Throughout this book, we've debunked the myth that going viral is simply a matter of luck or celebrity status. We've unraveled the science of virality, equipping you with the necessary tools and insights to become a viral sensation. It's a process that requires hard work, but you're now prepared to embark on this journey.

Now, it's *your* turn to put all this knowledge to work. Harness the power of the Hook Point Viral Content Model, Viral Formats, and the Communication Algorithm. With these tools, your content is on the path to success.

Remember, going viral isn't about mindlessly chasing trends or sticking to a rigid content calendar. It's about mastering the art of storytelling, captivating a broad range of viewers with knowledge about the right performance drivers and communication tools, and holding their attention with every post you make. This is the kind of content that algorithms love and distribute to millions of people.

Although the road to viral success may not be easy, it *is* simple:

- Do your research and analyze successful creators and videos.
- Find a format that resonates with your audience, and strive to become world class at it.
- Implement the Communication Algorithm to insert Feeling, Facts, and Fun into your content.

Finding the perfect formula for your content may take some trial and error, but with each attempt, you'll grow, learn, and improve. Keep your mind open and stay adaptable—these are the core traits that will help you master this approach.

So . . . go ahead, embrace this process, and don't be intimidated by the hard work or competition you'll face in the social media world. Yes, keep in mind that you're vying for attention among more than four billion other content creators in the world, but also remember that now you've got something most people don't: a scientifically grounded, repeatable strategy that will work now into the future, regardless of the platform or the type of content you're creating.

I can't wait to hear about your journey using these methods. Share your milestones, learning experiences, and the strategies that are elevating your brand—as well as how the transformative insights from this book impact your content. If you need further assistance, you can get in touch with my team and me at http://guide.hookpoint.com/. We'd be thrilled to connect with you and explore how to collaborate to fuel your social media growth and help you hit all your business goals.

So, I'll leave you with a challenge: Create the most viral video your industry has ever seen. Start researching, analyzing, and crafting your masterpiece. May your viral success be the proof of what can happen when you dare to think differently and tap into the science of virality.

I look forward to seeing your work popping up on my feed soon!

ACKNOWLEDGMENTS

First, I'd like to express my heartfelt gratitude to my literary agent, the late Bill Gladstone, who, in my opinion, was the best agent any author could ever have. Without him, this book would not have been possible. It still astonishes me that someone of Bill's stature—having represented more than $5 billion worth of book sales—took the time to pilot this project and support my journey as an author. I thank him for his unwavering dedication, and I miss him very much.

Thank you, Jeff King, for transforming my life with your teachings about the Communication Algorithm. Your support and guidance have meant the world to me. I cherish our conversations on communication and its profound impact on business, content, and our daily lives.

Thank you to the brilliant members of my team at Hook Point. Our growth and client satisfaction would not be possible without your unwavering hard work and dedication. A special salute to Paulo de Sousa, Melissa Huisman, Luke Evenson, Jose Brizida, Samantha Jane Simões Beedles, and Michael Glines for their various contributions and input on this book.

Last, but certainly not least, Tara Rose Gladstone, thank you for all your commitment, effort, and support in creating this book. Your knowledge and hard work have truly made it possible. I appreciate our collaborations and look forward to working with you on future projects.

ABOUT THE AUTHOR

Brendan Kane, the founder and CEO of Hook Point, empowers companies to achieve viral success without relying on luck. Kane has been a driving force behind significant breakthroughs in understanding virality and its impact on brands, influencers, and celebrities. With an unwavering commitment to research and tangible outcomes, he and his team have pioneered the Viral Content Model, revolutionizing the way we perceive and harness virality.

For nearly 20 years, Kane has been a trusted expert, guiding numerous prominent brands and celebrities to carve out their own routes to success. Through his guidance and the strategic model designed by his team, Kane's clients have attained notable accomplishments. Collectively, the Hook Point Viral Content Model and Communication Algorithm have generated an impressive $1 billion in revenue, tens of billions of views, and more than 100 million followers.

But Kane's influence extends far beyond the realm of business strategies. He has left a mark on the world of social media, with notable accomplishments such as developing the first-ever influencer campaign on YouTube back in 2007. His talents have been sought after by major corporations, and he has overseen marketing spends of $200 million plus, contributing to their unparalleled growth and success.

In the realm of celebrity influence, Kane has developed digital technology solutions for household names such as Taylor Swift,

Rihanna, and Adriana Lima. His insights and winning strategies have been leveraged by Fortune 500 companies and iconic brands like MTV, Yahoo!, IKEA, Viacom, *Vice* Magazine, and Skechers shoes.

Additionally, Kane served as vice president of Digital at Paramount Pictures and played a role in scaling one of the largest social paid media optimization firms, serving brands such as Disney, Fox, NBC, Netflix, Xbox, LinkedIn, and many others.

Kane embarked on a personal experiment that captivated the digital world. Implementing his own process, he achieved the extraordinary feat of generating more than a million followers in 100 countries in 30 days on his own Facebook page.

Kane's profound knowledge is shared through his bestselling books *One Million Followers: How I Built a Massive Social Audience in 30 Days,* and *Hook Point: How to Stand Out in a 3-Second World*. These works have become essential guides for aspiring creators and marketers, offering invaluable insights and transformative strategies for achieving success in the digital realm.

http://guide.hookpoint.com/

WE CAN HELP

My team and I have perfected the Hook Point Viral Content model, the Communication Algorithm, and the art of identifying Hook Points and Viral Formats for over 15 years.

We understand the significant time commitment required to identify the ideal Viral Format for a brand or business and to conduct in-depth research on the factors that drive its performance. That's exactly why Hook Point was founded; our team of innovative thinkers propels brands, corporations, thought leaders, and celebrities to success in highly competitive markets.

While most companies focus on maximizing attention, we command it. We discover what's unique about your brand and help you deliver it at scale. There are no templates or one-size-fits-all approaches here—just unexpected solutions that will delight your customers.

Investing with us to craft a unique Hook Point strategy is significant, but the results we achieve for our clients are substantial, and the return on investment is massive.

If you're interested in working with us,
visit https://hookpoint.com/.